The Devil's Marriage

Break Up the Corpocracy or Leave Democracy in the Lurch

Gary Brumback

authorHOUSE®

AuthorHouse™
1663 Liberty Drive
Bloomington, IN 47403
www.authorhouse.com
Phone: 1-800-839-8640

First published by AuthorHouse   2/15/2011

ISBN: 978-1-4567-1260-0 (sc)
ISBN: 978-1-4567-1259-4 (hc)
ISBN: 978-1-4567-1951-7 (e)

Library of Congress Control Number: 2010918917

Printed in the United States of America

Cover stock imagery © Thinkstock.

This book is printed on acid-free paper.

MORE PRAISE FOR THE DEVIL'S MARRIAGE

"NGOs have been fighting the Corpocracy one company at a time for 30 years...and losing. Brumback tells us why, gives us a battle plan, and issues a challenge to join forces to reclaim our democracy. This is the pre-eminent American challenge for the 21st Century. This book could not be more timely. Don't just read it. Take action. Now!"
---Michael Marx, PhD, Executive Director, Corporate Ethics International

"Gary Brumback has written a book that every disgruntled American should read. He identifies the source of our nation's most troubling problems (corpocracy), traces its history, and offers some practical albeit difficult solutions. Our democracy has been taken from us by unbridled corporate power. His book is a manual of sorts for those who wish to recapture the essence of what America once was—and can be again."
—Roger Terry, author, Economic Insanity: How Growth-Driven Capitalism Is Devouring the American Dream.

"Brumback makes a powerful argument for a radical democratic movement to take on corporate rule that Americans need to hear."
---Steven Hiatt, Editor, A Game as Old as Empire: The Secret World of Economic Hit Men and the Web of Global Corruption, and president of Edicetera.

"While you may not agree with his entire wide-ranging analysis, Gary Brumback's book is a tremendous tocsin that will rouse you from the malaise that plagues this country. We desperately need a democracy movement here in the U.S. to shake off the "corpocracy" that has colonized our culture and politics. This book has many good suggestions for building it."
-- Charlie Cray, Director, Center for Corporate Policy, and co-author, The People's Business.

"A devastating analysis of the relationship between government and business in America. Brumback's cutting insight and lively writing make his book a must-read for anyone who cares about the future of this country."

---S. Bartholomew Craig, Ph.D., Associate Professor of Industrial-Organizational Psychology, North Carolina State University and a former book review editor for Personnel Psychology: A Journal of Applied Research.

"From warfare welfare to health care, Gary Brumback identifies the biggest challenge to the great American experiment we face in this modern era. If you wonder why the two political parties in Washington D.C. are fast becoming indistinguishable from each other it is because corpocracy has them right where it wants them. Gary names this for what it is and tells us what is required to save free society from corporate take-over. Americans who wish not to be awakened every morning by a big screen Big Brother (our Chairman of the Board!) need to read this book."

---Jeffrey DeYoe, D. Min. Sr. Pastor, Worthington Presbyterian Church, Worthington, Ohio.

"In terms of its potential, Brumback's fine work is to political reform what General Smedley Butler's War Is a Racket is to the anti-war movement. Brumback's undermining of obsolete notions -- habitual ways of perceiving the electoral arena -- is refreshing, and if his recommendations were to be embraced we'd have a shot at citizens returning to the polls in large numbers."

-- Richard Martin Oxman, founder of California political movement, TOSCA

Contents

PREFACE

This is not a doomsday book because the corpocracy can be toppled by democracy power if only it can be mustered. This is not an ideological ranting. This is a wake-up call and a manifesto forged from ten years of extensive research and observations about America by a true American patriot worried that if the corpocracy isn't ended it will eventually end America.

The corpocracy is the marriage made in Hell between "our" government and large corporations. There is no real democracy in America today, no self rule, no government for, by, and of the people. Americans are ruled instead by an undemocratic regime, the huge and powerful corpocracy. Its rule is tyrannical and harmful. No sphere of American life is spared, whether it is the personal/social/cultural sphere; the economic sphere; the political sphere; or the environmental sphere. If FDR were to return and witness what is happening to us he might say we are living in a Fascist state.

The American Revolutionaries fought for a new democracy in a new land, a democracy of self-rule, not rule from afar. If they were to return today they would be revolted by what they see, tyrannical rule up close. Were Thomas Paine, who inspired the American Revolution with his pamphlet, "Common Sense" to return he would exhort us I'm sure to rely on our common sense and our moral obligation to "overthrow" the current regime (with all due respect Mr. Paine I'm not advocating a second, bloody American Revolution as the means to "overthrow" the current regime). A few years later Thomas Jefferson said he hoped "America would crush moneyed corporations" that were challenging our democracy. Were he to return he would say, "I warned you."

Why I Wrote this Book

Looking on and doing nothing while America is being dominated, exploited, and ruined by a powerful regime (i.e., the corpocracy) isn't an option for me. In a sense I am responding to John F. Kennedy's exhortation to all Americans: "Ask not what your country can do for you but what you can do for your country." Neither does jingoistic and dangerous patriotism ("America right or wrong") speak for me. What does speak for me is true patriotism ("America do right and no wrong"). The English writer and political thinker GK Chesterton (1874–1936) once said that "a true patriot would never say 'My country right or wrong.'"

What we can do for our country is to champion and pursue the political, legislative, judicial, and economic reforms that are needed to replace the corpocracy with an American democracy respectful of our founders and founding principles and equally good for the general welfare of all Americans living now and in the future.

I wrote this book for Americans who are disgusted with and distrustful of government. I wrote it as a wake-up call for Americans who for one reason or another don't see or understand the telltale signs of how the corpocracy is subjugating them and ruining America. I wrote it for the hundreds of NGOs, or non-governmental organizations each independently but insufficiently challenging the corpocracy in their own ways. I wrote it for all the activists and social movements that are or could be defenders of democracy. I also invite diehard members of the corpocracy and its allies to read it and to consider it an open confrontation of truth to power. Mice should never sit down at the table to negotiate with devilish cats.

Whenever I refer to the corpocracy the tone will sometimes be caustic or disdainful, hardly respectful, but never intentionally malicious. And it's pretty even-handed. Corporations, corporate executives, politicians, political parties, and even the judiciary are mostly indistinguishable among themselves (with the exception of the markedly different far right wing of the Republican Party), pursuing their own interests at the expense of the public's interests and the general welfare of the American people. In an interview with Amy Goodman on her TV/radio program Democracy Now! President Bill Clinton lost his temper, lashing out that her questions were "hostile, combative, and even disrespectful."[1] People in positions of power tend to expect and even demand the respect and trust of others, forgetting or ignoring that respect and trust must be earned from others, not owed by them. To be sure, one of Mr. Clinton's predecessors, the "Great Communicator," was loved by millions of people. They did not know or care that he passionately helped grow the corpocracy into what it is today.

A Quick Tour of the Book

The central theme holding the chapters together can be described in three sentences. Americans are being governed by an undemocratic and powerful regime that advances corporate and political self interests at a terrible cost to the American public. Current efforts to challenge the regime are totally inadequate. Only by following a strategic plan calling for systemic political, legislative, judicial, and economic reforms backed up by massive political pressure will Americans reclaim their democracy and regain greater control over their lives and general well being.

The first chapter gives an overview of the corpocracy. The corpocracy's many telltale signs are spotted and several explanations are given as to why they aren't yet very telling to most Americans. The corpocracy's allies, including foreign enemies that every regime needs, are discussed. The chapter closes by conjecturing on whether America is becoming a "ruiNation."

The second chapter recounts from colonial days forward the episodic history of democracy alternating with the corpocracy. The struggle between the two is now in the eighth round. America's scoreboard reads Corpocracy 5 Democracy 3 and on the ropes. You will be told about a tobacco road lawyer, Lewis F. Powell, who was a most unusual instigator of the corpocracy's current reincarnation before he was appointed by Nixon to the U.S. Supreme Court. When you finish this chapter, I implore you not to be complacent, thinking that the ups and downs of the corpocracy mean we just have to wait for its next downer. Massive street demonstrations over Vietnam didn't end the corpocracy, nor has the American blood and money wasted on Iraq and Afghanistan, nor has "Economic Katrina," the greatest depression since the Great One.

In the third chapter I ask and answer where today's opposition is to the corpocracy. The answer is that the corpocracy has divided and conquered its opposition. Several alternative forms of opposition are reviewed and rejected in favor of the proposal introduced in the next chapter.

In the fourth chapter a particular counterforce is proposed. I call it "democracy power," and it is made up of two sources of power. One would be a virtual network of the many NGOs each mostly challenging the corpocracy on their own. I call this virtual network the U.S. Chamber of Democracy (USCD). It would develop and carry out a comprehensive strategic "POW!" plan in unison with the second source of power, a new and very large coalition of the corpocracy's adversaries that I call the "People's Reignbow Coalition." It would be a melding of many different segments of the populace and would provide the political muscle/pressure behind each and every strategy. The question is raised as to whether this double-fisted democracy power will ever materialize. Whether it does is far less important than the goal of reclaiming our democracy, and as you will see throughout the rest of the book that goal need not depend on the particular form that democracy power takes.

Chapter 5 proposes telling the people about the corpocracy by priming democracy power in classrooms and the major media. The strategic initiatives described in this chapter are basically the mirror image of what Powell proposed in his manifesto to corporations to blitz the same two institutions in order to shape minds young to old about the virtues (as he perceived them) of the free enterprise system he so venerated and feared had been overtaken by liberals.

Satirical but serious chapter 6 proposes numerous strategic initiatives for closing the political/judicial circus of clowns that do the bidding of the corporate ringmaster. The clowns are the lifers and vote peddlers, the party twins, oval office puppets, the corporatized courts, the touts, the revolving doors and archways and their comers and goers, the burrowers, the vote hurdle makers, and the beastly bureaucracy.

Most corporate wrongdoing is legally rooted by "our" government in sham corporate charters, corporate personhood, and limited liability. Explaining them and proposing strategic initiatives for uprooting them is the subject of Chapter 7.

Chapter 8 examines the government's hands-off policies and practices that are soft on corporate crime, to put it mildly. I refer to them as lap dogs, escape hatches, pampering, and reckless deregulation. The chapter ends with a number of proposals for toughening up law enforcement on crime hatched in corporate suites.

Chapter 9 is about all the government's hand-outs to corporations. Remember the "Cadillac welfare queen?" Ronald Reagan conjured her up to show his disdain for social welfare while on the campaign stump. Do you know what he and subsequent puppets did once they were elected? They have starved the neediest and fed the greediest. That government won't tell us exactly how much corporate welfare is costing taxpayers tells us that the cost is astronomical, particularly the one feature of the corpocracy most likely to end America singlehandedly, warfare welfare. The chapter ends with proposals for turning off the government's spigot of handouts.

Besides Powell, there is one more individual who must be given credit for masterminding the creation of undemocratic capitalism that is yet another boon for the corpocracy. The mastermind was the late Milton Friedman, Nobel laureate in economics. Powell gave the corpocracy a battle plan. Friedman gave it an economic blueprint. It has proven to be good for the corpocracy, especially Wall Street, but disastrous for everyone else at home and away. This is all taken up in Chapter 10 along with proposing a very sweeping blueprint drawn from others' ideas as well as my own for establishing a form of capitalism worthy of a true democracy. In this chapter I direct you to Appendix C., Creative Economic Thinking from A to Z Minus E for Economists. Please don't overlook it. It is a synopsis of some of the best thinkers and their thinking on economics and capitalism. And they're not economists- a deliberate omission on my part!

Chapter 11, the last one, asks you to unleash your democracy power on your own and, much more essentially, to leverage your "Me" power by joining with all other true patriots to unleash your "We" power. If you are uncertain the corpocracy really exists, you might consider doing a reality check.

Acknowledgments

There are many footnotes. They are more than just a way to cite my sources, should you be interested in them. They also allow me to acknowledge all my sources that I have drawn upon for ideas, facts, and figures. In a way, "footnote" is sort of a metaphor-my standing on my feet on the shoulders of so many, many people. I am particularly indebted to the writings and insights of the following persons in alphabetical order: Aristotle (his skeletal shoulders), Peter Barnes, William Blum, John Cavanagh, Jamie Court, Noam Chomsky, Charlie Cray, Kevin Danaher, Charles Derber, Lee Drutman, Michael Edwards, Riane Eisler, Ralph Estes, Thomas Friedman, Jeffrey Gates, Thom Hartmann, Bob Herbert, Jim Hightower, Si Kahn, Howard Karger, Marjorie Kelly, Naomi Klein, David Korten, Paul Krugman, Evelene Lubbers, Jerry Mander, Ian Marshall, Elizabeth Minnich, Russell Mokhiber, Ted Nace, Ralph Nader,

Richard Oxam, Doug Pogue, David Sirota, Roger Terry, Naomi Wolf, and Danah Zohar. But no one named here and/or in my footnotes can be blamed for any errors or misstatements that may be in this book. If any are, I apologize for them. And if I missed any other shoulders, I apologize to their owners.

Dedication

I dedicate this book to the idea and the practice of real democracy and to democracy power as a way for all truly patriotic and dedicated activists, social movements, and nongovernmental organizations working to get rid of the Devil's Marriage that has taken our democracy from us and harmed our general welfare.

Special Dedication

If Thomas Jefferson were to return today I bet he would praise the one person the last 50 years or so who has consistently tried to "crush moneyed corporations," Mr. Ralph Nader. This book is especially dedicated to him. Had he been elected president I would not have had to write this book.

PART ONE. INTRODUCTION

Chapter 1. The Current Corpocracy: An Overview

autocracy
bureaucracy
corpocracy
democracy
kleptocracy
mobocracy (yes, it's a word)
monocracy
plutocracy
technocracy
theocracy
timocracy

The word "corpocracy" hasn't made it yet into the dictionary, unlike the other "cracies," or into public conversations as far as I know.[1] "Cracy" is derived from the Greek "kartia" for power. The corpocracy exemplifies regime power, the getting of more and more of it and the continuous abuse of it in serving its own interests at a terrible cost to public interests and the common good. Power, but a very different kind of power, is also a defining characteristic of "democracy."

There is such an inherent conflict between these two "cracies" that they can't co-exist in the same nation and they don't coexist in America. In America the corpocracy rules with tyrannical-like power. The self-ruling democracy power of the people has been taken from the people.

The Devil's Marriage

Where did the power of the people go?
To a marriage made in Hell did it flow.
Leaving democracy in the lurch,
Jilting Americans and much worse.

A corpocracy, Professor Charles Derber writes, is a "marriage between big business and big government [that] turns a formally democratic government into a vehicle for corporate ends" and leaves the American people with a "pseudo-democracy" (he also refers to the corpocracy as a "corporate regime" to reflect corporations' marriage to government; in this book, except when I need to single out either corporations or the government, I will use the terms "regime" and "corpocracy" interchangeably so as to be less monotonous).[2] This professor, by the way, isn't "bookish." He once walked off the campus and out into the street to protest the war in Iraq, and once was booked and jailed briefly for civil disobedience in supporting the "janitors for justice" protest in Boston in 2002.[3] He has thus experienced first hand how the corpocracy can strangle civil liberties. If only most Americans, especially politicians, walked the principles Professor Derber walks.

Not a Shotgun Wedding

The marriage was anything but a shotgun wedding. It was a wedding for the sake of mutual "badvantages" (advantages for all sorts of bad behavior, legal and illegal). Both partners compromised (some critics might say "corrupted") each other. Both got huge, unending dowries. Corporations (most but not all are U.S. corporations) get almost on a daily basis "power and profit gifts" in the form of favorable legislation, favorable regulations and deregulations, favorable judicial verdicts, welfare handouts, impunity from lawlessness, military help in global exploitation, and laissez-faire capitalism. And what do the politicians get? The Capital Hill bunch (aka "Corporate Hill") gets career employment in plush offices. The oval office puppets get brief prestige and mostly posturing power. And the robed bench sitters for life get to rule in favor of the corporate interests that helped to get them appointed. The first dowry far overshadows the second but neither partner can afford a divorce. They will stick together through thick and thin.

Self-Rule: Not in a Corpocracy

Self-rule is synonymous with democracy. It represents both a moral and a practical balance between the anarchy of no governance, or extreme individualism, on the one hand, and totalitarianism, or oppressive governance, on the other. In Abraham Lincoln's view the legitimate role of government in a democracy "is to do for a community of people, whatever they need to have done, but can not do at all, or can not so well do, for themselves-in their separate and individual capacities." His view may have reflected his interpretation of the framers' intent in writing the U.S. Constitution that it would "provide for the common defense [and] promote the <u>general</u> welfare---." I underscore the qualifier "general" because the Constitution is also intended to "establish justice," and there can be no social and economic justice in America when the welfare of all her people is hugely and shamefully uneven.

Self-Rule and Our Life's Equations

In a true democracy people in all walks and stations of life have self-rule or as much control as possible over their life equations. You, me, everyone has the same general equation. It may just be the most important non-mathematical equation anyone will ever see in their lifetime:

Our Selves + Our Situations = Whether/How Much
Health, Happiness, and Prosperity
We Have or Don't Have

The first input is our particular personal characteristics such as our needs, experience, abilities, motivation, values, and the like. The second input is our situations. We all encounter several spheres of situations along our path through life; personal/social/cultural spheres, a political sphere, an economic sphere, and an environmental sphere.

In a true democracy the outputs on the right side amount to an optimum level of general welfare for all Americans, not just the wealthiest ones.

In a corpocracy, the equation is much different. The corpocracy has considerable power and control over most Americans' life's equations and thus their general welfare. Here is what the equation looks like today for all but the wealthiest Americans:

Our Selves + The Corpocracy = Much, Much Less
Health, Happiness, and Prosperity
For Most of Us

"Life, liberty, and the pursuit of happiness" and the "promotion of the general welfare" are more than "just" declarations of the sanctity and importance of our life's equations. It's an affirmation of humanity and support for the general welfare in a civilized society. It's also why the American Revolution was fought. History books don't explain it this way, but the revolutionaries were liberating their life's equations from the Crown's oppressive rule, the first corpocracy on our soil of an America about to be born.

Now let's return to "a community of people" in Abraham Lincoln's words. There are many situations in the different spheres of our lives that affect our general welfare but that are beyond our "separate and individual capacities," that is, beyond our personal inputs in our life's equations, to control how well or how badly those situations affect us. Wouldn't most people prefer a democratically elected and publically responsive government over a corpocracy to determine their general welfare that is beyond their separate and individual capacity to control? The corporate partner of the corpocracy, of course, doesn't care about the general welfare, only about corporate welfare. And the political partner cares only about catering to its corporate partner.

The Telltale Signs of the Corpocracy's Tyrannical Power

Our life's equation obviously is an abstraction. But the corpocracy and its tyrannical power are real, very real. How do we know? How can we be sure it's not just some half-baked conspiracy theory? Most of this book is about the corpocracy's real existence, how it operates, what harm it does to America and Americans, and what must be done about it, but for now please look over the "telltale" signs listed in Table 1. These are signs of the regime's takeover of our democracy and subjugation of all but the wealthiest Americans in every sphere of their lives.

6

Table 1
Tell Tale Signs of the Corpocracy's Domination

-Over Our Personal, Social, and Cultural Spheres-

- Ceaselessly promotes materialism and consumption.
- Dominates and manipulates the mass media.
- Spews propaganda, half truths, and zero truths.
- Prevents truly universal, more affordable health care.
- Commercializes and privatizes education.
- Trains our youth as vigilantes.
- Commercializes religion.
- Invades our privacy.
- Callously forecloses on our homes.
- Uproots homes for commercial development

-Over Our Economic Sphere-

- Prevents the people's general welfare.
- Loots the people's treasury.
- Over taxes the many, under taxes the few.
- Wrecks havoc with the American economy.
- Profits from Economic Katrina.
- Creates unconscionable income inequality.
- Creates spiraling levels of unemployment.
- Provides only substandard wages.
- Outsources work and takes it off shore.
- Emasculates worker unions.
- Creates monopolies and Big Box stores.
- Causes the collapse of small business firms.
- Abandons communities in bad times.
- Advertises falsely.
- Gouges consumers with excessive prices.
- Creates unsafe/unhealthy products.
- Privatizes and manipulates scarce resources.
- Manipulates international trade agreements.
- Commercially exploits poor nations.
- Privatizes and degrades public utilities.

- Starves and privatizes social services.
- Excessively promotes consumerism.
- Devours and bankrupts honorable companies.
- Escapes accountability for lawlessness.

-Over Our Political Sphere-.

- Hijacks our Constitution
- Buys politicians.
- Dominates Supreme Court rulings.
- Hand picks judges.
- Erects voter hurdles.
- Lobbies intensely for its own special interests.
- Installs special interest office holders.
- Always trumps public interests with corporate interests.
- Controls laws and regulations.
- Stonewalls government investigations.
- Scams state and local governments for subsidies.
- Promotes and profits from U.S. militarism.
- Privatizes the military.
- Privatizes law enforcement.
- Weakens true security in breeding dissent.

-Over Our Environmental Sphere-

- Treats natural resources as commodities and waste dumps.
- Pursues unsustainable development.

Calling the regime's powerful dominance "tyrannical" isn't an exaggeration and doesn't mean an "Orwellian" control that goes so far as to lock up minds to keep them from going where trapped bodies cannot. Nor does the corpocracy's tyranny require the guns of a ruthless dictatorship. Let's highlight a few of these signs to illustrate the corpocracy's tyranny over us.

Consider two in our personal, social, and cultural spheres. First, this one: "Ceaselessly promotes materialism and consumption." Corporate marketing departments and their relentless advertising have turned American wants into needs and have led American youth and adults like sheep to unsustainable spending and waste. Now, this second one: "Spews propaganda, half truths, and zero truths." Except for the totally shaped (read duped) minds of many Americans, does anyone else believe the corpocracy's line, constantly presented in the major news media, that Iraq was invaded to find WMDs?

Consider just the first, very broad sign in the economics sphere that basically says it all for the rest in this sphere, "Prevents the general welfare of the American people." The middle class, the backbone of any democracy, gets "screwed" by the "corporatocracy" in various ways says prolific author and radio host Thom Hartmann (e.g., looting of the Social Security Trust Fund, disproportionately higher taxes, shrinking wages, longer work hours, etc., etc.).[4] Furthermore, adds the distinguished professor of social welfare, Mark Rank, "a clear majority of Americans will experience poverty at some point during their lifetime."[5] He refutes the popular belief that poor people are primarily responsible for their own poverty. Poverty instead, he contends, "is largely the result of structural failings at the economic, political, and social levels," affects us all, and is thus "an issue of vital national concern."[6] We should blame the corpocracy, not poor, jobless people.

Now consider this sign in the political sphere: "Hijacks our Constitution." A day that will live in infamy in the eyes of advocates of true democracy was January 21, 2010 when the corporatized majority of the U.S. Supreme Court handed elected public offices over to the highest bidders by ruling that corporations, unions, and other organizations could not be denied their "constitutional right" to "free speech."[7] The ruling flies in the face of the fact that "corporations, unions, and other organizations' aren't even mentioned in the Constitution and its framers were suspicious of corporations. These "associations of citizens," as the Court disingenuously called them now have the right to spend millions of dollars to advertise for political candidates who favor their special interests and to advertise against candidates who don't. Since unions and other organizations are paupers compared to large corporations the land's highest court helped guarantee America's continued and "legal" submission to rule by the powerful corporations and the politicians they pick and "employ." All told, though, when it comes to physically endangering and harming Americans, corporate free speech is the least injurious of the ten or more Constitutional rights that have been falsely granted to corporations over time.

And finally, consider two in the environmental sphere: First, this one: "Treats natural resources as endless commodities and waste dumps." Do you know what's in your tap water or why we have avoidable ecological disasters like the BP runaway oil well? Now, this one: "Pursues unsustainable development." More is not better. Better is better. Pursuing more on a grand scale leaves an open and growing wound on Nature.

Why Independence Hasn't Been Declared Again

> ---when [there is] a long train of abuses and
> asurpations [designed to] reduce [the people]
> under absolute despotism, it is their right, it is
> their duty, to throw off such government,
> and to provide new guards for their future security.
> ---Declaration of Independence

If the American revolutionaries were to return today they would be revolted by today's regime and disgusted with us for not being modern-day revolutionaries first posting a Second Declaration of Independence from the corpocracy and then revolting against it. The corpocracy's current version has been acquiring and abusing power for nearly four decades. The accumulated damage done to America, Americans, and their environment by the corpocracy over that period is incomparably and incalculably greater than that suffered by the colonists under King George's regime.

Why then hasn't there been a popular uprising to "throw off" today's regime? Why hasn't there been a Second Declaration of Independence? There are both obvious and less obvious reasons why.

Strong Corpocracy, Weak Opposition

King George's troops, fighting far away on foreign soil to defend the Crown's Corpocracy, were no match for the colonists' opposition unified and fortified by General George Washington and his Revolutionary Army. In stark contrast, the weak and fragmented opposition to the corpocracy of today would be no match for whatever level and kind of counterforce the corpocracy would marshal to hold onto its power. More is said about the current status of the corpocracy's opposition in Chapter 3 and a proposal is offered in Chapter 4 for beefing up the opposition and giving it a strategic direction toward reclaiming democracy once and for all.

Only Half-Telling

In their entirety the signs should clearly tell us that we are being subjugated, that we have lost our self rule, that the corpocracy is exacting a heavy and daily toll on America and American's lives.

But the signs clearly aren't telling enough. They may be sending "half-signals" to people like the "Half-Mad Hatters" of the Tea Party people movement, mad about big government, excessive federal taxation, excessive federal expenditures, an expensive healthcare reform law, and a distrusted Congress, but who apparently don't seem to see who's doing most of the sign making, namely, the corporate partner of the regime.

Or Barely Telling or Not at All

The signs aren't eye catching and action getting like "DANGER, RADIOACTIVE LEAK AHEAD!" The Devil's Marriage is a metaphor, the corpocracy and the end of democracy are abstractions, and none is like news photos of a dead vagrant face up on a busy sidewalk; a very long bread line; body bags from the war front; etc.

The signs aren't seen by people for whom believing is seeing. War hawks, war profiteers, and jingoistic patriots ("my country right or wrong") see and interpret the signs differently from doves and true patriots ("my county, do right, no wrong").

The signs are "an inconvenient truth" denied by people who would otherwise feel threatened or helpless if they didn't deny seeing the signs or rationalize them away.

They aren't seen for what they are by people who compare America favorably to the world's most impoverished and totalitarian nations.

They aren't seen by people who have become accustomed to them, taking them for granted as just the normal workings of commerce and politics.

They aren't seen by people who haven't directly felt their effects; who haven't had loved ones injured or lost from unregulated and unpunished actions of industries or from warfare to protect and expand the regime's hegemony; who aren't jobless; who---. You get the point. Experience the signs, suffer and remember them (although without necessarily knowing their origins). Only read about them, see them on TV, shrug and forget them (and just "go shopping" advised the swaggering President Bush to Americans as he ordered the military to invade Iraq).

They aren't seen by people with a particular upbringing. In one of the most enlightening books I've ever read (and I've read hundreds in my lifetime), <u>The Real Wealth of Nations: Creating a Caring Economics</u>, its author Riane Eisler, who is both a scholar of first order, with formal schooling in sociology, anthropology, and law, and an activist of first order, writes about her research on societies dating back thousands of years (I draw extensively on Eisler's book as we go along). One of her conclusions is that children reared in a very dominating setting come to know life as being a choice between dominating and being dominated.[8] These are people deprived of a true sense and respect for freedom and the equal rights of others. The corpocracy to them is a normal way of life.

They aren't seen for what they are by people for whom the signs are ambiguous, their origin misunderstood or confusing. During the height of "Economic Katrina" that erupted in 2008, that still exists, and that is the greatest depression since the Great One, a poll was taken of Americans asking them whether the biggest threat to our country was big government or big business. Most of them fingered big government, likely having been bamboozled by decades of corporate stealth, deviousness, and propaganda. But big government was "merely" the enabling partner with its accommodating legislation, deregulations, lax monitoring, and judicial verdicts that all favored Wall Street over a span of four decades. The Wall Street branch of the corpocracy was the real instigator. A sadly humorous example of being confused, to put it politely, is the person at a town hall meeting who yelled at a Congressman to "keep your government hands off my Medicare" and wouldn't accept the reply that Medicare is already a government program.[9] A different and sadly tragic example of the misunderstood effects of grafting Constitutional rights onto corporations will be brought up in Chapter 7,

They aren't seen by people worn down, preoccupied by the daily grind of living, just trying to make ends meet, to keep or to get a job.

They aren't seen by many people because the corpocracy's takeover of America has been gradual and for the most part done stealthily since 1971.[10] There is no "corpocracy membership directory," no "corpocracy newsletter" no annual "corpocracy conventions." And the tyrants don't dress like Hitler, Stalin, or Mao.

They aren't seen by many people because the corpocracy obfuscates, double-speaks, and falsifies. Take the misleading "Clear Skies Initiative" and the "Clean Water Initiative." They were lobbied and drafted by one partner and legislated by the other, allowing continued and hazardous pollution of our air, water, and sewage systems.[11] In just a period of five years companies have violated even those lenient laws over 500,000 times with impunity![12] The most egregious example by far though is the regime's propagandizing of its militarism and war making. We are not told that it is usually done to protect and expand corporate interests and to keep fear mongering politicians with their defense contract giveaways in office. Instead we are told about foreign enemies (every regime needs them) threatening our national security and are exhorted to be patriotically loyal (and submissive).

They aren't seen by people who didn't live during the most recent of the earlier corpocracies and who don't know their American history. The unvarnished truth about America is not to be found in corporatized school books.

They aren't seen by many people because they don't see the regime being hauled off to jail. Corrupt politicians are basically untouchable (except by the corrupters). And "our" government rarely imprisons corporate criminals and lets off criminal corporations with affordable fines if any are imposed and collected at all. Furthermore, most corporate wrongdoing is made perfectly legal by one or more of "our" three branches of government. Additionally, people see that there are many countries more corrupt and oppressive than the U.S. What they neglect to realize or acknowledge is that they are judging the U.S. on a comparative standard of "rotten apples in the world's barrel" rather than on an absolute standard of what a true democracy means.

And finally, they may be seen by people who are fatalistic, believe that matters must get worse before they get better and that America always recovers from its worst times, or who leave the problem's solution up to other people or to future generations.

While an increasing number of Americans are fed up with government, they aren't yet aware of or fed up with the primary sign maker, the corporate partner. I could go on and on about how real the "telltale" signs are but I will save the evidence for other chapters to come.

A Tacit Conspiracy
Not a Public Wedding

The marriage was not a public wedding. It was more like a tacit conspiracy between government and large corporations. Actually, there is another conspiracy, too, the one that exists throughout the corporate domain itself, within industries if not also among individual corporations themselves. To act together toward common goals is one definition of a "conspiracy."

And what are the conspirators' goals? To name a few: keeping its marriage intact; staying for a lifetime in public office; protecting corporations' fraudulent constitutional rights, not citizen rights; ensuring legislation, regulations, and judicial verdicts that protect corporate interests, not the public's interests or the general welfare; keeping the government's plentiful and endless hand outs; privatizing public services; controlling the mass media; keeping the marketplace free, not fair; and to expanding and protecting a profitable hegemony in other lands (corporations want global markets and politicians want global influence).

Being a conspiracy doesn't automatically mean the conspirators must operate secretly, although as I've said they obviously aren't going to publicize their conspiring. That being so, how do we know they conspire among themselves? There is plenty of sobering evidence. Corporations in the same industries and across industries often march in lock step together when they feel threatened or see opportunities for mutual gain through collaboration. Consider some examples.[13] First, the defense industry pushed for preemptive war with Iraq before Bush Jr.'s first administration and then was heavily represented among the war policy makers in the administration. Second there is the oil industry's secret collusion with the government on oil policies. Third, the National Association of Manufacturers launched a massive campaign to squelch lawsuits against manufacturers' for damages caused by their products. Fourth, perhaps nothing unites the corpocracy more than that of its bête noir, the labor unions, as witness their fierce lobbying against the Employee Free Choice Act. Fifth, witness the intense lobbying by the health insurance industry against any reform of health insurance.

There are also many venues crossing industrial sectors and even across continents that provide ample opportunity for schmoozing, conniving, and conspiring. Two prominent domestic venues are the Business Roundtable and the interlocking network of CEO corporate directors. Then there are international venues such as the Transatlantic Business Dialogue, the World Economic Forum, the World Bank, the International Monetary Fund, the World Trade Organization, the G8 club, and the ultra secret Bilderberg. Penetrating the CIA would be easier than getting inside Bilderberg. It is where the world's power elite meet annually.

Is the Corpocracy Turning America into a Fascist State?

Fascism should more properly be called corporatism because it is the merger of state and corporate power.

--- Benito Mussolini.

The liberty of a democracy is not safe if the people tolerate the growth of private power to a point where it becomes stronger than their democratic State itself. That, in its essence, is Fascism—ownership of government by an individual, by a group or by any controlling private power.

---FDR

These two people, Mussolini and FDR, certainly knew what fascism is. Mussolini presided over Fascist Italy. FDR went head to head with the Robber Barons and then not much later with the Fascists. His quote appears to characterize today's regime in America.[14] We are no Nazi Germany, but it also had its own corpocracy. Were it not for the support of its industrialists wanting to quash organized labor and to profit from the rearmament of Germany, Hitler's Third Reich might never have materialized.[15]

Naomi Wolf knows what fascism is. She was the political consultant to the Clinton and Gore presidential campaigns. She studied the history of Nazi Germany, and in her book, End of America, draws numerous parallels from the Third Reich to what has been happening in America; the recruiting, training, and deploying of a paramilitary force; the reliance on the threat of enemies to terrify, distract, and control the public; the surveillance of American citizens; the harassment of citizen groups; the targeting of individual citizens; the gagging of the press; the building and operation of an extra-legal prison system and the like.[16]

The Corpocracy's Allies

Touts and Shills
Cults Small and Large
Foreign Enemies
The Silent Majority

The regime has many allies it can depend on to further its interests: the touts and shills; the cultists; foreign enemies; and indirectly, the silent majority.

The Touts and Shills

They are a motley lot and the difference between a tout and a shill isn't always clear cut. Touts (that's what Winston Churchill called lobbyists) are hired and paid outside government to swarm inside and lobby it for the corpocracy, but politicians who are touted go along with it to stay in office. Anyone, any organization, any association can be a shill for the partnership. Even politicians or judges can be shills. As a matter of fact, if you want to call government the biggest shill I won't disagree with you.

A shill's focus is usually not as laser beamed as a tout's. Shills generally offer paeans to the corpocracy and its conservative, free-market ideological underpinnings. Think of shrill shills like ideologically blinded, ranting and raving radio talk show hosts as an extreme example. Touts, on the other hand, concentrate on getting specific power gifts for particular corporate members of the corpocracy, be they a particular corporation or a particular industry.

Would you consider the U.S. Chamber of Commerce a tout and shill? It's been called the "goliath of the lobbying world," making Big Pharma look like a piker.[17] From 1998 to 2007 the USCC reportedly spent nearly $370 million on lobbying expenses compared to Big Pharma's $127 million or so (and I don't think the source of these figures accounted for campaign financing).[18] Here's what the USCC has said about itself:

> Our core mission is to fight for business
> and free enterprise before Congress, the
> White House, regulators, the court of
> public opinion, and governments around
> the world.
>
> ---www.uschamber.com

Predictably, the USCC hailed the January 21, 2010 decision by the U.S. Supreme Court. "Today's ruling," said the executive vice president of the chamber's litigation center, "protects the First Amendment rights of organizations across the political spectrum, and is a positive for the political process and free enterprise."[19] Does he really mean the rights of organizations across the political spectrum or the rights of powerful and wealthy corporations to select and to dominate politicians?

The USCC reflexively and routinely opposes taxation, big government, and regulation.[20] In 2009 "its legislative priorities" were opposing a consumer financial-agency, a shareholder bill of rights, 'flawed health care proposals,' and a government cap-and-trade environmental proposal.[21] Its fight for business and free enterprise is downright impressive I have to admit. It knows how to win in court; although it's usually a business-friendly court to be sure. In one court term alone the Chamber filed before the U.S. Supreme Court not one but 15 friend of the court briefs.[22] Can you guess how many of the cases went the 15 friends' way? No, not all of them, just two short of all. I haven't bothered to look into those two, but I would guess they were shot down on technical grounds, certainly not on judicial/ideological grounds.

The USCC is very active during presidential elections. Its president reportedly said that his organization was planning to spend on the 2008 presidential election more than the $60 million it had spent on the last presidential election, that he was "concerned about anti-corporate and populist rhetoric from candidates for the presidency and about members of Congress and the media," and that he didn't plan to disclose any more than legally necessary the sources and beneficiaries of the funds to be distributed, arguing that "we are exercising our constitutional right to petition the government and we will continue to do so."[23] His remarks warrant two comments. First, he is right about USCC's constitutional "rights" (I call them "wrongs in Chapter 7), but only for as long as the infamous, corporate-friendly U.S. Supreme Court ruling of January 21, 2010 is not overturned (but it could be overturned eventually since the justices were bitterly divided five to four). Second, the USCC needs to be sure it does indeed legally disclose its "sources and beneficiaries" of the funds it distributes. The NGO, US Chamber Watch, recently filed a suit claiming that the USCC "violated tax codes by laundering millions of dollars meant for charitable work."[24] This relatively new watchdog group has strong union backing to scrutinize every questionable move of its adversary. The USCC, naturally, denies any wrongdoing in this case.

Shills that I'll lump together include: talking-head pundits and the rabble rousers shouting into a mike; "Erudites" squirreled away in think tanks authoring corporate gospel; and "front" groups, whose purpose is to mask corporate intent and consequences and call them what they are not.[see,e.g.25] Then there are in varying shades of shill the business and law schools that mint the new recruits for the managerial and executive ranks throughout the corpocracy and supply it with lawyers paid well to argue the legality of any corporate action no matter how harmful to our general welfare.[26]

The Cult of Growth

One of the most insidious cults is the "cult of growth," preferably fast growth, every quarter. The cultists in it generally aren't shrill shills but their views on and promotion of unbridled growth sometimes go to the extreme and the actions sometimes condoned for achieving growth go to the extreme. In this cult are mostly mainstream economists, management gurus, and speculative investors and their brokers. There is even a politically activist organization called the "Club of Growth" that is for bridled taxes and unbridled growth."[27]

Rapid and sizeable financial growth whether in terms of the economy as a whole, particular industries, specific corporations, or personal wealth, is seen as necessary and good. In reality much of financial growth is a euphemism for greed and a rationalization for all sorts of actions that may be on the right side of the law most of the time but are on the wrong side of ethics most of the time. This cult fuels much of the corpocracy's abuse of power by reinforcing speculative investing and a kind of "economic insanity."[28]

The Cult of the Cons

People in this cult are conservatives on the fringe but metastasizing. They mostly occupy the right wing of the once proud Republican Party that called Abraham Lincoln its first U.S. President.[29] This Party has become, says the Nobel laureate in economics, Paul Krugman, a strident group of malcontents "acting out of pure spite like a 'bratty 13-year-old.'"[30]

Cons spew provocative and deceitful exhortations and slogans (e.g., "let's reload," "don't tread on me," "freedom works"). They are against government solutions, particularly social welfare (so miserly it is dwarfed by corporate welfare) and, says another critic, are "endlessly worried that one's neighbor may be getting more than his or her 'fair' share."[31] They perpetuate the myth that people on the dole want to be on the dole and like staying there. They apparently want public services that benefit only them tangibly and want to be barely taxed for them. They regard any government efforts to improve our general welfare as totalitarianism or socialism. They call efforts to require physicians to counsel terminally ill patients "death panels."[32]

Consider two cons who have been in the slime light recently. A lieutenant governor running for governor on the con's slate recently "likened government assistance to the poor to feeding stray animals" and causing them to breed more.[33] A millionaire candidate running for governor of New York on the con's ticket in November 2010 reportedly has the Tea Party's backing and wants to "transform some New York prisons into dormitories for welfare recipients, where they could work in state-sponsored jobs, get employment training and take lessons in 'personal hygiene.'"[34] The aspiring governor seems to be thinking ahead of the corpocracy that is privatizing prisons as fast as it can, to creating a miniature Prison State. What next?

Wondering what makes malcontent cons tick I searched the literature looking for their psychological makeup (PMU). I found it in a big study of many smaller studies spanning 50 years. While there are always caveats about most research findings, a 50-year trail that doesn't detour would seem to lead straight to a durable conclusion; namely, cons by and large (there are always individual exceptions) and wherever they are (cons from 12 different countries were studied) resist change, are fearful, are aggressive, are tolerant of inequality to the extent of even endorsing it, are dogmatic, are intolerant of ambiguity and uncertainty, are hostile to outsiders, and are more comfortable with simplicity than with complexity.[35]

If this PMU is really true, PU! It's repugnant. But cons weren't totally born that way and I can imagine some of them have been duped along the way by the corpocracy and its demagogues. I'm convinced, moreover, that some cons at least could rejoin the kinder, more caring part of the human race if they chose to do so. Meanwhile, if the "Repugnantlican Party" should regain "control" of Congress, it will become even more subservient to powerful corporate interests that give lip service to democracy while being contemptuous of and harmful to the general welfare of the American people. I hasten to add that whenever the "Damnocratic Party" has "controlled" Congress" the slavish catering to the corporate member of the corpocracy has not diminished one iota. Neither of these two servile political parties control Congress; powerful corporate interests control Congress (and the White House, and the U.S. Supreme Court, and state capitals, legislatures, and judiciary). And it will forever be that way until we organize and activate a powerful opposition to the corpocracy.

Foreign Enemies

Professor Derber contends that "---today's regime "can survive only by practicing a foreign policy of bad faith that [he calls] 'marry-your-enemy.'"[36] Wars, hot and cold, military interventions, military occupations, and military base installations have been a staple of every one of America's four regimes. From 1893 to 1934 the U.S. occupied numerous foreign lands; some U.S. corporations collaborated with the Nazis; and since the end of WWII the U.S. has engaged in almost countless attempts and actual overthrows of legitimate governments as well as populist activists fighting against their own repressive regimes.[37]

A regime gets by with all this blatant militarism and needless bloodshed by scaring the American people with fear mongering, half truths and outright lies (or very bad judgment by President Obama in his military escalations), by evoking jingoistic patriotism, by blathering about building nations, and by slandering peace seekers as weaklings soft on the enemy. During the Cold War, for example, telling the American people there was an imminent threat of communism spreading to our Southern Hemisphere was sufficient cover for the regime to overturn legitimate governments, install brutal dictators, and protect and expand corporate interests there. Another regime tactic is relying on a voluntary armed service and secret operatives to blunt American opposition. The Iraqi and Afghanistan Wars would not have been started had there been a military service draft in place. Now, our war makers are secretly conducting "shadow wars" in dozens of countries.[38]

What is the point of all the killing, all the squandering of American money and goodwill, all the risking of more revengeful attacks reaching our own homeland? The point is simply and starkly this. Regime militarism fattens the defense industry, including beefing up its sale of arms (the U.S. is the world's top arms seller); opens up, protects, and expands corporations' foreign markets and exploitation of natural resources (oil and minerals) and cheap labor; keeps regime politicians in office; and distracts the American public from growing socioeconomic deterioration at home. With the exception of the Vietnam War ending President Johnson's political career, the personal costs to the regime's protected elite in their warring have been minimal. No corporate executive or public official I've heard of from the current regime has ever died on the battlefield. When they visit it for photo ops and whatnot they are heavily protected. During the Bush administration a member of a Congressional delegation's visit to an Iraqi bazaar said on TV "It is like any open-air market in Indiana in the summertime." Well, not really Congressman. You were wearing a flak jacket and surrounded by a mass of U.S. soldiers, and the day after you left 21 bazaar workers were kidnapped and executed.[39] What did you think of that Congressman? Did it cause you a few sleepless nights or did you go on being a politician as usual?

Sometimes America's enemies aren't directly cultivated by the regime but are an unintended consequence of its policies and actions, and yet the defense industry, the military establishment, and the career politicians still benefit. The origin of the terrorist groups, Al Qaeda and the Taliban, for instance, can be traced at least in part to the regime's overbearing and longstanding presence and exploitation in their lands. I can't imagine the regime having planned behind closed doors to create these terrorist groups. To do so would be a blatantly treasonous act (whether other war-related acts of the corpocracy seem treasonous I will leave up to your judgment). Some members of Congress have reportedly "invested in businesses in terror-sponsored states (treasonous?)."[40] Some have reportedly invested in companies profiting from the Iraqi war (treasonous?), causing one peace activist to exclaim, "No wonder we can't end the war!"[41] As columnist Frank Rich has noted, "---if there's to be a witch hunt for traitors, the top of our government is where it should begin."[42] Mr. Rich, are you calling a spade a spade?

The Silent Majority

Even if the silent majority saw the telltale signs as warning signs, what are the options? Write the administration and Congress? I naively tried several times and got nowhere. Vote for Democrats instead of Republicans? How much of a difference has there really been over the years? It's a shade of degree not kind between the two. They have both sold out America and her democracy for the sake of their political careers. Vote for another party? Which one? A winnable one has yet to materialize.

Is America Becoming a RuiNation?

All of the corpocracy's telltale signs taken together tell us that America is on the path to becoming a "ruiNation." Think not? Look again at the signs. Then read the rest of this book and maybe also do the reading I have done to help me write it (see the references in the Notes).

Among my readings have been the writings by some distinguished journalists and columnists like Paul Krugman and Bob Herbert. They, unlike shrieking and ideologically blinded radio hosts and writers of free-market screeds, are people who objectively and intelligently report on what they see happening in and to America. Their views are foreboding. Mr. Krugman observes that decades of antigovernment rhetoric spreading myths about social welfare queens and slothful government are taking America on the "road to nowhere."[43] Mr. Herbert observes that "the nation as we've known it is fading before our very eyes" as we pour billions after billions into "wars, endless wars" and that the Afghanistan War has become "a giant roadblock in the way of efforts to deal effectively with deteriorating economic and social conditions ---; [just] Look around at the economy, the public school system, the federal budget deficits, the fiscal conditions plaguing America's state and local governments."[44] Wars, endless wars in my opinion are the one single feature of the corpocracy most likely to ruin America.

Is it conceivable that the regime will eventually overplay its hand and the telltale signs will demand attention? Derber believes the regime's demise like that of the earlier corpocracies is eventually inevitable, being done in by its own excesses and the damage they do.[45] If that should happen this time, though, it will be a pyrrhic victory that also ends America as a viable nation. The end of the corpocracy by its own excesses could very well be catastrophic. Derber, by the way, is not saying that we should just wait and let the corpocracy self destruct. He is not waiting. As we shall see in Chapter 4 he is still an activist for democracy and against the corpocracy.

How Can We Break Up the Devil's Marriage?
A Preview of Chapters to Come

Organize the Opposition
Tell the People

Close the Corpocracy's Political/Judicial Circus
Dig Up the Corpocracy's Legal Roots
End Hands-Off Corporate Criminals
End Hand-Outs to the Corporate Welfare Queen
End Undemocratic Capitalism
Unleash Your Democracy Power

If the corpocracy's political, legislative, judicial, and economic badvantages were to be eliminated, the corpocracy would collapse without a shot having been fired. Most of the rest of this book is about how to eliminate them.

Some Closing Memory Ticklers and One Liners

"Corpocracy" isn't in the dictionary yet but is everywhere else.

Between extreme individualism and totalitarianism is democratic self-rule.

The marriage made in Hell wasn't a shotgun wedding; it was for mutual badvantages.

The marriage left the American people and their democracy in the lurch.

The corpocracy has taken over our life equations.

Let's call Capital Hill, Corporate Hill.

The corpocracy's telltale signs aren't telling most Americans anything, yet.

Jingoistic patriots ("my country right or wrong")

True patriots ("my county, do right, no wrong").

Experience it, suffer and loath it. Read it, shrug and forget it, and just go shopping.

The Tea Party: Half-Mad Hatters.

The double conspiracy; double paranoia or double reality?

Corporations want global markets and politicians want global influence.

What Mussolini and FDR said about Fascism sound like America today.

The USCC; can't beat their victories in the high (low) court, but victories for whom?

In varying shades of corpocracy shilling, business and law schools that mint new recruits.

Name the group that's for bridled taxes and unbridled growth.

The PMU of the cons is PU!

The "Repugnantlican Party?" The "Damnocratic Party?"

Enemies as allies? Yes, enemies as allies.

Members of Congress doing business with terror-sponsoring states?

End the corpocracy or let it turn America into a ruiNation.

Chapter 2. Earlier Corpocracies: A Review

1. The Crown's Corpocracy (Until 1776)
   1. Democracy
2. The Robber Baron's Corpocracy (1865-1901)
   2. Democracy
3. The Flapper Era Corpocracy (1921-1933)
   3. Democracy
4. The Cold War Era Corpocracy (1950-1980s)
5. The Current Corpocracy (1970s-Continuing)

Scoreboard is Stuck: Corpocracy 5, Democracy 3

The history of America is an episodic one, alternating between the rule of the corpocracy and the rule of democracy. The current corpocracy is by far the most omnipotent, omnipresent, and dangerous of all and shows no signs of relinquishing its power to a fourth rendition of democracy. This chapter gives a very, very short account of the rounds so far.

The Crown's Corpocracy

While this regime can't be counted as an American one, had it not existed America might not have been born. It is so ironic that the 1776 revolutionaries were not only revolting against the Crown but also against a miniature regime. Among its more notable members were the trading companies such as the Massachusetts Bay Company, the East India Company, and the Virginia Company. Four of the thirteen colonies in

America were actually established as trading corporations chartered by the Crown to help subsidize England's European wars and to yield profitable returns to British investors by monopolizing trade. This beginning was sort of a template for the subsequent regimes.

The biggest investors at the beginning weren't exactly the most "noble" of character; one of them, for example, had major interests in a piracy business. Nor were the corporations' British managers sympathetic to the hardships of the colonists in their simply trying to survive in a new and hostile environment. These managers were oppressive and ruthless in running their overseas operations. The most ruthless may have been the Virginia Company. It was called a "prison without walls" by the "gentleman" who promoted investments in the company.[1] Again, the Virginia Company was sort of a template for American corporations to follow.

It's hardly surprising that the Crown's taxes, import duties, and oppressive trading companies triggered the Boston Tea Party and shortly thereafter the American Revolution. Now that's one way to get rid of a regime! But it wasn't gone for long. Thomas Jefferson could see it stirring and told Americans:

> I hope we shall crush in its birth the aristocracy
> of our moneyed corporations which dare already
> to challenge our government to a trial of strength
> and bid defiance to the laws of our country.
> ---Thomas Jefferson

The Robber Barons' Corpocracy

> Corporations have been enthroned....An era
> of corruption in high places will follow. . .
> and the Republic is destroyed.
> ---Abraham Lincoln

Fourteen U.S. presidents later, the 16th one, Abraham Lincoln, made this dire prophecy shortly before his death. He was in effect foretelling America's first corpocracy of its very own, what Professor Charles Derber has called the "Robber Barons' regime."[2] The spoils of the Civil War had enriched its profiteers and political corruption had greased the way for the new industrialist tycoons to consolidate and expand their power.

They were called robber barons for their ruthless and rapacious business practices. They established the first true American regime. Through generous donations to no less than six U.S. presidents and the creation of the first powerful lobbies in Washington to pressure and lather Congress the Robber Barons and their corporations got in return subsidies, protective tariffs, protected cartels, and government suppression of labor unrest.[3]

But the robber barons overplayed their hand during an economic downturn, creating a public backlash and causing a new president, Theodore Roosevelt, to establish a Bureau of Corporations to regulate industry. He also took the unprecedented step of bringing anti-trust suits against more than 40 major corporations, deservedly earning the lasting reputation as the trust-busting president.

The Flapper Era Corpocracy

Hardly a decade after the trust buster left office the regime came roaring back in the 1920's with the Harding, Cooledge, and Hoover administrations in tow, giving the corpocracy carte blanche through laissez faire market policies except, of course, whenever an uncooperative market prompted the corpocracy to demand hands-on help from its government partner such as deregulation, the sending of federal troops to quell civil unrest, the lowering of surtaxes, and the establishment of yet more protective tariffs.

Up until Black Tuesday near the end of the decade when Wall Street crashed, the regime thrived from an expanding economy and the continued succoring from a complicit and compliant government. The excesses of those good times for the wealthy minority of the nation precipitated the Great Depression, followed by FDR's New Deal domestic policies and crack down on the regime. Even during WWII he didn't allow the defense industry sector to reassert itself. He imposed strict controls on it for the sake of the war effort. No president since then has done that in times of international conflict and war.

The Cold War Corpocracy

Less than a full-blown regime existed in the cold war period. The U.S. had three major enemies during this period, the Soviet Union, North Korea, and North Vietnam. This period was very beneficial to one particular part of the corpocracy, the defense industry, and to politicians who fanned the public's fears and parlayed defense funding into their reelections, an addictive habit that never ceases.[4] The period spanned four consecutive U.S. presidents, Eisenhower, Kennedy, Johnson, and Nixon. Their administrations, members of Congress, and the defense industry proceeded lockstep in promoting, justifying, and benefitting from the cold war and the two hot ones. When the final verdict of history is in, the Cold War period may very likely be judged America's darkest (with today's regime and its militarism arguably a close second), a time when the defense industry and the politicians shamefully fed off of each other at the risk of nuclear warfare, at the expense of many lives in other homelands spent in deviously justifying the halting of creeping Communism, and at the expense of other monumental costs to America, Americans, and America's good will internationally.

A Tobacco Road Lawyer's Legacy- The Current Corpocracy

Meanwhile, except for the defense industry, the bulk of the regime had never recovered from FDR, whom it loathed worse than any foreign enemy, for he and the U.S. Supreme Court of his time couldn't be high jacked and his New Deal policies were put firmly in place. But the upholders of democracy were completely caught off-guard by what was to transpire next, the emergence of the fifth regime, which Derber refers to as the regime of "born-again robber barons."[5]

It began with a wake-up call in 1971 to a moribund big business and to wealthy conservatives from a most unusual source. Lewis F. Powell was at the time a successful tobacco industry lawyer who specialized in securities laws and who had also been president of the American Bar Association. A staunch advocate of keeping government out of the affairs of business he had become alarmed over what he perceived to be a pervasive assault on the free enterprise system from the gamut of public institutions and the liberal elements of the public itself. Big business, he fretted, was taking the assault lying down.

So he wrote a memorandum, eventually dubbed Powell's "manifesto," to the U.S. Chamber of Commerce proposing that it lead a counterattack.[6] Business, he wrote, was "ill-equipped to conduct guerrilla warfare with those who propagandize against the system, seeking insidiously and constantly to sabotage it" and "have shown little stomach for hard-nose contest with their critics." He went on to lay out what amounted to a "battle plan," apparently to help business conduct "guerilla warfare."

He suggested numerous strategies targeting four major American institutions: education, the media, the political arena, and the courts. The strategies were all very aggressive. A few on paper at least seem militant and even paranoid and Orwellian in nature, to wit: It is "a long road and not for the fainthearted." "There should be no hesitation to attack [those] who openly seek destruction of the system." "There must be "constant surveillance of textbooks" and "monitoring of national television networks." Does that read like it's coming right out of some Orwellian pages?

This ideologue and corporate lawyer would become just a few months after firing off his manifesto a justice of the U.S. Supreme Court. Just think of that, a person like Powell taking a seat on the bench of the land's highest (or is it the lowest?) court. The Senate had been derelict in vetting Powell during the confirmation hearings, and even Powell had acknowledged years later to his biographer that he did not expect to be confirmed because of his close links to business (that was certainly putting it mildly). Powell joined the Burger Court that had just a few years earlier succeeded the liberally oriented Warren Court. It had favored citizen over corporate rights and very possibly influenced Powell in writing his manifesto about the courts.

His manifesto has rightly been called a "remarkable document, forming the seminal plan for one of the most successful political counterattacks in American history."[7] It triggered a tacit conspiracy of new conservative think tanks, conservatively activist legal centers and an awakened, alarmed, and determined corporate America that all worked together to achieve what former journalist Jerry Landay called the "greatest power grab."[8] And I would add that Powell demonstrated without a doubt the power of one. But the power grab could never have happened without a submissive government partner, beginning with the Carter administration and continuing with all successive administrations to this day.

So ends Part One, giving us an overview of the current corpocracy and a review of its earlier versions throughout the course of our history. What will be America's future? It will be very bleak unless America follows a Powell-like manifesto in reverse that unfolds in Part Two and Part Three.

Some Closing Memory Ticklers and One Liners

Corpocracy 5, Democracy 3.

And the scoreboard is stuck.

"Prison without Walls," Virginia Bay Co. then, America today?

Thomas Jefferson hoped moneyed corporations would be crushed.

Abraham Lincoln said we would be destroyed by corporations and corruption.

What would you pick as America's darkest period?

A tobacco road lawyer's memo jumpstarted today's regime.

So don't doubt the power of one.

Letting history continue repeating itself will end America.

PART TWO. THE CORPOCRACY'S OPPOSITION

Chapter 3. Where's Today's Opposition?

E Pluribus Unum: The corpocracy
E Pluribus Pluribus: The opposition

E Pluribus Unum, "out of many one," was the motto adopted by Congress in 1782 to symbolize the unity between the states and the federal government. It now symbolizes the unified diversity of the many different corporations and their industries and their union with "our" government to form the corpocracy. E Pluribus Pluribus, "out of many, many," symbolizes the status of the corpocracy's opposition. As long as this status continues so too will the corpocracy. It knows fully well that a divided opposition is a conquered opposition.

The Divided Opposition of NGOs

Because "our" government has failed so spectacularly to uphold democracy numerous <u>non</u>-governmental organizations or NGOs have surfaced over the last several decades (and more continue to pop up now and then) to oppose the corpocracy They pursue their objectives through a variety of initiatives such as educational programs, litigation, lobbying (miniscule compared to the corpocracy's lobbyists), organizing protests of one form or another, organizing political campaigns, and mobilizing supporters.

In browsing the websites of many NGOs I found 150 or so that seemed to warrant a closer look (see Appendix A for some of them). I then looked at their types and memberships, their funding sources and budgets (when published), the issues they address, their missions, their activities, and whether NGOs with similar issues, missions, and activities ever collaborate with or even talk to each other.

The NGOs vary considerably in their size. The smallest NGOs may have only a handful or more members. Some of the smallest ones don't last very long. They come and go. The largest ones have a million or more members and supporters. One, for example, has several million. But being large doesn't necessarily mean that the NGO's project initiatives are enduring or successful. They also come and go.

The smallest NGOs usually have the smallest budgets but not always. One very small NGO, for instance, posted a multi-million dollar budget. Many, however, seem to be operating on shoe-string budgets. Funding for expenses comes from individual donations or dues, foundation grants, and sometimes from the sale of products such as books, promotional materials, and the like. NGOs sometimes are desperate for funds after conducting expensive campaigns. I got an e-mail solicitation from one NGO saying it was over $1 million dollars in debt.

When I looked to see if NGOs with similar objectives coordinated their efforts or even collaborated on them, I found that in many instances NGOs didn't even acknowledge the existence of other NGOs having similar objectives. Unlike the corpocracy with its unified diversity, these NGOs are long on diversity and short on unity. There are a few exceptions where NGOs come together as ad hoc alliances or coalitions to achieve specific goals but generally they pursue their own agendas.[1] Had General George Washington's troops been as scattered and divided as today's NGOs are we would still be subjects of the Crown.

So the corpocracy has withstood the best shots the various and sundry NGOs have thrown at it over these many years. Yet, I'm not disparaging what accomplishments there have been by these hard working, genuinely patriotic, and conscientious NGOs. If they didn't exist we'd very likely have even a bigger and more powerful regime today. At the same time, though, it won't be ended if the NGOs don't get their acts together or unless some other alternative, formidable opposition emerges. The best the NGOs have done so far perhaps is to keep the regime from getting more omnipotent and omnipresent. Moreover, as the NGOs press ahead fragmented as they are they will be ill-equipped to counteract new defensive and offensive moves the regime will be certain to initiate whenever it is seriously challenged.

In the following quote, there is a stricken noun for you to guess and to guess who wrote the whole passage:

> ---independent and uncoordinated activity
> by individual xxxxxxxxxxxxx as important
> as this is, will not be sufficient. Strength
> lies in national organization, in planning,
> in unified action that is consistent and
> sustained for an indefinite period of time.
> ---Source temporarily hidden

The passage was not written by any prominent NGO spokesperson. There are only four letters in "NGOs." It was written by Lewis F. Powell in his infamous manifesto I've already mentioned (it's nearly impossible when the subject is the corpocracy not to mention his name, his manifesto, or his legacy). And what is the stricken noun? He was referring to individual "corporations."[2] Powell understood well the need for E Pluribus Unum among the scattered corporations of his day.

If I were to write a comparable manifesto (this book is sort of like one) to a counterpart national chamber (coming up shortly) and substitute in Powell's paragraph, *individual NGOs* for *individual corporations,* we can begin to see the challenge ahead in trying to end the corpocracy and reclaim democracy.

United Workers: A Bygone Era

Organized labor in its heyday helped to blunt the corpocracy's abusive power. That was some time ago. Although unions are partly to blame for their decline, it not coincidentally parallels the rise of the current corpocracy over the same period of time. The corpocracy's privatizing, outsourcing, off shoring, massive lay offs, legal stiffing, and worker intimidation have decimated unions. Today they represent only latent or potential opposition against the corpocracy and they couldn't prevail singlehandedly in any case simply because of the corpocracy's stranglehold on the country.

Grassroots Movements: Mostly Scattered in Back Yards

A totalitarian state is top-down rule by autocratic rulers. A democratic state is bottom-up rule by the populace loaning the power to be ruled by democratically elected leaders from the populace. The corpocracy, of course, is mostly like the former, with two tightly connected sources of power, one from big government, one from big business. The populace gets ruled by both and squeezed darn-near lifeless in between.

Grassroots movements are democracy in action, not democracy inaction. They usually start out and stay small-scale, limited to specific "back yard" issues that concern local communities or regions because their life equations are being adversely affected. If you were to catalogue all of the grassroots movements existing today you would need a lot of time unless you let someone else do it for you like I did. I found a long list already made of them and a plea from the compiler; "Please help alphabetize a few of these each time this list is edited."[3] I imagine the list would change/grow almost daily if there were a full-time compiler on duty.

One small movement gaining momentum and grabbing the headlines today is the "Tea Party" that I mentioned in the first chapter. They are mad about big government taking over their lives and being "Taxed Enough Already." These dissidents are able to mobilize speedily via the Internet protest groups around the country.[4] An offshoot of this loosely knit movement is the NGO, Tea Party Patriots, Inc., "a non-partisan, non-profit social welfare (emphasis mine) organization dedicated to furthering the common good and general welfare of the people of the United States." Their motto is "Ordinary citizens reclaiming America's founding principles."[5] As I already have said, the Tea Party people are "Half-Mad Hatters" in my mind because they ought to be even madder at the other half of the marriage made in Hell. If that point could be driven home to these people and they really are dedicated to furthering the common good (and not just the good of angry, disaffected pale-faced Americans) and reclaiming America's founding principles they might become very vocal and very active opponents of the whole corpocracy. Anything conceivable may be possible but probably not in the Tea Party's case as you will gather from what Charles Derber has to say in the next chapter.

Occasionally in our history grassroots movements have gone beyond the fringes and snowballed or fused into larger and wider movements such as the civil rights movement, the anti-Vietnam War protest movement, the women's equal rights movement, the labor movement, the consumer movement, the anti-globalization movement, the gay rights movement, the anti-abortion movement, and the environmental movement. They arose when more people gradually realized that troubling issues either adversely affected their life's equations too or were otherwise too widely consequential to be ignored. There is today no comparable social movement capable of seriously challenging today's corpocracy with the possible exception of the loosely knit anti-globalization movement (more about it in Chapters 4 and 10). Its sentiments and actions are against large multinational corporations, many of which are headquartered in the U.S.

State Power: A Risky, Unlikely Proposition

We have 50 states and only one United States. Could the 50 be a launching ground for reclaiming democracy for the entire nation? Joel Rogers thinks so. "Who controls state politics," he asserts, "controls American politics" (he seems to have left out the other marriage partner).[6] He is a professor of law, political science, and sociology at the University of Wisconsin and is also the director of the NGO, Center on Wisconsin Strategy. In each state there is the opportunity to organize and mobilize into concerted action a budding cadre of progressive politicians along with such groups as unions, community organizations, and local advocacy groups. Yet Rogers believes the opportunity is being largely overlooked.

At the moment state power seems to be hurtling around like loose cannons, or firearms (explained in a second). There has been a rash of states rushing to pass laws declaring states' rights in defiance of federal regulations as in the case of bypassing federal restrictions on firearms.[7] Several states' attorney generals are seeking to block implementation of the new federal health care reform law in their states.[8] The governor of Virginia signed a proclamation urging citizens to spend the month recalling Virginia's days as a member of the Confederate States of America.[9] Well, why don't you go back there Virginia governor?

I seriously doubt that there will ever be any constitutional amendments via Article V of the Constitution. It's not likely that 34 states can get there act together to make such a move. It might be easier for states angry over what they regard as excessive federal taxation, an excessive federal budget, and the new health care reform law to simply secede from the Union. Indeed, politicians in a few states have been threatening or at least posturing to secede.[10]

What if they left the Union and formed their own, let's call it the States' Union. There might be two Americas and two smaller corpocracies instead of one monstrous one. If Thomas Jefferson were still president he would immediately say again, "If any state in the Union will declare that it prefers separation ... to a continuance in the union .... I have no hesitation in saying, 'Let us separate.'"[11]

I'm not proposing that America be split into two Unions, but if it does it would be about 150 years too late. What I mean is that President Lincoln may have made a colossal mistake in entering the Civil War. His primary intent was to keep the union intact as a stronger defense against potential foreign enemies. Freeing the slaves was a secondary concern. Slavery probably would have ended peacefully without the bloody Civil War because plantation owners were beginning to realize that share croppers were economically a better option than slave holding and thus emancipation would not have been forced by the Union on slave holders. Concomitantly, racial hatred and prejudice might not persist to this day as reflected for instance in the cons' hatred of the first black American president and their obstructing his every policy initiative. With two Americas so divided each would not have been strong enough to do much warring around the globe. And with two Americas so divided, the corpocracy as it exists today might not exist today. So much for reverse history, we can all make of it what we will.

Traditional Revolution: Riskier and Not Wanted

A revolution typically is a nationwide movement that overthrows or seeks to overthrow the ruling establishment. The typical revolution is a ghastly, bloody sight, neither civil nor peaceful. Thank goodness for all Americans none is in sight. More people died from the American Civil War than from all other American wars and military excursions combined. Of course, if America continues marching to its war making drummer we will someday surpass the fatalities from the Civil War. If a typical revolution aimed at the corpocracy were to develop in the foreseeable future it would topple the corpocracy but it might also give rampant rein to the worst instincts of human nature, causing many to long for the corpocracy of old.

Start a Civil Revolution?

Steve Hamm, a *Business Week* writer, was taken aback by the bitter response of his 87-year old father, a lifelong Republican, to his son's opening telephone remark about the financial turmoil on Wall Street (this was one year before Economic Katrina). "I think we need a revolution in this country" said the elder Hamm.[12] Well, Mr. Hamm, according to Mr. Jefferson we are about 10 generations behind. Thomas Jefferson remarked some time after the American Revolution that "Every generation needs a new revolution." I suppose that's why he would have offered no resistance to defection by some of the states, not that there were many states all told at that time (only 16 if I counted correctly). And I'm assuming/hoping that both Mr. Hamm and Mr. Jefferson meant a "civil," that is, peaceful, orderly, non-violent kind of revolution.

Jeff Gates, in his book, <u>Democracy at Risk: Rescuing Main Street from Wall Street, A Populist Vision for the Twenty-First Century</u>, argues that considering what has been happening to our democracy "civil disobedience is highly appropriate, provided it's undertaken in Gandhian manner: with discipline, and with a willingness to take responsibility for [ones] actions---and with the full protection of the law as long as [one's] actions are aimed not at overthrowing authority but at changing laws and practices" (that aim is pretty much my aim for the democracy power plan and strategies that I spell out in the remaining chapters).[13] This is the same Mr. Gates, by the way, who offers in a different book unique, non-economist proposals for economic reform that you will learn about in Chapter 10 and Appendix C.

Marjorie Kelly in her book, <u>The Divine Right of Capital: Dethroning the Corporate Aristocracy</u>, published a year after Gate's book, wrote that "we need revolution not so much in terms of revolt but in---the sense of return" to our original rights as citizens of a democracy.[14] These include the rights to revoke corporate personhood and corporate charters and to alter public corporations because they are in legal fact public corporations. She goes on to offer a "manual for rebellion." It's not by any stretch of the imagination a plan to take up arms. Rather, she suggests numerous ideas for peaceful, lawful action by various sectors of society to consider, such as, for example, suggesting to business students that they "challenge the hidden bias in what they are taught" (can't get much milder than that unless the student needs to butter up the professor for a better grade).[15] I cite this particular suggestion because it's reminiscent in the reverse of one of Powell's suggestions in his "battle" plan.

A few years after Kelly's book was published, Kevin Danaher, author, activist, and co-founder of the NGO, Global Exchange, devoted one of his books entirely to the subject of powerful dissent. He writes about "forming fingers into fists" but not in a literal sense.[16] It's his clever metaphor for power through unity. Like Kelly, he calls for peaceful, lawful actions.

A few years after Danaher's book appeared David Sirota's book about a populist uprising was published.[17] He is a best selling author, a political organizer, a nationally syndicated newspaper columnist, and an activist in state and national politics. He claims there is a populist uprising that is frightening Wall Street and Washington. Frankly Mr. Sirota I don't see the evidence. Your book preceded Economic Katrina. It wasn't stopped by whatever uprising you saw and Wall Street and Washington aren't hiding in fear under their bed. Your book also preceded the Tea Party dissidents, but I would hardly call it a populist uprising at least yet. Nevertheless Mr. Sirota, I think your book ought to be widely read for the very reason that a massive political uprising uncoordinated and unguided by any strategic planning needs to be contrasted with the alternative, democracy power that I will start unveiling in the next chapter.

If there were ever to be a massive civil revolution let us hope it is a peaceful one like that of Vaclav Havel's "Velvet" revolution (although a dissident once told me it was too "capitalistic"). Mr. Havel called for a peaceful uprising in the former Czechoslovakia (now the Czech Republic) whose citizens were oppressed by a totalitarian Communist regime. Peaceful demonstrations by small groups of students, artists, and scientists were followed by massive demonstrations, a general strike, the major media's decision to join the general strike, and negotiations with the Communist-controlled government that subsequently acceded to a new government led by Mr. Havel.

He wrote about "the power of the powerless," about speaking truth to power, and about the importance of creating "parallel structures" such as a social culture, independent trade unions, independent educational institutions, and the like that together provide an outlet for the people who seek the truth and freedom while simultaneously challenging the existing regime. Mr. Havel believed that the "basic job of 'dissident movements' is to serve truth, that is, to serve the real aims of life---.[18]

History professor and author Barbara Epstein has written that "Telling the truth to power is or should be a part of radical politics but it is not a substitute for strategy and planning.[19] She is absolutely right, and in the next chapter I will propose what I suppose Mr. Havel and she might call something like a parallel structure for strategy and planning that could lead to democracy power.

Compromise? Don't Even Think About It!

If the opposition today is but a pest to the corpocracy, and there's no stiffer opposition on the horizon, perhaps the opposition today ought to seek a compromise, find some common ground and collaborate on joint changes in the status quo. No way!! The regime is too wily, too powerful, too unyielding to strike a meaningful bargain. It has set its course and is wed to it.

An example of an ill-advised, ill-fated collaboration is that of the Apparel Industry Partnership. It included several corporations, unions, human rights groups, and religious groups. The outcome was a total victory for the industry, "ratifying the very conditions that had led to the sweatshops in the first place."[20] The other "partners" walked away with nothing. They got suckered. Who, objectively, would have predicted any other outcome in the first place? Mice should never sit down at a table with a devilish cat. There may be a few success stories out there, but I suspect it would be premature to declare victory in any of them. They might turn out to be, in the words of philosopher Avishai Margalit, a "rotten compromise."[21]

The Answer to the Opening Question

Where is today's opposition I asked at the outset? We can now conclude that it's here and there in bits and pieces. Today's corpocracy will outlast the divided opposition of NGOs. It will barely notice scattered and miniscule grassroots movements. It will fight tooth and nail if it sees the opposition growing and growing tougher.[22] It would undoubtedly crush a violent revolution. But would it be any match for the opposition of tomorrow as envisioned in the next chapter if that opposition were ever to materialize?

Some Closing Memory Ticklers and One Liners

E Pluribus Unum: The corpocracy. E Pluribus Pluribus: The opposition.

Anti-cropocracy NGOs: Long on diversity, short on unity.

Grassroots movements are democracy in action, not democracy inaction.

Corpocracy-top down rule, democracy-bottom up rule.

But today's grassroots movements can be found in America's back yards.

Fight the corpocracy with state power? Don't be silly.

What if America's deadliest war, the Civil War, had never happened?

Would two Americas mean two smaller, weaker corpocracies?

Repeat 1776? Don't risk it.

Start a civil revolution? How civil?

Compromise? Don't even think about it.

Mice should never sit down at the table with devilish cats.

End a strong corpocracy and a weak opposition or see America ended.

Chapter 4. Organizing Tomorrow's Opposition: Democracy Power

Don't doubt the power of one.
But organize the power of many.

I ended the previous chapter by concluding that today's opposition with its fragmented, piece-meal challenges to the corpocracy is no match for it. It will continue to dominate all but the most powerful and wealthiest among us and that amounts to very few of us. It will continue to do so unless and until the opposition's power becomes an insurmountable challenge.

Democracy Power
A Comprehensive Strategy + Massive Political Muscle/Pressure

In this chapter I propose a democracy power made up of two parts that just might be such an insurmountable challenge. One part would be a new U.S. Chamber of Democracy. The other would be a new People's Reignbow Coalition. The USCD would be a central station for developing and carrying out a master strategic plan aimed at breaking up the corpocracy. The PRC would be a powerful political force behind each major strategic initiative as it is begun by holding massive but peaceful public demonstrations, lobbying, petitioning, boycotting, letter writing, and the like.

The U.S. Chamber of Democracy

Our core mission is to ~~fight for business
and free enterprise before Congress, the
White House, regulatory agencies, the
courts, the court of public opinion, and
governments around the world~~.
help America shed her corpocracy
and become a true democracy.
~~www.u.s.chamber.com~~
www.uscd.com.notthereyet

Several years ago I created the concept of "we/me power."[1] Applying it in the case of uniting the divided NGOs would mean blending their individual "me" strengths into a stronger "we" collective without sacrificing the individual NGOs' identities, progress, and potential. To that end I propose the creation of the "U.S. Chamber of Democracy," or USCD. You won't find it in the telephone directory, the Internet, or anywhere else other than in this book as far as I know. The USCD is an idea, not a reality yet. But that shouldn't matter at this moment. Ideas are often just heart beats away from action.

The USCD wouldn't be a bricks and mortar organization. It would be a virtual one, no real offices, and absolutely not organized into a hierarchical organization, the traditional and dysfunctional structure of the corporation. What would hold the new coalition of NGOs together would be a common vision, common goals, a strategic plan, the technology of modern communication such as the Internet and teleconferencing, and some important victories sooner than later that couldn't have been accomplished if the NGOs were still operating independently of one another.

Starting Up the USCD

A dozen or so NGOs would need to step forward to create the USCD and form a steering council. It would charter the coalition, give it a name-let's assume they do name it the U.S. Chamber of Democracy, develop a directory of all NGOs that might become potential members, and then aggressively recruit them. Ideally all of the NGOs I studied and any I missed that haven't been "corporatized" (explained shortly) would eventually join forces and then build liaisons with various social movements and other potential allies discussed later in this chapter.

The next steps would be to reach a consensus on what should be the USCD's vision; what it should look like organizationally; a strategic plan to guide its efforts; which NGOs would take lead roles in the different strategic areas; and on issues such as resource sharing and funding that if not resolved early on could unravel the new organization or at the very least impede progress.

The USCD's Vision

An early item on the agenda should be the search for a vision. The search should start by debating what an ideal democracy in America would be, and if the ideal isn't possible, what should be the right vision short of the ideal. Either it or the ideal vision would immediately give the USCD an uplifting advantage over the regime. Where is the regime's inspirational vision, acquiring more wealth and grabbing and abusing more power? That's a vision only a money and power monger could embrace.

The USCD's Organizational Structure

By organizational structure I don't mean a pecking order within a hierarchy where the biggest pecker is in the corner office! But the council does need to decide what should be the NGOs' roles within the USCD and their interrelationships within it. Without some form of organization the USCD would be just what there are today; a collection of independently minded and independently acting NGOs.

The USCD might be organized into several alliances having some commonality within each alliance. One possibility would be to group NGOs by what they do. There might be, say, a legal and regulatory reform alliance, a think tank alliance, an oversight/strike force alliance, and an outreach alliance. Each would have one or more roles and have a member on the council.

The alliance to reform the pertinent laws and regulations would have the most challenging task of all. The regime owns those laws and regulations. This alliance would probably have the fewest number of NGOs. To maximize its impact this alliance would need to zero in first on the reforms most critically needed.

The alliance of think tanks would have a lot of catching up to do with the conservative think tanks that sprouted up almost immediately after Powell's memorandum was publicized. Think tanks are the primary source of ideas to disseminate, to educate, and to spur action. Powel's call to arms spurred the creation of conservative think tanks such as the American Heritage Foundation, which has since its beginning been feeding the ideas of conservatism and free market ideology to Republicans, the most captive of the two major political parties.[2]

As its name implies, the oversight/strike force alliance would be the USCD's front line of scouts or regime trackers and strike forces of activists either associated with the USCD or with the People's Reignbow Coalition. This alliance would "serve notice" on the regime and its allies, would keep track of them, would go on either the offensive or defensive depending on the situation, and would, in effect, be a constant reminder about the USCD's existence and intent.

Either within this alliance or the legal and regulatory reform alliance would be a number of NGOs seeking the right kinds of cases and filing law suits against the corpocracy, either government and/or corporations. These NGOs would also need to specialize in their own legal defense, and they would be in demand since corporations and their industries would lash out, filing SLAPP suits, going to court, raising all sorts of legal arguments, and simply doing what corporate lawyers do best on behalf of their clients.

The last alliance, the outreach alliance, would be the largest (40% of the NGOs I looked at have this role) and would seek to recruit more NGOs, educate and arouse the general public, and then recruit and organize other potential allies such as social movements, various organizations and associations, and activists into the People's Reignbow Coalition. This coalition would need to have a widely respected and forceful leader come forward or be chosen. The coalition could either be an adjunct to the USCD or an integral part of it.

The critical nature of the outreach alliance cannot be overstated. Powell knew the value of outreach and the corpocracy and its allies know it and exploit it to the hilt in all venues, creating what a political scientist calls "supply-side politics" where the marketing of corpocratic themes is "so psychologically powerful" that it determines what the public thinks.[3] This alliance would need to respond in kind and amount. We need a "demand-side democracy!"

Another possible grouping of the NGOs would be by the strategic objectives they most have in common. In a moment I will suggest some particular strategic objectives. There would probably be overlap among the different groups because most NGOs will have several strategic objectives, although not necessarily giving the same priority to each.

However the USCD is organized, each NGO could assign itself to a particular alliance or choose to participate in more than one depending on the NGO's specialties (some 20 of the NGOs I looked at, for instance, have multiple roles that cut across two or more specialties). The status of each NGO would remain unchanged although collaboration among NGOs within the USCD and particularly within the same alliance would become the norm rather than the exception.

The POW! Plan

The council and the alliances would develop and ratify an overall strategic plan, which I have dubbed the "POW!" plan. It is a homophone of "Powell" and a metaphor for knocking out the corpocracy. While it's obviously not meant literally to pummel the regime, just as I'm certain Mr. Powell did not literally mean to call for "guerrilla warfare," the POW! plan ought to be even more aggressive than his.

Powell's memorandum to the USCC was more a manifesto than a detailed plan but did set forth some strategies. As already mentioned they targeted four major American institutions: education; television and other media; the political arena; and the courts. The USCD's steering council would be well advised to study his memorandum but then go far beyond it in detail, in scope, and in aggressiveness. The POW! plan can be thought of as sort of a mirror image of Powell's plan but with much greater detail. There would be a number of strategic objectives and more specific initiatives for each that when successfully completed would move us closer to ending the corpocracy's reign.

The steering council would need to determine the relative importance of each of the strategic objectives so that more resources could be allocated to the more important ones. A list of proposed objectives and more specific initiatives for each strategy could be drafted and circulated online as a questionnaire. NGOs could be asked what their current initiatives are; to rate the relative importance of the strategic objectives and the relative contribution the initiatives could make to each objective; to estimate the resources needed for each objective; and to report on the resources already available. An analysis of the answers could form the basis for a multi-year plan of action. For example, NGOs pursuing the same strategic objectives could be asked to form an alliance and collaborate on initiatives or at least to coordinate their efforts so that they are not duplicating them or acting at cross purposes. A realignment of effort would also be called for if any current objectives were being given either too much or too little attention in the view of the NGOs' opinions as reflected in the answers to the questionnaire.

Inventorying and Sharing Resources

The NGOs would undoubtedly vary considerably in the resources they have. As I've indicated, some NGOs have million-dollar budgets and millions of members. Some NGOs have shoe-string budgets and small staffs, including volunteers. Some NGOs are technologically savvy, and some aren't. Some have influential connections, and some don't. And some have developed educational and training materials, and some haven't.

But each and every NGO not corporatized presumably has at least two resources, an organized commitment to oppose the corpocracy and the demonstrated capability to sustain its organization and to work on one or more initiatives. Motivation and experience, narrow or broad, aren't meager resources. There are hundreds of possible initiatives that could be considered where there would be a need and an opportunity for every NGO to share its expertise. No one NGO has worked the gamut of possibilities. It would be an overwhelming task for even the largest and wealthiest NGO to attempt.

Before completing the strategic plan, the council would need to have each NGO inventory as part of the questionnaire its resources and indicate what and how much could be made available for objectives and initiatives in the plan that might involve that NGO. Two or more NGOs previously working alone on a given initiative chosen as a high priority for the USCD overall could now agree to collaborate and to pool some of their resources. If it turns out that some of the high priorities are being worked on by NGOs with the leanest budgets, then the wealthier NGOs would need to consider offering some of their funds for those priorities.

But the wealthier NGOs shouldn't be looked upon as cash cows. Moreover, carrying out the strategic plan would take far more resources than even they can contribute. The regime wasn't built up on the cheap and it won't be brought down on the cheap. The council, therefore, could make the coalition a tax-exempt organization and then solicit and obtain large, multi-year grants from wealthy, progressive foundations. Some NGOs already receive foundation support (one of them, Common Cause, is not tax exempt, but does have a tax exempt affiliate, the Common Cause Education Fund).

A dozen conservative foundations have been shoveling millions upon millions of dollars over the years into think tanks, advocacy groups, and other initiatives all intended to advance the regime in one way or another.[4] Paradoxically, progressive foundations are far wealthier than their conservative counterparts and presumably would be very supportive of the USCD but the funding for advocacy groups from these foundations has been relatively miniscule. This may be due to the foundations worrying about losing their tax exempt status and to the reluctance of advocacy groups to approach them.[5] Yet IRS rules provide considerable latitude in allowing tax-exempt funding even of advocacy groups seeking public policy changes.[6] Moreover, the conservative side certainly has not been inhibited by the IRS. Admittedly, the agency is part of the regime and just may be more lenient with conservative foundations. Regardless, the USCD would need to consider pursuing foundation support.

Mobilizing the People's Reignbow Coalition

When there's a loss
of political pressure
prime the democracy pump.

The metaphor, I think, is an apt one. Pumps are primed when there is a loss of pressure. Priming takes muscle. There is pathetically little democracy muscle in America today. It has been thoroughly outmuscled by the corpocracy.

The silent majority is an amorphous mass of Americans. Trying to prime it from scratch into a super coalition of democracy muscles might take endless pumping. Fortunately, I don't think we would have to start from scratch. While the corpocracy's telltale signs aren't yet at the hazardous warning level, they have helped to sew the seeds of discontent and active protest.

"Reignbow" is a homophone for the Rainbow Coalition, a generic term for any coalition of groups or parties opposed to any current regime anywhere. The Reverend Jesse Jackson, leader of the Rainbow Coalition in the U.S., garnered over 3 million and 6 million votes respectively in his 1984 and 1988 presidential bids. While his coalition is mostly of historical significance today, I give him credit for what he did. He, like Ralph Nader, was simply up against the corpocracy.

"Reignbow" is meant to connote a peoples' movement intent on wresting reign from the corpocracy and returning it to the American people. My idea of the People's Reignbow Coalition is to carry forward Charles Derber's proposal for "requilting the big tent."[7] By that he means politically realigning interest groups across a broad spectrum. He sees this realignment as a key to regime change. His tent would include religious voters ("fundamentalists, Christian activists, and social justice workers"); the Reagan democrats ("urban, ethnic, and immigrant workers); suburbanites and exurbanites ("software geeks, soccer moms, and outer-city minorities"); the base camp and aggressive progressives ("minorities, women, labor, and the new social movements"); and conservatives ("Southerners, small business, and pick up truck dads"). I suppose some if not all of the latter are the "cons" I mentioned in the first chapter. Anyone able to meld squabbling groups like cons and progressives, gays and gay bashers, pro-choice and anti-abortionists into a critical force strong enough to attack the regime would deserve the Democracy Quilter Prize. Go ahead and laugh. But remember, anything conceivable may be possible.

I have identified several potential segments of the populace along with some of the bits and pieces picked up from the previous chapter that conceivably might be fused into the super coalition. Here they are briefly in alphabetical order.

Activists and "Democracy Commandos"

Some activists obviously are already affiliated with one or more NGOs or these organizations wouldn't exist, but my guess is that there are countless unaffiliated activists who need to be recruited into a more organized campaign against the corpocracy.

Angry readers are an example I think of unaffiliated activists. Take a look at Table 4. Shown there is just a small sampling of comments submitted by angry readers of the New York Times about the news of the January 21, 2010 ruling.[8] Unite, all angry readers!

Table 4

Some New York Times Readers' Comments
About the Supreme Court's January 21, 2010 Ruling

The end of Freedom. We are now the United Corporations of America.

The United States of America (1776-2010)

Democracy is truly dead.

Decisions like this, in times like these, are how revolutions begin.

Where can I sign up for the "Revolutionary Party"? As an ex-veteran I am embarrassed to defend the so called American interest overseas; when in reality we are always defending the corporate interests overseas.

What are we waiting for? Seriously? Why aren't we starting a revolution?!

Can we impeach the Supreme Court?

Another nail in the coffin of American democracy.

Why bother even having elections? The one with the most money wins!"

Why not just bypass politicians and elect corporations directly to office?

This is the true end of freedom. Thanks, "conservatives!"

Jefferson's experiment has just about run its course. We don't have much time, people.

We are well on our way to becoming, on average, a rather illiterate, second rate economic power with a lot of weapons.

All working people are merely slaves who are free to move about.

Kiss democracy goodbye.

The American voter…that's a joke!

Corporate fascism advances onward.

What do you expect from a bought-and-paid-for judiciary?

Every future election is now decided.

Of the money, by the money, and for the money.

The people have just lost the power and the worst we will do is blog about it.

People, maybe we should stop typing and start marching.

Investigative journalist Eveline Lubbers in her book on <u>Battling Big Business</u> writes about "net.activism," the sophisticated use by activists of the Internet to challenge particular corporations, uncover and publicize secret information about the regime that is rightfully public information in the first place, and to connect to ongoing campaigns.[9] The USCD could put out a call to all net activists to unite and join the Coalition.

In my web browsing of the Internet I learned of the Gleitsman Foundation.[10] It awards citizen activists who "confront, challenge and correct social injustice." Since 1990 it has chosen and awarded nearly 40 individuals, Ralph Nader being one of the more notable ones. Would that several thousand of these individuals could be cloned!

Naomi Wolf in her non-fiction book, <u>Give Me Liberty</u>, proposes the idea of democracy commandos, groups of 10 to 20 people who individually or collectively write their elected representatives.[11] Her idea seems too tame for fighting the regime but could be raised several notches and expanded nationwide to a force of democracy commandos the regime couldn't withstand. To that end there ought to be "boot camps" established around the country to prime democracy power and channel it into the various strategic pursuits.

Aggrieved Victims

The most aggrieved are the millions of Americans personally and grievously victimized by the corpocracy in one way or another (e.g., people injured or killed in the corpocracy's wars, people victimized by the corporacry's devastating Economic Katrina, people injured or killed by corporate negligence, etc, etc,). A way needs to be figured out for identifying, cultivating, and mobilizing them and to do so in a sensitive way without exploiting their plight.

Angry Voters

This is certainly not a mutually exclusive group of people. At any one moment there may be millions of them and they can be found among some of the other segments of the populace being discussed here. They may be angry for the wrong reasons or vent their anger at only part of the corpocracy (e.g., the Half-Mad Hatters), but they are angry in any case.

Business and Public Servant Exemplars

An example of a courageous business exemplar is the story of a vice president of a large pharmaceutical corporation that undoubtedly is a bona fide member of the corpocracy. This executive was quoted as saying that he "joined this industry to save lives, not to take them, and that's the reason I've chosen to speak out" [against Big Pharma's practices].[12] More executives like that one need to be found and recruited!

Exemplary public servants who aren't the corpocracy's servants need to be identified and their active support solicited. They may be few and far between, but there are, for example, some members of the judiciary who aren't kept by the corpocracy. I'm thinking for instance of a federal judge who harshly rebuked a major corporation and rejected its lopsided settlement with the supine SEC.[13] There are also I think a few politicians who may be unfriendly to the corpocracy. I'm also thinking of two members of Congress who sought to impeach George Bush for his taking America to war in Iraq?[14] Other "outlier or outsider" members of Congress might be those receiving the perfect voting record score from the Americans for Democratic Action or receiving the lowest score on a yet-to-be developed "corpocracy ally index." This index might include such indicators as the volume of visits by touts, the number of tout-influenced votes, the percentage of campaign funds tied to the corpocracy, the number of political junkets sponsored by the corpocracy, and the like.

Consumers

The end of the Crown's corpocracy began partly through consumer activism, the Boston Tea Party. Ending the current corpocracy over 200 years later will probably require consumer activism on an unprecedented and organized scale. The successes in consumer education and protection achieved in the 1960s and 70s largely due to Ralph Nader have since been eroded by massive deregulation and by massive marketing efforts that have infected the American people with a massive case of consumption.

Being on Mr. Nader's alert list, I recently got an e-mail from him titled, "There's No Consumer Power." He was referring to the fact that "there was no room for a Financial Consumers Association in the 1500 pages of the financial regulation bill the Senate had passed." Mr. Nader, you know as well as I do that there will never be consumer power again like you marshaled long ago until someone like you marshals it again.

Nevertheless, consumer sensitivity, resistance to, and protests about marketplace exploitation are on the rise. Most consumers, for example, carry out from time to time personal or collective boycotts of offending brands. I have spotted several consumer-oriented NGOs and there must be hundreds more. They need to join or align with a new peoples' coalition and the millions of unorganized, individual boycotters need to be mobilized as well. Additionally, the most offensive corporate members of the corpocracy that sell to consumers need to be identified and specifically targeted by groups of boycotters.

The Corporcracy's Outliers and Outsiders

This potential segment may seem like an odd one but bear with me. The corpocracy is a motley lot. There are hundreds if not thousands of corporations in numerous industries that are probably "card carrying members" of the corpocracy. Although most large corporations tend to be corrupt and corrupting, no corporation is inherently bad as some critics seem to suggest, so there must be some corporations that are outliers and outsiders.[15] Outliers are any corporations that don't meet all of the four criteria I have in mind for "vetting" corporations. Outsiders are any corporations that don't meet any of them. What are the four?

One is size. The logic of this criterion is simply that the bigger the corporation the more potential it has to abuse its power. Another would be whether the corporation's behavior is represented by any of the telltale signs. Another would be bad publicity. Since a large corporation is a masterful PR machine and can manipulate the media, getting bad publicity means it must really be so bad it can't be hidden or explained away. A fourth would be whether the corporation is being tracked by any NGOs that track corporations because of their abusive power and bad behavior in general and possibly also whether, in the process of the tracking, the corporation might get a high "corporateer quotient" based on such indicators as the "percentage of total expenditures spent on political contributions and trade lobbying."[16] Corporations pegged as an ally of true democracy would then be solicited as a corporate sponsor or adjunct to the new super coalition. I realize it may be unrealistic to think one or more corporations in each industry would risk becoming an outcast.

Creative Arts

Creative people in the field of arts and letters ought to be tapped for creating works critical of the regime. It is from this field that some memorable broadsides have been aimed at regimes. Novelists of a bygone era like Charles Dickens, Sinclair Lewis, Mark Twain, George Orwell, George Bernard Shaw, and much more recently the late novelist Kurt Vonnegut come to mind. On the current scene there are, to mention three social critics, movie director and filmmakers Oliver Stone, Michael Moore, and Robert Greenwald. A "novel" idea might be for one or more NGOs to recruit and commission a "stable" of artists to pen and perform works aimed squarely at raising public awareness and anger over the regime.

Front-Line Volunteers

There must be thousands upon thousands of volunteers across the country ministering to the needy through soup kitchens, bread lines, holiday dinners, donated clothing stops, and what have you. The paradox of their service is that while it does ameliorate temporarily the effects of poverty, at the same time it provides a ready-made conscience salve for those who never experienced it first hand or who, much worse, had a hand directly or indirectly in making poverty worse. There will always be soup kitchens and their kind as long as the corpocracy exists. I would guess volunteers realize they are treating symptoms rather than the underlying socio-politico-economic disease itself. They need to be rallied to give some of their time to challenging the corpocracy rather than unwittingly helping to prolong it.

Growing and Fusing Grass Roots Movements

In recent American history there have been various nationwide movements that through their political pressure and litigation have achieved their goals by and large of gaining civil rights for people who had been denied them, or in the case of one antiwar movement succeeded in ending the Vietnam War. Then there are the more limited grass roots movements that I discussed in the previous chapter. While the specific objectives of large and small movements may seem different from one another on the surface, I think they all in large to small ways are seeking to replace some or all of the corporcracy's interests with the peoples' interests. Furthermore, these movements are a good recruiting ground for a broader attack on the corpocracy, but they need to be united and fused into a broader coalition. How to do this is way beyond my know-how boundaries. Fortunately, there are people who know a lot about grass-roots growing.[17]

In the previous chapter I mentioned the "Half-Mad Hatters," or the Tea Party, as one of several grass roots movements. I asked Professor Derber if his tent was big enough to include them. Here is his answer verbatim.

"Gary - I see no way of uniting with the Tea Party-it's outside the big tent. In fact, it's threatening to pull up the stakes and blow up the tent. Anyone concerned with restoring democracy must worry first and foremost that the Far Right could not just support corpocracy but actually replace it with something even worse: some form of Fascist Lite stem or a soft theocratic state. If the economy continues to worsen, the parallels with Weimar Germany in the 1920s become very scary - and the first concern of all progressives should be to ward off this nightmarish spectre. Now, admittedly, the Tea Party is very diverse - and a few Tea branches close to Ron Paul might become allies of the Democracy, Not Corpocracy movement. Ron Paul's domestic agenda is frightening, but he's wonderful on foreign policy. He opposes the Empire, virtually all wars, and all intrusions on civil liberties. So some tactical alliances with a few of the more sane elements of the Tea Party, mostly restricted to Ron Paul's anti-war brand of Tea Party, might bring one of the Tea Party branches very partially into the tent. But beware of most of the Tea Party, whose goal is a state far worse than our current corpocracy."[18]

The same day I got his e-mail answer I learned that the Republican Far Right was stoking "destructive anger" and doing well at the primaries---"by playing on some people's fears of Hispanics and Muslims, by painting the president as a dangerous radical, [and] by distorting the truth about the causes of the recession."[19] Derber, with his premonition about the "Far Right," has a far better sense than I do of what is happening in and to America. I'm a neophyte observer compared to him even though he is my junior by many years. He was far better trained than I on political and economic matters and he's been at them much longer while I was an organizational psychologist trained and experienced in working on other matters. If his assessment is valid, then the challenge becomes even greater. We must fight the corpocracy while keeping our eye out and be prepared to respond to whatever the extremists on the right end of the political spectrum are doing that could create "a state far worse than our current copocracy."

The anti-globalization movement may just be a sleeping giant if it can be steered toward America's corpocracy for an extended confrontation. Astonishingly, there apparently are some 10,000 anti-globalization NGOs world-wide. Would that they could become a branch of the People's Reignbow Coalition or vice versa!

Millennials

The millennials are the first generation of adults in the new millennium. They are, according to the Pew Research Center, "confident, self-expressive, liberal, upbeat and open to change."[20] They have been hit hard by Economic Katrina and for that reason alone might be open to joining a broad coalition of people seeking to end the corcopracy's reign.

Organized Religion?

Our republic for over 200 years has been a secular one. Despite Christian conservatives' relentless efforts to make school books say so, we are not a Christian nation, nor are we a Jewish nation, a Muslim nation, or any other religion nation. Organized religion tends to be exclusionary, divisive, contentious, and sometimes violent. Allies against the regime need to fight it, not among themselves. So my inclination would be to cautiously approach any prospective religious groups of whatever faith knowing at the same time that there must be some out there doing good work and not for the regime. Obviously it would be far better for the Republic if religion aligns with the foes of the regime rather than with its allies. Co-authors Si Kahn and Elizabeth Minnich in reminding us of the colonial days when the Puritans collaborated with the Crown's regime to create the Massachusetts Bay Company point out that "Religion gave the corporation the authority, the corporation gave religion the money, and the Crown gave both the right to use force to control peoples' lives."[21]

Peace and Feminist Groups

If the cold war regime followed by the current regime, the Iraqi War, the Afghanistan War, and various and sundry military excursions here there and everywhere tell us anything it is that America does not excel at peace-building. Peace groups in America abound, but they need to be united. They would seem to have a natural compatibility with feminist groups. War making is almost entirely male war making. Women helping to break the glass ceiling help to liberate women at work. Women helping to break the corpocracy help to liberate America.

Professional Associations

> Make crime pay.
> Become a lawyer.
> ---Will Rogers

I finally decided against creating a checklist of professional associations and giving readers the opportunity to check whether they thought the associations were friends or foes of the regime. Ferreting out some of the friends ought to be no-brainers, the ones who have basically sold out to government grants and/or corporate interests, but others might possibly be touchy and tough, and I'm not sure I would want to go public with my choices. I'll gladly turn the task over to the USCD's outreach alliance should it ever materialize!

Responsible Corporate Owners

Institutional investors now own the greater share of corporate America. Some have become very aggressive in their demands on corporations. One Wall Street takeover lawyer thinks they are "even more dangerous" in driving corporations to sacrifice long-term value for short-term results.[22] But there are some institutional investors that seek socially responsible or morally ethical investments even if they mean deferring financial gains in the short run. These investors each of which have their own lists of taboo investments (e.g., shunning the defense industry) are expected eventually to become "mainstream" and are the ones that need to be cultivated.[23] Their lists might help verify the vetting of outliers and outsiders.

Senior Citizens

Senior citizens are the fastest growing segment of the U.S. population, totaling close to 40 million people and always still counting. Very recently a small group of "grannies" (along with some elder gentlemen) for the 330th consecutive Wednesday staged in New York City an hour's protest against America's wars.[24] All senior citizens like them need a leader among themselves to champion and spearhead the super coalition.

Small Businesses

Small businesses are sometimes called the "backbone of the U.S. economy," although this metaphor ought to be qualified. The backbone needs stiffened.

About 99% of all enterprises in the U.S. are small business firms, not the large corporations making up the corpocracy. A fraction of these small firms do depend for some if not all of their livelihood as suppliers to or contractors with the corpocracy and thus probably couldn't be counted on to bite the massive hand that feeds them despite being bullied by them at the same time.[25] The many small business firms that are members of the USCC would probably be difficult to recruit also, but the bulk of small business firms represent an untapped and potential ally. They just need to be mobilized and organized more.

Two NGOs that seek to protect and promote the interests of small business firms are the American Independent Business Alliance and the Business Alliance for Local Living Economies.[26] They need to be recruited into a super coalition. The biggest advantages of having small businesses as an ally are their pervasiveness, their entrepreneurial spirit, their savvy, and their boost to local economies. The latter is particularly important because the corpocracy will sacrifice local economies whenever necessary. Just as a USCD could be an alternative to the USCC, community-based enterprises such as those fostered by AMIBA and BALLE could be an alternative to local chambers of commerce and could be among the charter members of local chapters of their own national organization.

Social Entrepreneurs

Social entrepreneurs are like business entrepreneurs. The difference is that social entrepreneurs apply their innovative ideas not to starting a business but to rectifying social injustices and solving other problems such as environmental degradation. Social entrepreneurs are thus also like citizen activists but unlike many of the latter go beyond protesting to creating ways to make positive social changes. Social entrepreneurs may not necessarily target the regime but they certainly work on problems caused partly or totally by the regime.

Social entrepreneurs aren't exactly a new breed of reformers. They have appeared on the scene occasionally for several millennia here and there throughout the world. In recent times, however, social entrepreneurship and its practitioners have grown by leaps and bounds. According to one of the modern-day pioneers of this development, "we are in the midst of a rare, fundamental structural change in society: citizens and citizen groups are beginning to operate with the same entrepreneurial and competitive skill that has driven business ahead over the last three centuries."[27] I think that is an entirely exaggerated claim but we shall see.

The Super Wealthy?

Do I hear you laughing? Including members of this group as advocates for eliminating the corpocracy would never have occurred to me had I not gotten very recently one of Ralph Nader's e-mail alerts telling me that "with corporations able to amass trillions of dollars to advance harmful corporate interests, a small number of enlightened mega-rich elders putting their money and smarts behind broad redirections in our country supported by majorities can generate very compelling dynamics for a functioning democratic society." Mr. Nader, I'll wait and see what unfolds. I really can't imagine two of the super wealthy, Warren Buffett and Bill Gates, actively challenging the corpocracy.

Unions

Organized labor in its heyday helped to blunt the corpocracy's abusive power. That was some time ago as I have already noted. Unions ought to be a natural enemy of the corpocracy for the opposite is certainly the case. The U.S. may be the only developed country where its courts and legislators favor the corpocracy over unions. This travesty must end. Union membership may have declined, but there are still some 15 million organized workers, not a trifle number. It would be sheer folly to ignore organized labor. Soliciting their support is crucial. I know that organized labor makes the corpocracy and its allies froth at the mouth, but organized labor is a hallmark of a true democracy.

The idea occurred to me that there needs to be a "labor ready" (not to be confused with the day worker employment firm of the same name) union of unemployed but employable people in the U.S. I searched the Internet and found that there already is one nicknamed "UCubed" because it organizes from the ground up, starting with "cubes" of people who have the same zip code address.[28] UCubed is only a few months old but is growing rapidly, has issued press releases, and written op-ed articles for newspapers. If the millions of jobless join UCubed it will be a force the administration and Congress will find hard to ignore. But might it work at cross purposes to a broader-scale challenge of the corpocracy? It might. If UCubed succeeds in getting millions employed they may be reluctant as vulnerable new employees to take on the corpocracy. Nevertheless, an overture to UCubed on behalf of a broader-scale democracy force ought to be made.

Democracy Power: Possibly the Knock-Out Punch?

Democracy power as I have envisioned it here would be unlike any counterforce the corpocracy has ever faced before. The USCD's strategic objectives and initiatives would guide both its activities and those of the People's Reignbow Coalition. The latter would be the first nationwide movement of massive political muscle to be guided by a comprehensive strategic plan under the auspices of a unified organization of NGOs.

Strategic Objectives

The goal of the POW! plan is to break up the Devil's Marriage. There are eight broad strategic objectives and numerous initiatives in the plan. Carrying them out successfully would eliminate all the corpocracy's badvantages and it would collapse.

> Organize the opposition (this chapter).
> Tell the people (Chapter 5).
> Close the corpocracy's political/judicial circus (Chapter 6).
> Dig up the corpocracy's legal roots (Chapter7).
> End hands-off corporate criminals (Chapter 8).
> End hand-outs to the corporate welfare queen (Chapter 9).
> End undemocratic capitalism (Chapter 10).
> Unleash your democracy power (Chapter 11).

I will illustrate now how the two sources of democracy power might work in tandem to achieve one strategic initiative; that of digging up the corpocracy's mother root, corporate personhood. Digging it up would really hobble the corpocracy, sort of like bringing it to its knees for an extended count.

Instead of numerous NGOs challenging corporate personhood on their own as they are doing, the USCD would start coordinating the attack as part of the fourth strategic objective in its POW! plan. The alliance of think tanks would start preparing amicus briefs, legal background papers, op editorials and the like against corporate personhood. The legal and regulatory reform alliance would start searching for cases to litigate against the U.S. Supreme Court's ruling for corporate personhood and/or for legislative actions to overturn or counteract the ruling. The Reignbow people would apply massive, and I do mean massive, political pressure in various ways (e.g., petitions, massive demonstrations, etc.) all aimed at uprooting corporate personhood. Such a coordinated and concentrated counteroffensive short of a civil revolution just for one strategic initiative mind you may be necessary because corporate personhood is a foundational pillar of the corpocracy and because the latter is so powerful and entrenched. The corpocracy, I guarantee you, will not surrender its personhood (more like its manhood considering all the unbroken glass ceilings) without a fierce fight. You will read about several possible initiatives for uprooting corporate personhood in Chapter 7.

Democracy Power's "Debut"

If the USCD and the People's Reignbow Coalition were to become a reality, this combo force would need to debut itself to the general public by sending out a bevy of messages through a variety of mediums. The message and medium would depend on the audience.

Promotional messages could be broadcast to the public at large and include an invitation to join the People's Reignbow Coalition and to become actively involved in one or more ways, perhaps starting with the signing of the Second Declaration of Independence to be described momentarily. Letters with a similar message could be sent to specific segments of the general public that might be potential allies but have yet to join the coalition.

Politicians would be a unique audience. Letters to them could introduce the USCD and the People's Reignbow Coalition and the combined campaign to end the marriage made in Hell, seek endorsements of the POW! plan, and request the signing of the Second Declaration of

Independence and the cancelling of their Declaration of Dependence. That will be the day!

Letters of an entirely different nature could be written by the oversight/ strike force alliance and sent to targeted members of the corporate partner and its allies. Common to all of these letters would be an announcement about the campaign and the organized forces behind it. Notices to corporations that have already been confronted by activist NGOs would reflect that fact and should a) present an assessment of each corporation's corpocratic actions along with a request for a self-assessment to be made such as completing the "corporateer quotient" questionnaire developed by Jamie Court, b) make the case for why the corporation should reject the corpocracy and undertake self-reform, c) advise repairing major harms its actions have caused, d) advise resolving whatever longstanding or current issues have been raised by activist groups, and e) offer advice on corporate reform.[29] The notice would close by requesting a response within one month and saying the response would influence the campaign's next steps. My guess is the return rate might be zero or close to it but again, anything conceivable may be possible.

The Second Declaration of Independence

America's first Declaration of Independence declared that the Thirteen Colonies were independent of Great Britain and then went on to list grievances against the King. A second declaration is sorely needed today that might read something like this:

The Second Declaration of Independence

The history of America's corpocracies is a
history of tyranny over the people of these
United States. The proof of this is not in
doubt. It is therefore solemnly published
and declared that the people of these United
States shall resume their self rule through a
true democracy free of the regime's tyranny.

The first Declaration was meant not only to tell the King to shove off but also to persuade reluctant colonists to sign on and to unite in the struggle against the King. All but 20% or so of them did, and perhaps it's prophetic that those who didn't were predominantly upper class landowners and business people who worried that they would lose their property rights and status if a new republic were to succeed. The hold outs were an ominous sign for democracy's development, an auspicious sign for land and business development. I fully expect that if such a letter were to be sent to all elected and appointed officials of all branches and levels of government the response would be similar to that of the pre-revolutionary hold-outs. And the response would itself be a Declaration of Dependence on the corpocracy.

Anything Conceivable May be Possible, But

So far in this chapter I have taken you through some ideas and wishful thinking. Will the ideas forever remain ideas and never see the day light of action? It's a question that sometimes haunts me.

I want to tell you about an e-mail I got from Doug Page in response to an article I published in the e-newsletter, *Dissident Voice*.[30] I did not know Doug before then. He is an octogenarian "promoting active non-violence" in his local community of Reedley, CA and also an organic farmer. He was once a union lawyer, a former mayor of Walnut Creek, CA, and a 1960 Democratic Candidate for Congress. When someone like Doug writes me, I sit up and take note!

"Gary," he wrote, "I think your article in *Dissident Voice* is brilliant and right on as to analysis and specific steps to be taken. It is basing this effort on NGOs that seems a weak link to me."[31] His critique of my idea of a USCD is that in his opinion NGOs' existence depends "NOT on "solving the problem" but on continuing to get funding to work on a continuing problem.

Another person whom I will sit up and take notice when he writes me is Charlie Derber (he wrote me before this chapter had been revised). "The idea," he said, "of unifying the NGOs and the more general project of integrating the fragmented opposition [to the corpocracy] is right on the mark!"[32] But then he added that many of these NGOs are "pseudo-corporations in non-profit clothes," cited numerous examples, and referred me to a book by journalist Christine MacDonald who exposed the corrupting of prominent conservationist NGOs by well-known corporations.[33] He went on to suggest that I "highlight [social] movements more [while] at least noting the limits of many NGOs." He told me he has "been working with a group called The Majority Agenda, a new NGO that is trying to integrate the labor, peace and environmental movements while reaching out on a whole-system change agenda to the mass public."[34]

I am assuming that the pseudo NGOs would show themselves by shunning any overture to create the USCD, a proposal that Derber obviously likes but with reservations. His suggestion that I put more emphasis on social movements actually led to my idea of the People's Reignbow Coalition. It was not in my earlier drafts. I will also be watching to see how the Majority Agenda progresses.

I have also asked a few people in the NGO community if they thought the creation of something like a USCD was plausible. Most answered that it would be plausible but also very difficult to create. One person advocated periodic meetings and conferences to build a consensus around a range of strategies before seeking to create a super coalition. Another person mentioned the obstacle of turf wars among the badly fractured community of NGOs, but then suggested that a solution might be to build a large fund of money and then distribute the funds after specifying initiatives eligible for the funds.

Because the USCD may never happen, or the People's Reignbow Coalition for that matter, in the remaining chapters I won't rely on either of the two fictions as the proposed agents of change. While I will refer in subsequent chapters to the POW! Plan, any one or more NGOs and grassroots movements on their own are welcome to implement it. Conceivably, some smaller scale version or variation of the USCD and the People's Reignbow Coalition or some entirely different form of opposition may emerge. Ghandi didn't have a USCD. Neither did the Rev. Martin Luther King. Neither did the Vietnam War protesters. Neither did Vaclav Havel. But they did have their own versions of democracy power. So I will cling to the idea of democracy power, whatever form it takes. You can be sure, though, that I won't stop promoting the USCD/PRC form of democracy power.

Some Closing Memory Ticklers and One Liners

Democracy Power? Yes, democracy strategy + democracy muscle.

Organize NGOs for "we/me" democracy power.

The U.S. Chamber of Democracy. You heard about it here.

The Peoples' Reignbow Coalition. You heard about it here.

Democracy boot camps?

Any professional organizations or organized religions unfriendly to the corpocracy?

Women helping to break the glass ceiling help to liberate women at work.

Women helping to break the corpocracy would help to liberate America.

Soup kitchen ladlers, ladle less and protest more!

U.S. only developed country with a government hostile to organized labor.

Tea Party turning into a Fascist Party?

Let's sign the Second Declaration of Independence.

How many politicians would sign it?

How many would cancel their Declaration of Dependence?

Anything conceivable may be possible.

Declare and reclaim independence or declare dependence and lose America.

PART THREE. UNLEASHING DEMOCRACY POWER: THE POSSIBILITIES

Chapter 5. Telling the People

Tell the truth
The whole truth and
Nothing but the truth
Every day, everywhere

Joseph Goebbels, Hitler's propagandist reportedly said, "If you tell a lie big enough and keep repeating it, people will eventually come to believe it." The counteroffensive of the POW! plan's strategic objective is to tell the truth big enough, widely enough, and often enough about the Devil's Marriage that a critical mass of the people will eventually come to believe it, make it a habit of their thinking, and go on to act upon it. This strategic objective is the mirror image of the Powell plan to blitz the classroom and the mainstream media.[1] The intent is to stir the American people into breaking up the Devil's Marriage and reclaiming their democracy.

Prime Democracy Power in Classrooms

Educate and inform,
the only sure reliance for
the preservation of our liberty.
---Thomas Jefferson's letter
to James Madison, 1787

Powell's Proposal to Teach Free Enterprise

Powell understood perfectly how intensive and extensive shaping of the young mind could sew the seeds for the reforms he advocated. He proposed several initiatives for blitzing classrooms even down to the secondary education level.

He believed that the college campus was the "single most dynamic source" of the attacks on free enterprise and had been for several years. He also blamed professors in the social science faculties "known to be unsympathetic to the enterprise system" who were shaping their young students' minds.

A "priority task for business and the U.S. Chamber of Commerce," Powell believed, was to counter the "liberal" bias on campus with a multifaceted strategy that included these proposed initiatives: Establish prominent scholars in the social sciences who believe in the free enterprise system. Give incentives to induce these scholars to be as passionate and productive as liberal/leftist faculty members in publishing their scholarly writings. Create a "Speaker's Bureau" to deploy polished speakers who would "articulate the product of the scholars." Insist on "equal time on the college speaking circuit" for those speakers. Continuously evaluate the textbooks of social sciences in order to ensure a fair and factual balance. Correct the "most fundamental problem," that of the imbalance of many faculties." Parlay rapport with graduate schools of business into greater influence there in the "essential training of the executives of the future."

Powell didn't stop with higher education. He stooped into secondary education, although he didn't go into specifics: "Action programs, tailored to the high schools and similar to those mentioned [for higher education], should be considered." He proposed that the implementation of these programs be "a major program for local chambers of commerce," but that the "National Chamber" would retain responsibility for the "control and direction" of the programs. Ironically, the robber baron regime helped promote compulsory public education as a way to ensure less individualistic and more compliant workforces.[2]

Powell's Legacy

Big business and conservative intellectuals took Powell's proposal for blitzing classrooms and proceeded over the years to "incorporate" much of education. At the university level the takeover can be seen in curriculum content, in the teaching of classes, in the commercializing of faculty research, in soliciting partnerships with universities for war-related research, and even in the ownership of some universities.[3] Ultraconservative corporate foundations alone reportedly give millions of dollars annually to influence political science, law, and economics departments at numerous universities.[4] The corpocracy's heavy hand is greatest naturally in business schools where students are imbued with the free-enterprise spirit, myopically trained in financial management, and then graduate ready to do whatever is necessary to help corporations maximize short-term profits. It surely is not a coincidence that most business wrongdoing is committed by members of the managerial class, the destination of most business school graduates.[5] Enron, for example, was annually hiring 250 newly minted MBA's during the 1990s.[6]

At secondary and primary levels the influence of the corpocracy and its think tanks is seen in the privatization of schools, in the profitable selling of standardized tests, in curriculum content, in sponsorships, in the piping in of sham educational broadcasts run by marketing corporations, and in school hallways lined with vending machines.[7] To give you an example of "Corporcracy High," the arch conservative and corporate funded Ayn Rand Institute uses high schools as a "major battleground" to advance the ideas of unfettered capitalism.[8] It does so by giving hundreds of thousands of Rand's books to high school teachers and by sponsoring annual high school essay contests. I will never endorse book burning, but Rand's books tempt me! Instead of high school students being given a dose of Rand, democracy would be better served if they were given a heavier antidote of civics. Most flunk a miniature version of the test immigrants seeking U.S. citizenship must pass.[9]

The POW! Plan

We don't want to regress to a dark ages with the corpocracy as High Church! But we're mighty close to it. Journalist Charles Pierce calls us an "idiot America" where stupidity or ignorance is glorified (I was basically an idiot about the corpocracy until I set out to learn about it) and says an old and wise friend told him that "the only question that any American citizen is required to answer is "Do you govern or are you governed?"[10] And journalist James Surowiecki seems to be calling many Americas "greater fools" for being financially illiterate.[11] Keeping the masses ignorant, submissive, and consumptive is exactly what the regime wants and achieves, starting at the lowest school levels possible.

In Table 5.1 are listed some initiatives illustrating what might be done to prime democracy power in classrooms. Most of the initiatives are the mirror image of those in Powell's proposal. As he did with his, I'm not going to spell out the specifics here. I will leave them for any interested parties such as the NGOs that are already and independently working on educational initiatives (note that I said "independently" reaching).

Table 5.1
Some Illustrative Initiatives for Priming Democracy Power in Classrooms

-In Getting More Ready-

-Beef up think tank production of educational material

-In Colleges and Universities-

-Establish prominent scholars in business schools who believe in democratic capitalism and have published about the corpocracy's power.
-Create a "Speaker's Bureau" to deploy polished speakers who would articulate the case for ending the corpocracy.
-Insist on "equal time on the college speaking circuit" for those speakers.
-Continuously evaluate the textbooks of business schools in order to ensure a fair and factual balance.
-Correct the the corpocracy bias of many faculties.
-Liberalize and humanize business school education.
-Educate students in other professional schools (e.g., law) on the corpocracy.
-Encourage student dissidence, especially in business and law schools.

-In Secondary and Primary Schools-

-Expand educational programs on responsible citizenship in a democracy.
-Review public educational materials for biases toward the corpocracy and pressure school boards and publishers to eliminate those biases.
-Ask book stores to set aside and highlight space devoted to

all books about the corpocracy and the diminishment of our democracy.

-Counter corpocracy propaganda in literature aimed at the public schools.

-Declare public schools off limits to corporate advertising.

-Pressure local authorities to reverse the privatizing and chartering of public schools.

-Pressure school authorities to stop allowing the profitable standardized testing of students and to instead enrich curricula and teacher pay.

Out of curiosity I looked at three NGOs actively working on initiatives reaching into the classroom. The student action campaign of one NGO has produced documentary films and programs "to educate campus communities about important social justice issues and expose students to careers in public interest advocacy."[12] The second NGO provides resources teachers can use in teaching "about issues surrounding trade justice and fair trade."[13] And the third NGO has numerous initiatives to increase understanding of and commitment to civic engagement among students in state colleges and universities.[14]

If just the first few NGOs on my list are so active there must be many more initiatives being undertaken by the hundred and some remaining NGOs on my list and others not on it that focus on the education of students about problems in our society created or aggravated by the corpocracy. It's unfortunate that all this work isn't coordinated and guided by an overarching strategic plan.

Blitzing the Media

The media act as a megaphone for those in power---.

---Amy Goodman[15]

Powell believed strongly in free enterprise, but apparently not for a free press, and he wanted the media used as a megaphone with big business as the mouth piece for free enterprise. While he considered "reaching the campus and the secondary school as vital for the long run" in reviving free enterprise, he saw reaching the public as "generally more important for the shorter term."

Powell's Proposal for Blitzing the Media

His answer to his rhetorical question, "What can be done about the public?" was a very general proposal that the USCC orchestrate a media blitz that would include not just television but also radio, the press, the newsstands, and, of course, a "sustained campaign of paid advertisements to inform and enlighten the American people." To gear up for this blitz, he recommended as the "first essential establishing the staffs of eminent scholars, writers and speakers, who will do the thinking, the analysis, the writing and the speaking," and as the second essential having "staff personnel who are thoroughly familiar with the media and how most effectively to communicate with the public."

Powell's Legacy

Corporations and the blossoming conservative think tanks took his proposal and ran with it. And they have succeeded immensely. Muckrakers who had exposed corporate fraud and inspired progressive-era reforms are muzzled by the mainstream media today.[16] What we get now instead is propaganda, half truths, and zero truths. Most of the mainstream networks' viewers, for example, believed the administration's explanation for the Iraqi war while only about 20% of the public networks' (PBS/NPR) audience were fooled.[17] What we have today, author Robert McChesney says is "rich media, poor Democracy."[18] What we also have today I say are loud voices drowning out reason and true patriotism.

The POW! Plan

Over the years numerous independent outlets have emerged as an alternative to the rich media (see some examples in Appendix B). They need to be encouraged to ramp up their decibel level and expand their space even more in repeatedly telling the American people about the regime and in recruiting and organizing allies against it. One or more of them, for example, need to create and broadcast a TV miniseries on the Devil's Marriage that might jolt Americans into action. Other media initiatives are suggested in Table 5.2.

Table 5.2

Some Illustrative Initiatives for Blitzing the Media/Internet

-Educate and Inform the Public About-

-the devil's marriage and what the corpocracy is.
-how democracy and corpocracy differ.
-what the corpocracy's telltale signs are.
-what the corpocracy has done to America.
-how the corpocracy controls all spheres of our lives.
-all the corpocracy's allies.
-the political/judicial circus.
-the wrongdoing of corporations on most-admired lists.
-the "most wanted lists" of corporate scofflaws.
-the corporate welfare queen and her "food stamps."
-the corpocracy's sham charities and philantrophy.
-public "serpents" masquerading as public servants.
-the counter offensives of the corpocracy and its allies.
-the corpocracy's dependence on public inaction.
-anti-corpocracy movements and NGOs.
-all the possible strategies/initiatives to end the corpocracy.
-what a corpocracy-free America would look like and do.

-Some Other Initiatives Using the Media/Internet-

-to build public support for all anti-corpocracy measures.
-to recruit and organize allies for democracy power.
-to create a StopCorpocracy.org as a one-stop web source.
-to announce Golden Fleece awards (see Chapter 9).

The American people not only need to understand the corpocracy's telltale signs but they also need to be told what a regime-free America could be like: no one living in poverty; everyone employable holding jobs earning at the very least a living wage; everyone having affordable health care and a quality education; no homeless people; no slum housing; no gangs marauding inner cities; no more unregulated harmful products or an environment to worry about; and no more wars or lesser military conflicts to pay for in money and lives. These would not be signs of a utopia. They would be signs that the Devil's Marriage has been broken up and that the trillions of dollars wasted on corporate welfare, including warfare welfare (see Chapter 9) would now be available for protecting and promoting the general welfare of all Americans.

It's unmistakably clear to me that the mainstream media and through it the regime are being challenged almost on a daily or weekly basis by the independent media. It's also unmistakably clear to me that all of this energy and activity ought to be better organized and coordinated. Very few NGOs specializing in educational efforts even acknowledge each other, let alone do any collaborating. Additionally, I wonder if they are mostly preaching to the choir and need to seek innovative ways to broaden their audiences such as through more creative use of visual arts like the politically activist videos produced by Brave New Films.

Another part of the Powell legacy is the political/judiciary circus. It is taken up in the next chapter.

Some Closing Memory Ticklers and One Liners

Tell the truth big enough and keep repeating it so people will come to believe it.

Keeping the masses ignorant, submissive, consumptive-a corpocracy agenda.

Let's not regress to a dark ages with the corpocracy as High Church!

Does the thought of burning Ayn Rand's books tempt anyone?

What we have today are loud voices drowning out reason and true patriotism.

End the lying corpocracy or it will end America.

Chapter 6. Closing the Corpocracy's Political/ Judicial Circus

> How many clowns
> can get out of that car?
> The party twins.
> All the lifers and vote peddlers.
> All the oval office puppets.
> All the touts.
> All the burrowers.
> All the hurdle makers.
> The car has revolving doors!
> And archways!
> Who's driving the car?
> The big beast?
> No, the corporate ringmaster.
> What's the car pulling?
> A bench with robed clowns.

What's going on here? P.T. Barnum would know. Mark Twain would know. Will Rogers would know. Late night comedians would know. They would know it's not simply a carnival, here today, gone tomorrow. It's the biggest tragic-comic circus playing throughout America, with the main cast of characters performing in Washington, DC. It's been going on for decades, and Americans are paying dearly for it.

The circus is another part of Powell's legacy. In his memorandum under the section heading "the neglected political arena" Powell began with what might be a Freudian slip of the tongue, writing that "in the final analysis, the payoff -- short-of revolution -- is what government does."[1] Make of it what you will, but to me government payoffs are synonymous with the dowry of government power gifts to the corporate partner in return for its keeping the politicians in office. Political power, he advised, must be constantly cultivated, even used aggressively, determinedly, and without embarrassment. He didn't give any specifics and concluded this section of his manifesto by telling the USCC that while it may be reluctant to do so it needed to "consider assuming a broader and more vigorous role in the political arena." This is one arena where the USCC didn't hesitate to get involved and hasn't lost any zeal over the years.

Powell also noted that there was a "neglected opportunity in the courts" and that given our constitutional system "especially with an activist-minded Supreme Court (emphasis mine) the judiciary may be the most important instrument for social, economic, and political change." He then noted that "American business has been much less astute in exploiting (emphasis mine again) the judiciary. I can't overstate how much this is a chilling revelation from a soon-to-be Supreme Court justice that foretells what will unfold over the next few years and continues to this day, namely the corpocracy's creation and manipulation of an activist and sympathetic judiciary.

Since he wasn't a politician, Powell probably succeeded beyond his wildest dreams (with the likely exception of his anticipating making future judicial decisions to his liking and considering that as a Supreme Court justice he voted his free enterprises biases).

Closing the circus will be a monumental challenge if we are to return to a true democracy for the common good. The circus clowns are smart, wily, tough, and tenacious.

Reform the Political Party System

> No one party can fool all of the people all
> of the time. That's why we have two parties.
> ---Bob Hope

Some possible strategic initiatives for reforming the political system include dumping the party twins, creating or revitalizing an independent party, reviving progressivism, adopting a form of deliberative democracy, and pursuing federal ballot initiatives. Whatever the initiatives pursued, it is imperative that politics as usual is changed into politics as unusual whether through changing politicians or forcing politicians to change their ways.

Dump the Party Twins

The two dominant political parties, Democratic and Republican, are simply two sides of the corpocracy's expensive coin (with the Republican side being the most corporatized, obstructionist, repugnlicant). If you look for mention of any political parties in the U.S. Constitution you won't find it. The Framers disdained the very notion, warning that political parties simply invite factionalism and could create all sorts of mischief and civil strife. How prescient they were! The U.S. was governed for over 20 years before the first political parties emerged.

Suppose we could create some modern version of the way we governed ourselves those first 20 some years. Consider what my scholarly/artistic/ activist friend Richard Oxman is trying to do to change our political paradigm in a legal and nonviolent way.[2] He has created a small movement and given it the acronym, TOSCA, for Taking Over the State of California. Goodness knows this state has become nearly ungovernable and seems about ready to fall into a budget quake. Richard proposes having twelve unaffiliated, non-politician citizens serving as Governor of California. There would be a figurehead candidate elected to satisfy the traditional political paradigm but all major decisions would be made in complete transparency by the non-political twelve. While he is currently recruiting people in the other states to create their own TOSXX, he doesn't want to slow his work in California that is his greatest priority for now.

There are several politically oriented NGOs. They need to find or figure out a good answer to what to do about political parties as we know them today whether it be helping Oxman to advance his TOSCA and TOSXX or to come up with and pursue some other options.

Revive Progressivism

There reportedly are about 80 members of Congress belonging to a "progressive caucus" (to some "progressive" is just another label for "democrat"). That leaves the bulk of Congress, the remaining 85%, in the non-progressive caucus, the caucus most bound to the corpocracy.

A dozen or so NGOs are actively involved in reviving progressivism, a philosophy and practice that seem suited for a political approach to reclaiming democracy although I'm sure progressivism isn't progressive enough for some people. One of the NGOs, Democracy for America even has a National Campaign Academy for training socially progressive candidates to run for office.[3] What's striking immediately is all the other NGOs are doing roughly the same thing, which seems to beg for their coordinating, and collaborating with each other and following a strategic plan.

Some of the earliest tenets of progressivism called for giving the American people a more direct role in their government by, for instance, voting directly on proposed laws rather than voting on politicians who propose and make laws. Taken to their logical extension such tenets conceivably could even lead to replacing "politicians" with "citizen "delegates" comparable I suppose to what Oxam is trying to do. But obviously we are dealing with more than a word game here. What we are dealing with is the idea of and the effort to revive our earliest American custom of electing citizens, not would-be lifers, who govern on behalf of their fellow citizenry for a short period of time and then withdraw to become regular citizens once again. Granted, the idea of replacing politicians with citizens who delegate to each other on some kind of selective and term-limited basis the continuing responsibility of governing America may seem idealistic and unwieldy, yet Oxman for one isn't deterred from trying to put the idea into practice. How the idea might be further elaborated and tested certainly warrants being explored further. The late Supreme Court justice Felix Frankfurter once said that "In a democracy, the highest office is the office of citizen."

Try Deliberative Democracy

Stopping short of the early progressive model that bypasses politicians in voting on proposed laws is a model known as deliberative democracy that appeared in 1980.[4] In this model a representative sample of the public is selected to deliberate an issue and then to conduct a poll among themselves to choose a public policy option. The results can be used to inform public officials on the issue and sometimes is a stand-in for a traditional vote on the issue. Political scientist professor and philosopher James Fishkin who was instrumental in developing the non-traditional form of opinion polling has recently published a book reporting on numerous applications in the U.S. and elsewhere of the deliberative democracy process.[5] To what extent it ever takes hold nationwide remains to be seen. Had this process (or something like Oxman's proposed process) been used instead of the non-deliberative, hedonistic and reckless direct voting by Californians "to tax themselves like libertarians and subsidize themselves like socialists" the state would not be crumbling as it is today.[6]

A different variation of deliberative democracy I think is the idea of "direct decrees" by the people as expressed in federal ballot initiatives. An amendment to the U.S. Constitution would be required I think to implant the process, and the three executive branches of the federal government could not be bypassed in the process. This idea is promoted by the NGO, National Initiative for Democracy.[7] Supporters of the idea argue that many states already have ballot initiatives. That does not seem like a good argument to me. State initiatives can and have yielded regrettable changes with California being an illustrative case.

I suppose there are many other conceivable ways to let the "will of the people" be expressed and established. I'm not an expert on self-rule so I can't speak to other possibilities. What I do know absolutely is that self-rule is preferable to corpocracy rule and there must be a way found to end the latter.

Create or Revitalize an Independent Party

Perhaps nothing suits corporate interests better than America's two-party iron-clad grip on politics and political discourse. Both the Republican and Democratic parties are patsies for corporate interests. In her book, Grand Illusion: The Myth of Voter Choice in a Two Party Tyranny, Theresa Amato, former campaign manager for Ralph Nader and founder of the NGO, Citizen Advocacy Center, says that unless one has been running a political race outside the two primary parties, "it is impossible to imagine the injustices of the two-party-tilted electoral process.[8] Third parties, not unlike thwarted eligible voters, run into all sorts of legal and other hurdles.

Nevertheless, third parties don't give up for trying. In the history of U.S. politics there have been some 800 third parties in all. Nearly 20 have nominated presidential candidates in recent times. Officially establishing a third party seems no more difficult than getting a driver's license and there's no quiz to take. What's nearly impossible is to get third party candidates elected. The Libertarian Party, espousing laissez-faire government and individual liberty, apparently has more people in office than all other third parties combined but fortunately has never put one in the oval office (I say "fortunately" because this political group doesn't seem to understand or appreciate the implications of Lincoln's "community of people"). Ralph Nader certainly gave his party a shot at the office. Had he won I wouldn't have had to write this book.

Two parties that embrace various positions against the corpocracy and for more direct participation by the citizenry in legislation and other political matters are the Progressive Party and the Populist Party. Of the two, the first seems to be the more active and robust. The politically active NGOs could decide whether to pursue their agenda within the context of the two major parties or to promote one or the other of these two independent parties and along the way to try and get Ms Amato's proposed federal reforms implemented. As I mentioned, there is the non-party, miniscule Congressional Progressive Caucus, but its influence so far has been minimal. Maybe we need a political reform to establish open primaries, giving people outside the corpocracy a crack at being voted into office.

Oust the Lifers and Vote Peddlers

> We have the best Congress
> money can buy.
> ---Will Rogers

Politics was never meant to be a professional calling and career in America. Before political parties emerged politicians were considered citizens first and foremost and they voluntarily left office instead of running for reelection. Politicians are more likely now to retire from or die in office than to be ousted from it by the voters.

End Politics as a Career

Having experienced first-hand despotic rule, the founders of our new democracy weren't about to provide for imperialism again in designing our Constitution. They were students of history and could not fail to note and appreciate that a political feature of ancient Greece and Rome was rotation of office, or term limits. Thomas Jefferson, no less, urged limiting tenure "to prevent every danger which might arise to American freedom---." I would bet a dollar to a doughnut that Mr. Jefferson had in mind the equivalent then of today's corpocracy.

Establishing term limits would be one tactic for ending political careerists. Quixotically, our Constitution and its amendments are SILENT on the matter of term limits for all elected offices but the U.S. presidency, and that apparently was all the leeway the U.S. Supreme Court needed to rule in a 1995 case that states couldn't impose term limits on their U.S. senators and representatives and that a constitutional amendment would be required to establish term limits.[9] Nonsense. Four dissenting justices thought so, too. States, on the other hand, are free to impose term limits on politicians elected to state offices, and several states have done just that. Some others have tried but have been thwarted by their legislators or judiciary

An argument often heard against term limits is that political offices would always be held by neophytes. There is some merit to this argument as evidenced in cases like that of California.[10] Term limits don't negate the political influence of corporate interests but do, I should think, make their influence more difficult to satisfy. Another argument with which I sympathize is that should a new breed of politicians come along hostile to the corpocracy they must come and go just as quickly, but worth happening I think to get rid of entrenched and beholden lifers.

Heavy political pressure ought to be put on members of Congress to pass a law limiting their terms. About 70% of the general public is reportedly in favor of term limits.[11] This poll "simply" needs to be turned into "poll"itical pressure. The 104th Congress did try twice, half-heartedly, and failed to legislate for a constitutional amendment allowing for term limits on its members. If Congress were pressured enough it could circumvent the Court by either decreeing a self-imposed term limit or passing term-limit legislation without seeking an amendment. This, of course, might lead to a showdown regarding the equality of powers and their separation. Admittedly, this tactic may not have a ghost of a chance. Politicians don't want to end their careers voluntarily. I guess I can't really blame them on that.

End Campaign Financing

To stay in their cushy positions through one reelection after another politicians have learned to be consummate vote peddlers catering to the corporations' touts that collect favors expected after the corporate campaign financing put the peddlers in office. "Nothing," says one U.S. Senator, dominates the life of a senator more than raising money. Of any free time you have, I would say fifty per cent, maybe even more," is spent on fund-raising;" and "you're dialling for dollars" says a former Senate majority leader.[12]

The bottom line is that money flowing to campaign coffers is like water flowing to its lowest level, sewer politics, regardless of obstacles put in its path. Does the thought of "bribery" enter your mind? If you follow the money trail as the authors of <u>The People's Business</u> have, you will see, they say, that a "pattern of influence will inevitably emerge" when major votes on issues affecting particular industries are compared to the campaign money and follow-up lobbying by those industries.[13] How could this pattern not emerge? Would any sane person think corporations finance campaigns as a way to strengthen democracy and not themselves? If there were no issues, no huge profits, and no political careers at stake, you can take money to the bank there would be much less money for corporations and their touts and much less security for politicians. An indirect benefit to corporations incidentally, is that donations to politicians, particularly to the lifers, buoy share price by giving comfort and assurance to shareholders of politically favored corporations.[14]

Now and then throughout the course of our history there have been attempts to prevent the sale of public office through vote peddling during political campaigns. The yin and yang between democracy and the corpocracy in the fight for and against campaign finance reform would be comic if democracy weren't the loser. The struggle's history is long and full of enactments, rulings, reversals, circumventions, violations, and lax enforcement. It doesn't make for very easy or interesting reading, so I have put the highlights in Table 6.1 and will simply leave the history at that.

Table 6.1

<u>The Yin and Yang of Campaign Financing Reform</u>

1907. Congress bans campaign donations from corporations.
1907 to 1966. More statues enacted to toughen the restrictions.
1971. Congress puts earlier reforms into The Federal Election Campaign Act (FECA) and starts public funding of federal elections.
1974. Congress amends FECA and creates the Federal Election Commission (FEC).
1976. Supreme Court strikes down campaign financing limits.

1979. Congress streamlines FEC's monitoring and expands role of political parties.

2000. Supreme Court "elects" George Bush.

2002. Congress bans "soft money" but increases contribution limits.

2006. Supreme Court reaffirms unconstitutionality of spending limits.

2007. Supreme Court loosens restrictions on campaign advertising.

2008. Congress mulling bills allowing corporations' direct donations to candidates.

2010. Supreme Court rules in favor of selling elections.

The Supreme Court is the biggest obstacle to Americans regaining control of the campaign process and its outcomes, yet the Court has never been unanimous in its opinion on the matter. So the door is slightly ajar for a strategy to seek the Court's rejection of corporate personhood by marshalling all the resources available to arrange for getting an indefensible test case on its way up to the Court. To quote Powell in reverse in his charge to the USCC, "the greatest care should be exercised in selecting the cases in which to participate, or the suits to institute. But the opportunity merits the necessary effort." As a last resort (other options are discussed in Chapter 7), an effort to prosecute or impeach judges who vote for corporate interests through biased interpretations of the Constitution and other laws could be initiated, but that might not happen until the 12th of Never.

Meanwhile, there have been various proposals to at least curtail or offset corporate financing of campaigns such as boosting the Federal Election Commission's enforcement role (which might run afoul of the January 21, 2010 ruling), providing substantially more money from publicly funded campaign financing, and requiring broadcasters who are given free public licenses to give candidates free air time. But these proposals, which have "loopholes a jet can fly through," are no substitute for totally banning corporations from flooding campaigns with donations.[15] Neither are voluntary disclosures by corporations of their political spending a substitute.[16] Whom do they think they're kidding, anyway? An aggressive push for a total ban is sorely needed, including having the ban upheld as constitutionally legal.

An ancillary initiative to ending campaign financing, since unlimited terms aid incumbents the most, would be to eliminate gerrymandering that creates "designer districts" of "safe seats tailor made for incumbents."[17]

In an analysis by Common Cause of the redrawing of political boundaries in California first by incumbents and later by three retired judges under a court-imposed mandate, reelection of incumbents declined in both U.S. House and state legislative races. This NGO has launched a nationwide redistricting plan by working in multiple states to build statewide coalitions to develop state redistricting plans.[18]

Cut the Oval Office Puppets' Strings

Two-term limits keep U.S. presidents from being life-long residents of the White House. But that's plenty enough time and more for them to do damage. Whether in the oval office one or two terms, they are corporate puppets and might as well be on its payroll, except it's cheaper for corporations to have presidents stay on the tax payer's roll.

The corporate strings are taut and short. The puppets wage war urged on by the defense (war) industry and other corporate interests. Besides warfare welfare they dole out all sorts of other corporate welfare. They deregulate public constraints on corporate power. They promote the exploitative, undemocratic form of capitalism on behalf of corporations, and especially the big firms on Wall Street. They make judicial appointments that please corporations. They open the revolving door and let it keep spinning with corpocrats coming and going. They use the bully pulpit on behalf of corporate interests. They issue "signing statements" to end run new corporate-hostile laws and regulations (not that there are many to end run). They set in motion the policies that paved the way to Economic Katrina, etc., etc.

What about President Obama? Won't he be different? His first year came and went with a totally inadequate response by his administration to Economic Katrina and the blockading by health care/insurance self-interests of any substantive health care reform. In building up military forces in Afghanistan and elsewhere he has shown the lessons of Vietnam and other American military aggressions were lost on him. In sum, he may turn out to be just another puppet of a different color. The only way to end puppet presidencies is to end the corpocracy and elect presidents committed to true democracy and the general welfare.

Out the Touts

I've been tout fishing
On the banks of the political sewer.
And with just one cast
Look at what I caught
One of the biggest touts of all!

BIG PHARMA

What has Big Pharma, second to none in the tout sewer, gotten for its money?[19] The Center for Public Integrity answered this question by looking at the Congress-Drug lobby track record from 1980 until 2006. I have paraphrased their findings in Table 6.2.

Table 6.2

Big Pharma's Return on its Touts*

-defeat of mandatory discount pricing.
-protection of drug patents in trade agreements.
-joint research patents with public institutions allowe.
-Medicare price negotiations with companies prevented.
-government list of preferred drugs prohibited.
-availability of generic pediatric drugs delayed.
-faster government drug safety reviews.
-company recommended reviewers allowed.
-bill to make generic drugs more accessible defeated.
-bigger hurdle before government warning letters issued.
-approval of some drugs just from animal testing.
-medical device makers get favorable considerations.
-unapproved uses of drugs gets journalistic license.
-restrictions eased on direct-to consumer advertising.
-tax credits given to makers of orphan drugs.
-licensing of new sites for making drugs eased.
-continuous review of approved new sites ended.
-pre-clinical trial data allowed for patent application.
-criteria for awarding patents for genes relaxed.

- price control proposals dropped by government.
-companies allowed to pay fee for faster reviews.
-faster review of drugs for life-threatening diseases.
-distribution of drug samples allowed.
-easier for brand-name makers to sue generic makers.
-government promotes university-industry partnerships.
-industry allowed to tap research at subsidized facilities.

---

*Adapted from the Center for Public Integrity, www.publicintegrity. org.

In June, 2009, Big Pharma pledged to contribute $80 billion in discounts and other savings over the next decade as part of the administration's health care reform initiative.[20] Let's not be fooled or overcome by gratitude. It's estimated the American people spent $3.3 trillion since 1980, and Big Pharma will reap even more profits if reform extends coverage to millions of uninsured.

The sewer is full of touts besides Big Pharma. Name an industry that doesn't have a school of touts. So when any of them comes through a Capitol Hill door the public's interest in getting legislation and budget allocations for the common good gets thrown out the window.

In 1970 before Powell's manifesto, only 175 corporations in the U.S. had registered lobbyists.[21] Enter the manifesto. Powell had complained in it that "few elements of American society today have as little influence in government as---the lobbyist for the business point of view before Congressional committees---or in the legislative halls of most states and major cities."

His complaint was heard loud and clear. Ten years later, 650 corporations had registered lobbyists, 20 years later, 16,000 some, and then more than doubling just five years later in 2005 to nearly 35,000 touts according to one account.[22] One giant corporation alone had over 130 lobbyists on its payroll one year.[23] The cost to the corpocracy of its touting over the years, nearly $20 billion from 1998 to 20007, seems staggering until one realizes the corpocracy wouldn't be spending that amount foolishly if it weren't getting its money's worth.[24]

State politicians get their share of touts, apparently another 17,000 some altogether, and are finding it doesn't hurt to have their own lobbyists pleading for more favors from the federal government.[25] Lobbyists for the health care industry alone gave nearly $102 million to state political campaigns across the country, exceeding the amount given to campaigns at the federal level.[26]

The Nation's capital, naturally, is overflowing with touts. Because there are so many and because the two galleries of Congress can hold only so many spectators without collapsing, the touts who need to attend crucial public hearings pay "line sitters" who are law school students, bicycle messengers, even the homeless, to camp out overnight to get gallery tickets.[27] The gallery guards let in anyone with a ticket, even known corporate scofflaws as was the case one time with ticket holders representing 20 corporate defrauders of the government.

Because of purportedly stricter regulations imposed recently on tout activity the number of touts on record has started declining but it is an illusory game of numbers.[28] The regulations have merely driven the touts "underground," and the regulations are flexible and the enforcement negligible. What else would we expect from tout-addicted politicians who make the rules the touts expect them to make and draft for them?

"The stricter" rules, moreover, don't rule out "inside" touts. When you think about it for a moment, all legislators are touts, too, inside touts who tout their clients' interests to other inside touts when legislation is being considered. Some legislators tout their own business interests. One U.S. senator, for instance, besides getting plenty of donations from the financial services industry, has a multimillion dollar real estate business and has plenty of clout when it comes to legislation affecting his own interests as well as those of his industry clientele.[29]

It remains to be seen just how soft or tough President Obama will be on the touting crowd. Lobbyists have even steadily increased their spending since he took office. His requiring touts to more fully report their lobbying expenses and actions isn't nearly tough enough. The comical "Bedfellow Disclosure Bill of 2005" requiring greater transparency would simply amount to nothing more than more paperwork. Assessing a lobbying tax would be almost laughable. Corporations can easily afford the tax. A lobbying tax couldn't begin to balance all of the corporate welfare flowing from the government.

The best way to deal with the touts, but never a sure way given the powerful and resourceful corpocracy, would be to take money out of politics. And I don't mean by this not giving legislators substantial pay increases, which might be justified if they were forced to become short-term office-holders. What I mean would require totally barring corporations, its touts, or any other intermediaries from giving anything of value to legislators. If you can believe this statistic, 90% of the American people reportedly favor "not giving anything of value" to legislators (it's not hard to guess who make up the 10%).[30]

Another option short of ridding government of touts is to blunt or counterbalance their influence on legislation and regulations by ensuring that all public interest groups are involved as extensively and as intensely as corporate touts when legislators and regulators are drafting their laws and regulations. Preferably, every time a lobbyist representing any industry meets with members of Congress and/or their staff, a representative of a public interest group should be included. If it is excluded or prevented from meaningful input, legislators should be sued for misrepresentation.

Plug the Burrower's Holes

Now you see them, now you don't. Once the puppets are out of office their favorite appointees are quietly made civil servants. Candidate Barack Obama promised on the campaign trail to stop the practice. We should demand that he does.

Lock the Revolving Doors and Archways

Now you see them here. Now you see them there. Who are they and where are they coming and going? They don't stay put like the careerists do. They are the self-serving clowns coming and going, the shufflers back and forth through the so-called, perfectly named "revolving door." To author and activist Jim Hightower these shufflers are among the "thieves in high places, steadily and quietly pilfering" the essence of our democracy."[31] There are actually three kinds of revolving doors.

One is for corporate officials and lobbyists who go through to appointments in key government posts to ensure corporate interests aren't denied by the American people. The Bush administration for instance appointed at least "100 top officials who in their prior lives were lobbyists, attorneys, or spokespeople in industries" they oversaw."[32] One of those top officials was a former oil industry executive, revolved into a new Vice President in the West Wing, who was appointed by Bush to be "in charge of drafting its closed-door energy policy."[33] Another shuffler right behind the VP had been a former state's attorney general known for his disdain of government-run consumer protection programs who then quickly selected for the agency's general counsel a former corporate defense lawyer for corporations in suits against their wanton disregard for product safety. Those two officials did what they could to turn the Consumer Protection Agency's into the Corporate Protection Agency.[34] I could go on with the rest of the 100 obnoxious cases but I will spare us.

There's the government-to-industry door through which public officials, having gotten experience and valuable contacts from the inside in keeping public interests at bay, go to industry and parlay their experience and contacts into furthering corporate interests in exchanges, usually private, with the government.

And finally, there's the government-to-lobbyist door through which former legislators, their staffs, and executive-branch officials pass on the way to lucrative positions in lobbying firms to lobby their former colleagues. A former member of Congress left to head Big Pharma with a yearly salary estimated at $2 million and was reportedly lobbying against allowing Americans to buy cheaper drugs from Canada.[35] For such a sickening and reprehensible act Americans may need to take some Canadian medication.

Besides the revolving doors there are the "archways," the metaphor author Naomi Klein uses for the passage of people who used to occupy top posts in the government, left for lucrative positions in the corporate world, then left it but stopped short of going through the revolving door.[36] Instead they remained outside as influential advisors to top government officials and in so doing avoided conflict of interest rules (which have never stopped conflicts of interest among the revolving door people). She cites members of the Defense Policy Board as an example. Those folks helped pedal the Iraqi War.

Let's put to rest right now the argument that appointing people from corporations and their allies to influential government positions helps make government do a better job of legislating, regulating, and enforcing measures to protect the American people from powerful corporate interests. I'm not stupid. I know what happens when foxes guard chicken houses

The Revolving Door Working Group, an NGO, has proposed numerous initiatives for locking or slowing the passageways to and from public offices for people with self serving private interests. The first proposal on the NGO's list is to "strengthen self-policing by executive and legislative branches."[37] But can we expect a corporatized government to police itself any more than we can expect it to police corporations? I seriously doubt it. Doubts can also be raised about the rest of the proposals on the list.

I think we can assume that President Obama will keep the doors and archways passable for at least awhile. No sooner had he been elected than he let Rahm Emanuel revolve in to become Chief of Staff, a very, very powerful position. True, Mr. Emanuel left Congress to take the job, but prior to being a Representative from Illinois, he had excelled in representing the banking industry.[38] Mr. Emanuel isn't the only outsider/insider on Obama's team. Its members say a columnist, typically served in the Clinton administration and then went off to places like law and financial firms.[39]

So we can forget Obama. Until all the corpocracy's badvantages are removed we can expect the doors and archways to remain open.

Knock Down Voting Hurdles

> I don't want everybody to vote.
> Elections are not won by a majority
> of the people. They never have been
> from the beginning of our country.
> They are not now. As a matter of
> fact, our leverage in the elections
> quite candidly goes up as the
> voting populace goes down.
> ---Paul Weyrich

Thank you "radical right strategist," Paul Weyrich for your candid remark at a 1980 training session for 15,000 conservative preachers in Dallas (just imagine being cooped up with them).[40] Mr. Weyrich has reinforced my conclusion that the fewer the voters the easier it is for the regime to influence the outcome of elections. Voting hurdles help achieve that end. They misrepresent the voter, deter the voter, deny voting, or derail honest voting. Voter disillusionment is the only self-imposed hurdle but it is reinforced by the actions of the regime making eligible voters feel it's futile to vote.

Voter misrepresentation occurs when a candidate wins the popular vote but loses the Electoral College vote, a perfectly legitimate but terribly unfair outcome. I'm not going to get bogged down here in a discussion of half a dozen or so alternatives to the ridiculous Electoral College such as instant runoff voting, direct vote with plurality rule, etc. There are far worse problems and possible solutions to cover in this book.

Voter suppression is mostly achieved directly through regulatory, legislative and administrative skullduggery, although occasionally illegal tactics are used such as Republican operatives jamming a Democratic phone bank.[41]

Other noteworthy hurdles are unjust voter eligibility criteria that bar otherwise eligible voters from voting, vote tampering that corrupts honest votes, and understaffed and incompetent personnel at polling places that complicate or distort the voting.

The Supremely Corporatized Court, not long ago in a 6 to 3 vote upheld Indiana's voter identification law, allegedly the strictest in the country. The majority said the law was not unconstitutional, would improve the election process, would deter fraud and shrugged off counter arguments that prosecuted fraud is rare to nil; and that an unjustified, nontrivial burden was being imposed "on people who are old, poor or members of minority groups and less likely to have driver's licenses or other acceptable forms of identification."[42] I have no doubt that in conservative Indiana the real motivation for the law in the first place was to bar otherwise eligible voters from voting for the opposite party (alas, Indiana is my home state). Does the silent majority of Americans really want to return to the Jim Crow era of poll taxes and literacy tests that kept Black voters from the ballot box?

So what's to be done about these hurdles? The answer, to knock them down, is easier said than done (obviously the same goes for closing down the rest of the circus). The different hurdles call for different counter measures. Direct vote with plurality rule would require a Constitutional amendment, the biggest hurdle of all. Unjust eligibility criteria would require legislative reform or litigation. Illegal tactics such as jamming phone banks would need to be monitored and swiftly countered when they arise, an appropriate action for law enforcement authorities if only they would enforce the law.

Shrink the Big Beast

The cons are fond of saying "starve the beast." They are referring, of course, to big government. They want to cut public budgets, public services, and the number of public servants to the bone. I understand their gripe although their solutions are worse than the problem. The beast isn't as big as the cons' stereotype of it. Government expenditures in the U.S. as part of its overall economy as measured by gross domestic product are rather small compared to the ratios of other Western countries, and you would have to run into about seven strangers before you found a government worker if my figures are correct. Nevertheless, that's not many strangers and it does seem inconsistent that a government that seems to do so little (e.g. regulates so little, enforces so little, and privatizes so much) is as big as it is. So I am convinced that the beastly bureaucracy could stand at least some trimming, but not starving. The corpocracy is a big reason we have big government. The corpocracy absurdly but purposely spawned a gargantuan Department of Homeland Security, including a "hidden world [of nearly 1300 government organizations and nearly 2000 private companies] growing out of control."[43] The corpocracy, private and public beast together, will never starve as long as they can keep provoking terrorism.

Let's imagine that a citizens' commission and a task force of experts is established (by whom or what left deliberately unsaid here) to deliberate on and recommend the appropriate role for government in our society, a role that would strike a balance between too little and too much government once freed from corporate influence, and ways to streamline the structure and administrative staffing of the federal and state legislative and judicial bodies and to improve their performance. In addressing the first issue the task force would determine what America really needs that requires a collective effort best done through government such as national security and what America really doesn't need such as endless wars (making some of these determinations would parallel other taskforces' initiatives proposed in Chapters 9 and 10).

The commission and task force would produce a joint report, get it published, and then distribute it widely to the media, to the public, and especially to government. The government's response would then need to be monitored and political pressure applied if the proposed government reforms are being stalled or rejected.

Restore Justice to the Corporatized Courts

Verdicts of the corporatized U.S. Supreme Court in the last ten years or so have favored corporate interests over public interests in rulings that made it easier to buy votes; loosened antitrust restrictions; severely limited punitive damages; made it harder for workers to sue employers; made it easier to seize private land; made it harder for shareholders to sue for corporate securities-related fraud; and made it harder to obtain patents.

In other words, whenever the politicized high court hears a corporate case with highly paid lawyers pleading them at the bar, the ordinary citizen can expect to get soaked. Lady Justice is neither blind nor her scales balanced!

It's an idealistic myth to think that justices and judges put on their robes of impartiality. Let's call them what they are, robes of partiality. Additionally, besides their own predilections, their deliberations are bombarded by arguments and counterarguments from well-paid corporate lawyers. In a speech to state judges, retired Supreme Court justice Sandra Day O'Connor worried that courts are losing their autonomy.[44] Wasn't she on the same bench with Powell and the others?

Powell was a perfect example of a former corporate lawyer who, once on the U.S. Supreme Court, continued as a corporatized justice. He significantly influenced the court's decisions rolling back the expanding judicial interpretations of federal securities laws. He was a consistent defender of corporations' constitutional right to free speech. In a 1972 decision, which reversed a Hugo Black decision nearly a quarter of a century earlier, he successfully argued that mall owners could prohibit the free speech of activists distributing flyers on public issues and then four years later wrote the majority opinion that corporations had the right to speak out on public issues; and in 1980 he again wrote for the majority opinion a "fervent defense" of corporations' free-speech rights.[45] Corporations owe him an enormous debt of gratitude for that defense, and it surely must have fortified the corporate-sided reasoning behind the January 21, 2010 ruling.

Burger's Court, the one Powell joined, was eventually succeeded by the Rehnquist court and then the Robert's court of today. In comparing the two, one Washington lawyer commented that the "Rehnquist court was really quite a good forum for business---but the Roberts court is even better," and an executive vice president of the USCC "declared the Robert's court as "<u>our</u> (emphasis mine) best Supreme Court ever."[46] At the close of the first full term of the Robert's court, the New York Times editorialized that "time and again the court has ruled, almost always 5-4, in favor of corporations and powerful interests while slamming the courthouse door on individuals and ideals that truly need the court's shelter."[47] Legal journalist Jeffrey Toobin has portrayed Roberts as a "No More Mr. Nice Guy" who "has sided with the prosecution over the defendant, the state over the condemned, the executive branch over the legislative, and the corporate defendant over the individual plaintiff."[48] Mr. Toobin might as well have called Roberts the "Chief Justice for the United Corporations of America." Roberts sealed that epithet with the January 21, 2010 ruling.

But let's never ever forget the day when the Rehnquist court stooped down to become the sleaziest court of the land, the high court of supremely low integrity, by defying the majority of voters in handing over the 2000 presidential election to George W. Bush so that he could become yet another oval office puppet (but I'm almost certain Gore would have been one, too).

Corporate control over the judiciary doesn't stop with the high court. It seems that corporations and their industries own the judiciary at any level.[49] Recall that the National Association of Manufacturer's, for instance, launched a project to elect state judges friendly to its client corporations in cases of tort suits. In nearly four fifths of the states judges are elected rather than appointed to the state's highest court. Its seats are open to the highest bidder, with some candidates spending $2 million or more. As we might expect, the USCC is in the thick of the election battles and winning them for their kept judges almost every time.[50]

Indebted justices don't forget their benefactors. In one state, for example, justices ruled in favor of corporate litigants who were contributors to their successful reelection campaigns 70 percent of the time.[51] I will repeat, the scales of justice are neither balanced nor is the lady holding them blindfolded when corporations go to court.

If the public ever stormed up Capitol Hill en masse and demanded that the Constitution be honored, corporate interests might never again be represented before the high court.

Another radical way to democratize the courts would be through impeachment of kept judges. The Oregon Democratic Party's central committee tried to do just that when it overwhelmingly voted in 2001 to launch a drive to impeach the five U.S. Supreme Court justices who gave the election to George W. Bush.[52] The impeachment never materialized however, yet it is still most needed, and can still be done even after a justice leaves the bench.

Ending or altering term limits for the judiciary would undoubtedly make courts more democratic, but the Constitution grants life tenure to justices of the U.S. Supreme Court. As for lower courts, term limits and other initiatives such as creating citizens' grand juries to prosecute wayward justices have been on state ballots but to my knowledge none has passed.

Some legal scholars have proposed sidestepping the constitutional issue by shunting the more senior justices to secondary roles and by more frequently appointing new justices.[53]

Jean Edward Smith, professor and prolific author, advocates another tactic to "bring the court to heel," namely, changing the number of seats on the bench.[54] FDR, you may know, tried but failed to do just that.

Whatever the tactic considered, there needs to be continuing efforts to create opportunities for appointing or electing judges who would uphold the ideals of justice and the rule of law rather than being "activist-minded" (recall Powell's manifesto) and exploitable by corporate or any other special interests.[55]

Pursue Miscellaneous Legislature Reforms

From time to time there have been various initiatives proposed and some undertaken to reform the way the legislature works. They amount in my opinion to palliatives and facades. I will mention just one dealing with the U.S. Senate's legislative rules so as not to waste more words or your time. The U.S. Senate could, but won't, end perhaps the biggest log jamming rule, the filibuster. I don't think it really matters much though if they do or don't. The filibuster rule hardly accounts for the corpocracy's rule of America. I'll throw in this wishful thought, having some group step forward and sue Congress for malfeasance of public duty. If the group needs to show it has standing as a plaintiff, it can stand on the backs of all of us who are misrepresented and ill served by our legislators.

Will the Show Ever Close Down?

The regime will keep the show open and busy until and if we close it down. U.S. Presidents won't do it for us. They come and go as part of the show. Congress won't do it for us. They stay doggedly and deviously in the show, and to expect them to reform themselves is wishful thinking. Corporate members of the corpocracy certainly won't do it. No, permanently closing the show will require a very large "take-down crew," countless initiatives coalescing into major strategic actions such as those described in this book, and a series of legislative reform efforts that finally start leading to successes. All this can be either a cause of pessimism or optimism about America's future.

Some Closing Memory Ticklers and One Liners

So many clowns in one very expensive car!

The real lifers aren't the ones in prison but probably should be.

Politics was never meant to be what it's become, a career.

Elect citizens, not wannabe lifers.

Libertarians just don't understand Lincoln's "community of people."

It would be cheaper were we still under British rule!

A "pattern of influence." Is that like bribery?

Does anyone really think corporations donate money to improve democracy?

Corporate strings to oval office puppets, taut and short.

Obama may be just another puppet of a different color.

The U.S. Supreme Corporate Court.

The scales of justice? Not balanced. Lady ain't blindfolded.

Tout fishing isn't a misspelling.

Nor are the banks of the political sewer a misplaced metaphor.

Name an industry that doesn't have an army of touts.

When touts go into the Capital, the common good is thrown out the window.

Can you imagine being cooped up with 15,000 conservative preachers?

Taking the corpocracy out of the circus would take the corpocracy out of America.

Had Nader won this wouldn't be a book.

The poll favoring term limits needs to be turned into "poll"itical pressure.

Starve the beast? First, take away the corpocracy's double dowry.

Close down the circus or it will close down America.

Chapter 7. Digging Up The Corpocracy's Legal Roots

-Much of corporate wrongdoing is perfectly legal-

Without three legal roots deeply planted by its government partner corporations would not be nearly as powerful and harmful to the general welfare and some would probably fail to survive. The three are sham charters, corporate personhood, and limited liability.

Uproot Sham Charters

Public corporations are granted the right to do business through charters issued by the states where the corporations are incorporated. During the Crown's corpocracy corporations like the brutish British East Indies were chartered by the king. Wanting no more of that, the framers of the Constitution left it up to the states to do the chartering instead of requiring a uniform federal chartering. That decision proved to be a terrible mistake for it eventually led to sham charters. A few states got the idea that by loosening their restrictions they could attract more business, and soon there was a race to the bottom of charter laxity. It wasn't too long before any corporation in any state could get a charter just for the asking and go off and operate as they pleased.

Freed from any restrictions on size and with trust busters nowhere in sight, any corporation can seek to become monolithic and monopolistic. Freed from any expiration deadlines, any corporation can "outlive its own crimes and atrocities" and can wait out more restrictive administrations eventually replaced by more laissez faire ones.[1] Freed from any restrictions on the very nature of its business, a criminally convicted corporation can "disguise itself, run and hide, or reorganize into a whole new entity to stay in business."[2]

While Delaware still is the champion charter maker, Virginia may be the most lax, having allowed, for instance, a group of anti-tobacco activists to get a charter for their new tobacco company, "Licensed to Kill, Inc.," even though it was clearly stated in the articles of incorporation that the company's purpose would be to make and sell products that kill millions of people worldwide.[3]

But it's never too late to correct the Framers' mistakes. If they could return I am sure they would make the corrections themselves. Some possible ways to uproot sham charters include federalizing chartering uniformly; selectively federalizing chartering for certain industries or corporations; and fighting criminally wayward corporations by seeking to have their charters revoked.

Federalize Chartering Uniformly

Uniform federal chartering across all industries with air-tight restrictions on crucial features such as the public purpose of public corporations, corporate size, corporate conduct, and the like would indeed be one way to help beef up corporate accountability as well as to dilute corporate power. The problem, of course, is that moving a mountain might be easier to do. Nevertheless the Constitution's supremacy clause lets federal law trump state law.

The idea of federal chartering is hardly new. I imagine the Framers toyed with it and then decided to defer to the states. Proposals for it actually did appear in the two political parties' platforms at the beginning of the 20th century, and the idea was later revived by Ralph Nader and some of his colleagues in the late 70's.[4] Some federal chartering does exist today but it's miniscule and relatively innocuous. The mortgage lenders Freddie Mac and Fanny Mae are federally chartered for instance. But they are troubling examples. They can't seem to stay out of trouble, stacking their boards with political cronies, and lobbying intensively to sidestep regulations.[5] If nothing else they underscore the point that federal chartering isn't a sine qua non by any means even if doable.

Selectively Federalize Chartering

An option short of blanket federal chartering would be to establish federal charters for certain individual corporations, as in the case of Freddie Mac and Fannie Mae, or very consequential industries such as the defense industry, banking industry, insurance industry, and the pharmaceutical industry to mention just a few (perhaps I should have listed all of them). This option might at least be a start toward eventual blanket chartering.

Selectively Attack Charters and Chartering

Another option is to fight criminally wayward corporations by seeking to have their charters revoked. One provision state legislators haven't removed from their corporate chartering statutes is that of charter revocation. It is an option I think in every state and has been since the beginning of the chartering system shortly after the American Revolution. The option seems to be exercised mostly though at the small fry for small offenses that displease the state for one reason or another (e.g., delinquency in paying fees) but never at the big fry. States' attorney generals would cave under political pressure if they would even hint at revoking a big corporation's charter.

A telling experience is that of POCLAD (Program on Corporations, Law, and Democracy) and allies of this NGO that mounted an offensive to have the California charter of the oil corporation, Unocal, revoked. The state attorney "dismissed the petition out of hand."[6] Because there are 49 other like-minded attorney generals and any goodly number of 9,000 or so large corporations (having 1,000 or more employees) running afoul of the law whenever necessary, it would be tempting to dismiss this option as out of hand also. But sharpened, more targeted, and with greater pressure behind it the tactic might work very slowly but surely.

Yet another option is "merely" a defensive one to keep state charters, which vary in how "shamful" they are, from getting even less restrictive, at least on paper. The NGO, Reclaim Democracy, warns that corporate lawyer members of the American Bar Association extol its "Model Corporation Act" while at the same time are stealthily succeeding in "modernizing" state charters by getting legislatures to further dilute their already flaccid charters before concerned citizens become aware early enough to mount a successful counterattack.[7] This NGO tells about an exception in its experiences, namely its helping to mount a successful counterattack in

Colorado and then provides guidance through its website to citizens of other states where the corpocracy apparently has yet to strike. I don't know how meaningful the success is if Colorado never enforces its restrictions on large corporations, but I don't mean to belittle the effort made. It's a way to hone skills for larger battles.

Corporations aren't chained to their original state charters, of course, and can shop around for the most forgiving ones. Some large corporations have gone so far as to brave opprobrium at home for disloyalty by shucking their state charters and reincorporating off shore. This practice, known as corporate inversions, prompted Congress to include in legislation for creating new jobs clauses that are intended to remove the tax incentives for these inversions. The clauses, however, are ambiguous as their writers undoubtedly intended and it remains to be seen how much of an effect it will have on inversions.[8]

I realize that my review of several options for uprooting sham charters doesn't lead to a very optimistic outlook for replacing them with bona fide restrictive charters as one means to control public corporations. But it's not a reason for despair. Where there is a will there is a way, and the will has some ways.

Uproot Corporate Personhood

Not prescribing a federal charter in the Constitution was one mistake too many for the Framers to make. But then they did it again by not outlawing in the Constitution constitutional rights for corporations. Corporations aren't even mentioned in the Constitution. It's absolutely unimaginable that the Framers meant to give corporations Constitutional rights but somehow forgot to do so. They had a vivid memory of the Crown's oppressive and ruthless corporations.

So, how you might ask, if you don't already know the answer, did corporations get Constitutional rights? They got it by judicial chicanery or fraud through what surely had to be a tacit understanding between Chief Justice Morrison Waite and his court recorder in the infamous 1886 ruling in favor of the Southern Pacific railroad company over Santa Clara County, California.[9] Justice Waite, perhaps pressured by the Robber Barons and by a broader campaign of business interests at the time, prevented the issue of corporate personhood from being deliberated by commenting at the outset of the hearings that he and his colleagues on the bench took corporate personhood for granted and so they weren't going to consider the issue in their deliberations. The case was thus decided by the justices entirely and formally on other grounds. Afterwards, Waite, who presumably knew of the court recorder's significant railroad interests, and probably with an encouraging wink, let the recorder decide whether to insert the comment into the record. It got inserted. Both Waite and his recorder should posthumously be given a "Corpocracy Award."

In the opinion of one commentator the "outrageous" Santa Clara decision "has done more to damage our liberty and freedoms than any other single ruling in the history of the country---and paved the way for rendering the people subservient to corporations."[10] That is exactly my opinion also, but I would have to disagree with the commentator on one point. It wasn't a bona fide court ruling. To repeat, it was a recorder's insert after the verdict was made, not a deliberative part of it. It was judicial fraud of the first order, a High Crime of the High Court.

The Supreme Court's preposterous, un-constitutional, un-American, and dangerous ruling on January 21, 2010 for corporate free speech was just the latest in a long string of Constitutional violations the corporatized Court committed in granting corporations other Constitutional rights derived from corporate personhood; namely, the corporation's right to a) due process, b) be free from unreasonable searches, c) a jury trial in a criminal case, d) compensation for government takings, e) be free of double jeopardy, f) jury trial in a civil case, g) commercial speech, h) political speech, i) dissociate with others' speech, j) equal protection, and k) compensation for regulatory takings that aren't available to real people.

Shielded by the Supreme Court corporations are allowed to get away with all sorts of harmful wrongdoing. Sometimes the consequences are deadly as in cases when the corporcracy's right to be free from unreasonable searches is involved. The corporatized Court, for instance, ruled in 1978 that the government's unannounced inspections of work sites, which the manufacturing arm of the corpocracy particularly despised, was unconstitutional and had to be stopped. Search warrants had to be issued instead and only for good cause. What happened afterwards was predictable, even, I would think, to the callous court (captive its members are but obtuse, no). The aftermath of that ruling was the death, maiming, or poisoning of thousands of workers from accidents on the job, many of which were preventable had unannounced government plant inspections been allowed to continue.[11]

Corporations haven't been granted Constitutional "rights." They have been granted Constitutional "wrongs" by a succession of wrongful arguments by corporate lawyers and wrongful decisions by the judiciary. As absurd as it seems, uprooting corporate personhood amounts to having to expunge the word "corporation" from the Constitution that's not even in it, and yet it just may be the most formidable challenge of all initiatives to curb corporate power and its abuse. Corporations have built a veritable fortress and offensive of think tanks, tout farms, political slush funds, and whatever else to keep and expand corporate constitutional rights. It will take relentlessly pursuing a battery of initiatives like those briefly discussed next to take away those "rights."

Amend U.S. or State Constitutions

The 10th Amendment of the U.S. Constitution could be restored to its original intent of giving considerable power to the states, including authority over corporations. It has been argued that this legislative initiative would "magically end all forms of financial contributions" by corporations.[12]

Or the original Constitution itself could be amended. One legal scholar has proposed a two-paragraph amendment declaring that corporations aren't persons.[13] Not being a legal scholar, I think I could draft a one-sentence amendment. But whether adding one sentence or two paragraphs, changing the Constitution seems almost futile. Some 18,000 amendments have been introduced in Congress in the course of our history, and less than 30 of them have been ratified.[14] The chance of a personhood amendment even getting to the ratification stage is thus slim, but its chances might improve if amendments to state constitutions are first pursued and achieved. [15]

Change Corporate Charters

Corporate personhood could be declared null and void through individual charters for selected industries and/or corporations.

Pass Anti-Personhood Legislation

Another option, and one "urgently" recommended by Charles Derber, is to pressure Congress to pass legislation asserting that corporations do not have any constitutional rights. Derber sees this option as necessary in order to "free America from corporate rule."[16] I know of no such legislation ever being introduced in Congress, and we can be sure if such legislation were to be introduced and eventually passed corporate lawyers would find ways to challenge it in the courts.

Pass Prohibitive Ordinances

A fourth option is to work at the grass roots level to get local ordinances passed refuting the Constitutional rights of corporations seeking to impose themselves on municipalities. This option has been tried successfully in a few local jurisdictions. The city of Turlock, California, for example, passed an ordinance barring Wal-Mart from building a store there. The world's largest retail corporation sued. An appeals court ruled that the city's ban didn't infringe on the corporation's constitutional right of equal protection, and the California Supreme Court declined to review the case.[17] The difficulty with this option is that there are thousands of municipalities. Each time an ordinance revoking corporate personhood is passed the ordinance most likely will be challenged in court. Moreover, one way or the other judicial rulings at the lower levels usually don't generalize beyond the specifics of the local jurisdiction's case.

Shepherd a Test Case to the Highest Court

A fifth option would be to seize upon a specific case that clearly and only challenges corporate personhood, shepherd it all the way up to the U.S. Supreme Court, and present an air-tight argument that convinces the majority of justices that corporations do not have constitutional rights.[18] As I have said, corporations owe Powell an enormous debt of gratitude for his "fervent" defense of the corporate free speech. It surely must have fortified the corporate-sided reasoning behind the January 21, 2010 ruling. We need several mirror image lawyers facing the bench and fervently making their case that corporations don't have vocal chords or tongues!

The difficulty with this option, of course, is that a case must first be found or created, it must wind its way up through several judicial levels, and the tainted judiciary at each level must be convinced not to favor the corpocracy. Were the same conservative majority as that of January 21, 2010 to be sitting on the supreme bench any test case would probably be doomed

Target the Judiciary

The premise of this option is that corporate personhood is fraudulent, that perpetuating it is an unlawful act and causes incalculable, widespread harm to the American people and democracy, and that an aggressive, prosecutorial counter offensive is thus justified. The only reason it has yet to be taken as far as I can tell is that the flawed doctrine of judicial immunity is an intimidating barrier. But it's high time not to be intimidated. This option would involve petitioning municipal, state, and federal prosecutors as the case applies to prosecute members of the bar and the judiciary whose arguments for corporate personhood result in verdicts favoring corporations. Prosecutors who decline to file suits ought to be sued themselves for malfeasance.

An alternative to prosecuting the judiciary would be to change its membership or role through initiatives such as those discussed in the previous chapter. The slim five-to-four January 21, 2010 ruling for instance could someday turn into a four-to-five ruling via presidential replacements of departing corporate servants with truly impartial justices beholden only to the Constitution and true justice. If President Obama has the opportunity I hope he would do just that.

Pursue Miscellaneous Options

In the meantime a few legislators reportedly are working on legislative proposals to counter or impede application of the January 21, 2010 ruling. These proposals include prohibiting political advertising by certain corporations such as those that hire lobbyists, get corporate welfare, or have offshore operations; prohibiting campaign groups and corporate-related groups from using the same advertising firms and consultants; require shareholders to approve political expenditures; require chief executives to personally sponsor political commercials paid for by their companies or intermediaries; and expand and strengthen the public political campaign finance system.

Uproot Limited Liability

States initially gave their chartered corporations limited liability only if they provided public services, but with the advent of sham charters, any chartered corporation gets limited liability. State legislators in effect have given shareholders, who are the owners of corporations, a moral waiver. It limits owner liability in cases of corporate wrongdoing only to the potential loss of their initial investments and does not extend to potential costs of the damage done by the wrongdoing. Investors are thus free to buy shares in corporations without having to worry about whether increased share value will be gained through corporate wrongdoing and its harmful consequences to individuals or to society at large.

Tort law supposedly allows individuals harmed by willful or negligent corporate actions and products to sue corporations for monetary compensation. But over the years tort liability has been chiseled away by the judicial doctrines of contributory and comparative negligence, the fellow servant rule, and assumption of risk.[19] These doctrines can sometimes enable the corporation to escape liability altogether or to at least blunt it. For instance, an employer's lawyer may argue in court for relief of liability if a worker sues who is injured on the job but accused of being careless. Corporate lawyers have been trouncing trial lawyers.

The regime is trying through sham tort reform to expand limited liability even further. For example, the FDA "by fiat" (which means by order or permission of the oval puppet) shielded makers of flawed medical devices from law suits until the old reliable Supreme Court ruled 8-to-1 to make the fiat a judicial order from on high.[20]Another way in which corporations limit or totally avoid their liability has been to end-run the Seventh Amendment of the Constitution by getting Congress and the Supreme Court to force consumers and employees with grievances to forego their Constitutional right to a trial and submit to binding arbitration. Corporate contracts have thus taken priority over our Constitution.[21]

Intuitively, one might argue that shareholders are too far removed from the actual decisions and operations of corporations and thus shouldn't vicariously be held fully liable. There may be some merit to this argument for very small shareholders but not for large ones like mutual fund investors. Another argument for not ending limited liability has been that to do so would dry up the purchase of corporate stocks and thus also shrivel capital for corporate investments, but that argument doesn't hold much water. Studies have shown that unlimited liability when and where it has existed doesn't affect stock purchases.[22] Furthermore, corporations only get investment capital from the stock market when selling stocks initially, which doesn't happen often, and many corporations are awash in cash anyway and don't have to depend anymore on shareholders buying corporate stocks.[23]

Three possible approaches to uprooting limited liability are to make shareholders more accountable, to step up litigation of tort cases, and to step up legislative efforts.

Make Shareholders More Accountable

Since sham charters ushered in the doctrine of limited liability, rewriting charters to make shareholders more accountable for corporate wrongdoing and its consequences would be one option to consider. Another would be to make regulatory changes that put more of the risk of liability on shareholders. They could, for example, be assessed with liens when the liability costs become known or stocks of corporations incurring the expenses from lawsuits and judgments could automatically be marked down. Investors would have an incentive to buy insurance to cover the risk of liability judgments and possibly might become more responsible as owners in overseeing the management of the corporations they own.[24]

Step Up Litigation of Tort Cases

The USCC and its Institute for Legal Reform have spent millions on publicity campaigns and lobbying to erect all sorts of road blocks to the filing of tort claims for personal injury or death.[25] Litigation of tort reform cases may be the most important counteroffensive because the courts are a big road block. In the opinion of one attorney courts "have really written opinions that say not just that businesses should ultimately win, but that these cases should go nowhere from the very beginning."[26] The courts along with the rest of the regime are in effect telling the American people "buyer beware-if products and services that hurt or kill you, you bought them." If tort "reform" law is allowed to stand, it puts us that much closer to the law of the jungle, or as one former judge put it, will let corporations "kill with impunity."[27] Pressure also needs to be put on Congress and the White House to "un reform" tort reform.

Sluggish Spade Work Ahead

Anti-corpocracy crusaders are progressing at a snail's pace at best in digging up the corpocracy's entrenched roots. Meanwhile, the corpocracy's dowry from the government isn't shrinking nor is its powerful and harmful influence over America and American life.

Some Closing Memory Ticklers and One Liners

Shameful state charters? Remember "Licensed to Kill, Inc."

The shams let corporations become Leviathans.

The shams give corporations immortality.

The shams give corporations criminal disguises.

Corporate personhood gives corporations vocal chords and tongues.

Constitutional rights for Corporations? More like Constitutional "wrongs."

High crimes from the High Court? Waite and Bush rulings, two of many.

Un reform tort reform.

Buyer beware. A big understatement.

If it kills you, you still bought it.

Uproot the corpocracy or it will uproot America.

Chapter 8. Ending Hands-Off Corporate Criminals

"Hands up corporate crooks!"
Not really
Unless it's in a movie

While legal wrongdoing by corporations overshadows in prevalence and even harm illegal corporate wrongdoing, that is, corporate crime, ending it must also be a strategy in ending the corpocracy. If the corpocracy's legal roots were uprooted, one result would be that the corporate crime rate would suddenly soar!

Hands-off corporate crime by the government results in exactly what even simple-minded people like me would expect, an open-invitation to corporate crime whenever corporations need or want to do something wrong, which seems to happen daily.

Daily? Well, yes, if we consider all forms of legal as well as illegal wrongdoing. As for the latter or corporate crime, we really don't know how much of it all told there is. Like mushrooms, corporate crime thrives in the dark. Government also keeps us in the dark. It spews out annual statistics on crime in the streets, but except for one instance doesn't track and keep statistics on crime in corporate suites, which ought to tell us something about its prevalence. The one instance was in 1979 when it issued its "first and last report" (emphasis mine) revealing that in just a two year period (1975-1976), "approximately two-thirds of large corporations violated the law, some of them many times."[1] That apparently was too much of a revelation and too much law enforcement for corporations to tolerate.

They were beginning to flex their muscles at the time of the report and ever since with the help of its marriage partner has blindfolded, muzzled, and handcuffed law enforcement. Author Ted Nace was right in titling his book "Gangs of America," and he wasn't writing about street gangs.[2]

So for any more recent accounts of corporate lawlessness we must look outside the government to people who track corporate crime. One of them, Russell Mokhiber, for example, called the 1990's the "decade of rampant corporate criminality.[3] Corporate lawlessness continues unabated and "does more damage" asserts another private watchdog and anti-corporate crusader, Ralph Nader, "to people's health, safety, and economic resources by far than crime in the streets."[4] I have been compiling haphazardly and sporadically for several years incidents of corporate legal and illegal wrongdoing in all industries. So far I'm up to nearly 2000 incidents. I'd get nothing else done if I tried to compile daily reports of new ones. Since corporate crime thrives even better in the dark can you imagine how many more people like Mokhiber, Nader, and I would find sleuthing with big floodlights?

The Nature of Corporate Crime

It doesn't take a rocket scientist to explain corporate crime. It always happens when certain personal factors and certain situational factors, or badvantages (temptations and pressures), come together.

First, needless to say, there must be corporate people predisposed to cut ethical and legal corners. They tend not to think of themselves as criminals, particularly because of all their rationalizations, and they usually aren't seen by their associates, family, and friends as criminals. Most of these people are in the upper reaches of corporations. They tend to have one or more of these characteristics; greed, irresponsibility, a lack of virtue, materialistic values, moral frailty, narcissism, and narrow-mindedness. These people are simply more vulnerable to the temptations and pressures of corporate life. Changing the personal nature of corporate leadership is a responsibility of corporations, their directors, and owners. Hiring, if they can be found, more virtuous corporate leaders might go a long way to stemming corporate crime. I have written elsewhere about how this might be done and so won't do so here.[5]

Second, there must be badvantages within the corporation. They always exist. Ignoble expectations and upside down rewards are classic examples. I have also written extensively elsewhere about them and so will not do so here.[6]

Third, there must be badvantages outside the corporation. A hands-off government is a huge badvantage with its lap dogs, escape hatches, pampering, and deregulation. They are the subject of this chapter.

Books upon books have been written about corporate crime. This chapter can only skim the surface, and I am heavily indebted to people like Russell Mokhiber and Ralph Nader and related NGOs for their work in monitoring corporate crime and in proposing detailed preventive measures. Much of this chapter draws upon their work.

No More Hands Off Corporate Crooks: Unleash the Watch Dogs

A watch dog guards against intruders and theft. A lap dog lets thieves pet them. The last time a watch dog monitored corporate criminal behavior seems to have been when that 1979 report was made. A few years later Ronald Reagan was swept into the oval office and all watch dogs were swept out and replaced by lap dogs, a reckless policy that has continued through subsequent administrations of either political party (only time will tell whether the Obama administration replaces the lap dogs with watch dogs). Regulations not deregulated but inimical to corporations have simply been ignored or regulatory staffs and budgets slashed and the health, safety, and welfare of the public put on the chopping block.

Cataloguing the incidents of lap dogging by regulatory and other enforcement agencies since the start of the Reagan administration would require many volumes. I briefly considered doing it and then decided some private eye ought to do it and title the catalogue "Beware of the Government's Lap Dogs." Sections in it could start like this: "Do you know what's in the meat you eat? Meat inspectors don't." "Could this pace maker stop your heart permanently? Don't expect medical device inspectors to know." "Could you get killed on this job? Don't expect occupational health and safety inspectors to know." "Could this drug prescription be toxic? Don't expect the drug inspectors to know." Would this be too risky an investment? Don't expect the SEC to force rating agencies to rate honestly. And so on for each and every industry. Just reading the catalogue might be enough to persuade readers to join an anti-corpocracy NGO or protest movement.

At the very minimum the American people ought to be able to rely on their government to protect their health, safety, and welfare from being endangered by corporate lawlessness. But their government is not their government and it is too busy being petted by and petting corporations.

Unify the Private Eyes

I would guess that Mokhiber and Nader might appreciate having their efforts and those of scattered here and there watchdog NGOs coordinated and intensified with one or more watchdog NGOs assigned to each industry and criminal profiles in each industry published regularly. It might help too if an independent body of citizens representing consumers, workers, tax payers, and other public interest groups were established to monitor each industry and to regularly report on the findings to Congress.

Unify the Public Eyes

All public watchdogs ought to be in one agency, not scattered asunder. It's preposterous that there are over 50 regulatory agencies regardless of whether they are doing any real regulating. They need to be consolidated. One way to accomplish this would be to subdivide the Department of Commerce (anathema to Republican administrations that have wanted to eliminate or neuter it) into a corporate sub agency, a non-corporate sub agency, and a third one for all crosscutting matters; abolish the regulatory agencies; put all regulatory functions into the appropriate sub agencies; and oversee them with a regulatory czar who is a civil servant, not a political appointee.

Publicize Violations

The U.S. Department of Justice (more appropriately named the Department of "Injustice") needs to be pressured to track and annually publicize not only the prevalence and cost of corporate crime but also all specific cases and how they were handled by the agency. A copy of the 1979 report ought to be taken to the U.S. Attorney General as a reminder and protestors stationed at the AG's door step demanding that a detailed accounting be publicized widely each year on what wayward corporations by name have been doing, what the harm done was, and what if anything was being done by the government in response.

Maximize Disclosures

Needless to say criminals don't voluntarily disclose their crimes. Non disclosures can never be prevented but efforts can be taken to maximize disclosures.

One widespread effort of questionable value in my opinion is the sprouting of what must be hundreds of sunshine laws and model disclosure standards. Unless law enforcement agencies get serious about detecting, prosecuting, and substantially penalizing nondisclosures, toothless laws and model standards may amount to nothing more than paperwork and bamboozling of the public.

The disclosure requirements of the Sarbanes-Oxley law of 2002 are totally inadequate and need to be expanded and strengthened.[7] They apply only to financial reporting, and financial fraud is only a part of corporate crime.

The sacrosanct doctrine of attorney-client confidentiality needs to be liberalized so that convincing disclosures of crime aren't withheld.[8] Corporations under criminal investigation ought to be required to waive confidentiality.

Legislative attempts need to be renewed to make management's failure to disclose material infractions and harmful practices a federal crime.[9]

Whistleblowers are vulnerable watch dogs. Existing law inadequately protects them from corporate retaliation. People who have an inside view of corporate crime and blow the whistle need to be better shielded by the government from retaliation.

Prosecute the Lap Dogs for Malfeasance of Duty

Law enforcement agencies should be prosecuted for malfeasance of duty in not discovering, not reporting, and/or not prosecuting any cases of corporate lawlessness.

No More Hands Off Corporate Crooks: Seal the Escape Hatches

Cataloguing corporate crime that's already happened, watching to see if it happens again, and catching the corporate criminals when it does would be a good start if only the criminals didn't go scot free through escape hatches. I've spotted seven of them so far: legal and regulatory loopholes; protective judicial doctrines; amnesty; special immunities; the business judgment rule; fugitiveness; and the corporate corner office.

Escape hatches are often easy to find or create. They are out in the open just waiting to be used. Whenever they aren't, corporations can turn to their hired Houdinis, or lawyers, for help. Once they go to work finding or creating escape hatches the game is up-for justice that is.[10] It's Corporation 1, Justice 0, in almost every instance as public-interest lawyers Ralph Nader and Wesley Smith amply documented in their book on how corporate lawyers "pervert justice."[11]

Plug the Loopholes

Loopholes are the most common type of escape hatch and probably occupy most of corporate lawyers' time. Loophole lawyers, says one legal affairs writer, "fuel white-collar crime," by writing "gilded, watermarked cotton-fiber letters to their corporate CEOs saying that a particular [act contemplated] is legal."[12] The rubber stamp undermines prosecutors' arguments, which they are forced to make given the irrational and impractical doctrine of criminal intent, that corporate executives who possess the letters had a "criminal intent" to commit the illegal act.

To a certain extent loopholes are inevitable, and no law or rule, no matter how tightly written can probably ever be free of loopholes. Opportunities for corporations to stay on the right side of the law but on the wrong side of ethics are as limitless as the ways for corporations to exploit them. We would drown in laws and regulations if every conceivable opportunity and every conceivable illegal behavior that might follow were to be proscribed in detail and unambiguously so. But even where narrower loopholes do exist, corporate lawyers would simply have to do more looking and wriggling. They seldom need to do this, however. Corporate touts usually succeed in getting laws and rules deliberately written with loopholes large enough for the proverbial truck to drive through them.

The best approach for plugging loopholes is a proactive one, preventing them in the first place. Corporate touts could be barred from peddling loopholes and helping to draft them into pending legislation or they could be rebuffed by commissions of public interest groups in their crafting of laws and regulations. Other tactics might include holding loophole lawyers more accountable and pressuring judges to give less deference to the so-called advice-of-counsel defense."[13] Finally, a citizens "corporate loophole" commission might be established to find, publicize, and pressure politicians to plug all existing loopholes that have let corporate criminals slide through them with impunity.

Stop Judicial Protections

The corporatized court is a great friend of criminal corporations. The judicial doctrine of criminal intent that I've already mentioned, judicial doctrines in the practice of tort law, and the business judgment rule are all great escape hatches for these corporations.

The judicial doctrine of criminal intent is a good example of legal sophistry that says being motivated to commit a crime is immaterial, while intent to commit a crime is material. Now, I'm a psychologist who thinks the difference between motive and intent is gossamer thin if different at all and that both require the judiciary and the jury to be what neither they nor anyone else can possibly be, psychics who pretend to read minds.

The doctrine is a foundational part of case law and will be tough to end. Yet it's not impossible. I'll cite one of three examples, a real oddity, that indicate this escape hatch might be sealable. Strict penalties may be imposed for the taking of migratory birds "even if done utterly by accident."[14] If accidental "birdnappers" can't escape, why let corporate criminals? Congress could be pressured to abolish the use of the doctrine altogether. It could be replaced by what I call the criterion of nexus. If a connection of any kind can be reasonably demonstrated between criminal acts and executives, who more often than not don't actually commit the acts, then prosecutors should charge the executives with a criminal act and seek to have them convicted and punished. One obvious connection is simply that the executive, especially a senior one like the CEO, is in charge of the corporation and responsible for what it does and doesn't do ("the buck stops here"). Another connection is evidenced, for example, when executive expectations of achieving clearly unrealistically high outcomes were clearly made but were silent on the means of achieving the outcomes. The criterion of nexus, it should be emphasized, doesn't require mind reading.

Another alternative would be to get the doctrine's use limited as narrowly as possible or to subordinate the requirement to show *mens rea*, or guilty mind, to the requirement to show *actus reus*, or guilty act.[15] Still another option would be to get Congress or the Department of Justice to issue a crystal clear definition of what the doctrine means and what constitutes sufficient evidence of its existence. I have yet to see a crystal clear definition and conclusive evidentiary proof in print. That it's probably forever elusive should tell us that the doctrine should forever be ended.

In cases where corporations violate tort law, what is still left of it, the judicial doctrines of contributory and comparative negligence, the fellow servant rule, and assumption of risk are additional examples of judicial escape hatches.[16] The business judgment rule is another commonly used escape hatch that judges defer to in letting corporate directors off the hook for bad judgments and sometimes criminal actions of corporate management. The rule is usually a cover up for complicit directors who feign ignorance.[17] These escape hatches need to be targeted for sealing.

End Amnesty

In certain circumstance corporations acting criminally may be granted amnesty. Telecom companies, for instance, were granted retroactive amnesty from massive prosecution for invasion of privacy in the administration's surveillance operations seeking to ferret out possible terrorists.[18]Amnesty is a central part of the Department of Justice's "corporate leniency" policy. It and amnesty must be ended through public pressure, litigation, or any other appropriate means.

Block the Safe Harbors

Special immunity, or a "safe harbor" away from prosecution, is sometimes given throughout an industry or profession. More than half the states, for instance, have immunized the auto industry from prosecution for not paying certain legitimate claims.[19] Congress, the states, and the U.S. Supreme Court have all given safe harbor to accountants for instances of securities fraud.[20] Let's block those harbors with public pressure for administrative and legislative changes.

Close the Ports to Fugitives

When corporate executives are wanted by foreign countries for corporate crimes committed on their soil, and our captive government refuses to allow their extradition, the criminals become fugitives but apparently only in the eyes of the plaintiff countries.[21] Scofflaw corporations are also fugitives when they incorporate offshore. They ought to be barred from government contracts and fugitive executives ought to be extradited. Since corporations loathe bad publicity, any and all of them that have escaped should be broadcast as escapees from the law or crooks on the loose! Put posters of them in post offices! Slap them on billboards! Put their pictures on grocery bags! Get equal air time for Justice and blast them on radio and TV!

Raid the Corner Offices

Refuge in the corporate corner office, the last escape hatch, is the only one not hatched by the government. From their lofty perch atop layers of subordinate managers and non-managers higher level managers can convey ignoble expectations (e.g., "do whatever is necessary," "wink and nods," feigned ignorance, and the like) and then let underlings who carry out the criminal acts take the heat if caught. It takes real determination and persistence for the criminal justice system to put the top guns on the hot seat. In an illustrative case a company caught dumping carcinogens into a major waterway offered up a series of underlings for sacrifice, each of which was rejected by the judge. He persisted and finally got the company's CEO and chair on the stand.[22] A rare judge, that judge.

Two kinds of reform, one inside, one outside are needed here. On the inside, corporations need to be persuaded that hierarchical organizational structures with their top/down commands and controls will forever keep corporations from excelling and will, without corporate self-reform, lead to their downfall if they someday are deprived of the corpocracy's many badvantages. I have written extensively elsewhere on corporate self-reform.[23] On the outside all of the reform measures covered in this chapter plus public pressure need to zero in on making corporate executives accountable for crimes spawned from their office suites whether by wink-and-nods or other forms of "ignoble expectations." The criterion of nexus is simply the corner office and the criminal act wherever it was actually done.

No More Hands Off Corporate Crooks: Stop Pampering, Start Punishing

The U.S. Supreme Court upheld California's tough "3 strikes and you're out" law, letting stand two consecutive 25-year terms to life imprisonment with little chance for parole of a man convicted of stealing nine videotapes worth $150 after two earlier offenses.[24] Now that's more like bloody overkill and certainly not a case of pampering or coddling the criminal!

Consider, in stark contrast, pampered corporate criminals. If they only stole videotapes I wouldn't be writing this chapter. Neither, I'm sure, would the commentator on and chronicler of corporate crime I've already cited, Russell Mokhiber, editor of *Corporate Crime Reporter*, be doing what he's doing. I happened to spot on the Internet a speech he gave not long ago. It was short, snappy, and one of the best speeches I've ever read on any subject.[25] Two of the lessons he said he learned in his years of reporting were that corporate crime is more costly and damaging in the harm it causes than that caused by all of street crime combined; and that corporate crime is often violent, causing roughly three and one/half times more deaths annually than murders. In other words, by any stretch of the imagination corporate crime is not petty theft. Yet the paucity of its prosecution and the puniness of its punishment are beyond any stretch of the imagination except that of the corpocracy.

The best way to get tough on corporate crime is to stop the pampering and to start punishing, really punishing, the corporations and the crooks inside them. The Department of Justice, though, throws up one obstacle after another to meeting its own hypocritically stated goal of punishing corporate criminals. The thrust of any offensive to turn pampering into punishing, therefore, should be aimed at that federal agency, but not without also pressuring Congress for tough anti-crime legislation that neither the executive nor the judicial branch can circumvent.

Numerous proposals for meaningful punishment of corporate crime and criminals have been made in the literature and on the websites of a few NGOs although not as far as I could tell for preventing each and every one of the following ways the Department of Justice pampers corporate criminals: non-prosecution; "deferred" prosecution; mitigation; double-disclaimers; plea bargaining; non-criminal alternatives; and wrist slapping.

End Non Prosecutions

The sine qua non of pampering is simply not to prosecute. Despite two arguments that try to justify this practice, non prosecution is a blatant as well as an unlawful cop out by our non-law enforcing captive government. One argument is that only persons can commit crimes. The argument is ludicrous when made by defenders of corporate personhood, but that is really beside the point. Much more to the point is that the persons responsible for the crime occupy official positions legitimized by the corporation; the crime is usually intended to benefit the corporation; the harm done is magnified by the overall presence and power of the corporation; and the organizational history and culture conducive to the crime will likely remain even if the individual culprits are removed. The second argument is that indicting corporations would put them out of business and in doing so would hurt innocent shareholders, employees, creditors, and other stakeholders. But few corporations have ever been put out of business by being indicted. Nevertheless, advocates of this argument point to what happened to the consulting firm hired by Enron, Arthur Anderson. It was indicted, folded with some 28, 000 employees left unemployed, and then was subsequently acquitted by the U.S. Supreme Court. The ruling, however, turned on technicalities that didn't really exonerate its culpability. Moreover, the firm's history and culture of wrongdoing had made it ripe for self-destruction. According to one law professor, "the firm was already dead." [26]

Government will sometimes go to extreme lengths not to prosecute corporate crime, as in cases of what I call "phantom substitutes" and Mokhiber calls "empty closets" or "defunct entities."[27] Instead of having to give a "death sentence" mandated by its own harsh (on paper only) rule of excluding corporations that defrauded Medicare from doing further business with it, the prosecution has a phantom or defunct unit plead guilty (I guess the phantom can write and talk) and gives it the death sentence. The "parent" criminal, meanwhile, continues to milk the cash cow.

The Department of Injustice currently has given itself entirely too much discretion in choosing whether to prosecute. Non-prosecution might be limited to cases where the harm done is relatively miniscule and no-repeat pledges are required and tied to heavy penalties if not honored. There should be no other exceptions.

End Deferred Prosecutions

If it doesn't think it can get away with not prosecuting criminal corporations, government resorts to "deferred" prosecutions, but they eventually evaporate into non prosecutions. Ever since the Arthur Anderson case the trend has been for criminal corporations to be offered "deferred" prosecution agreements and the public gets hoodwinked yet again. The agreements aren't publicized, so the corporation avoids damage to their reputation. Sometimes the court appoints a monitor with authority to impose internal reforms, but the monitor usually turns out to be cozy with the corporation. In any case, most often all charges in deferred agreements are dropped after the agreement "expires." That's why some legal experts refer to these agreements as a "get-out-of-jail card."[28]

There should be no exceptions, however, for deferred prosecution agreements. They should be totally banned. In their place, criminal corporations should be fully and rigorously prosecuted with no double disclaimers or plea bargaining allowed, and, where appropriate, put on tough probation that includes a bona fide outside monitor or trustee, ouster and severe punishment of the offending executives, a court-ordered restructuring plan, and publication in the major media of the corporation's crime and punishment. Executives involved in any really serious corporate crimes should be prosecuted as criminals under the principle of "do crime, do time."

Severely Limit Mitigation

Punishment, the saying goes, must fit the crime. Mitigation of punishment, contrary to conventional wisdom, can never tailor the fit simply because the harm done by the crime can't be sufficiently mitigated. It's already happened, and victims can seldom be made whole again. Mitigation, therefore, always amounts more or less to coddling the corporation and its criminals. Non-prosecution amounts to carrying mitigation to the extreme. A less extreme example is a provision in the corporate sentencing guidelines (eventually made advisory rather than mandatory by a U.S. Supreme Court ruling) that allows for fines and other penalties to be reduced up to 95% if the corporation's gets a low "culpability score" by having adopted and begun implementing a compliance program prior to the offense. Now obviously the program failed or there wouldn't have been an offense in the first place! And that isn't surprising because compliance programs tend to be window dressing anyway. Moreover, having a compliance program tends to give corporations a sense of immunity and brazenness.[29] My disparaging view isn't shared, naturally, by the judge who chaired the commission responsible for the guidelines. In her topsy-turvy view, the mitigation is a way to "reward organizations."[30] Does that seem to you like a gross misjudgment by her?

A tough, mandatory, not advisory, sentencing standard needs to be put into law that won't offend the U.S. Supreme Court but that will terribly offend the scofflaws (the Court worries that any mandatory standard would violate due process by disallowing juries from considering mitigating or extenuating factors). The Congress should hand the other two branches a law that spells out unambiguously within it what factors could legally be considered and to what extent for each level and type of crime. There should be absolutely no mitigating or extenuating factors permissible for recidivist corporations and their crooks.

End Double Disclaimers

A common tactic of corporate crooks to avoid the consequences of being tried and convicted in court is to settle out of it by telling the prosecution they "neither admit nor deny guilt."

The logic of double disclaimers eludes me. Two contradictory conditions can't apply to the same case. The double disclaimer apparently means guilt but the prosecution doesn't want to go to the trouble of trying to prove guilt in court. Being allowed to make the double disclaimer is obviously a real benefit for the disclaimer. The only costs are usually token fines or fines that are easily affordable and thus shrugged off as a cost of doing business. Without the disclaimer, corporations, their directors, and management would face severe penalties and greater liability to private lawsuits.

The double disclaimer breeds public cynicism about justice being served when it's relaxed for powerful corporations. Confessions, whether accompanied or not by apologies, followed by punishment are, after all, time-honored ways to deal with transgressions and ought to be a mandatory part of punishment of criminal corporations and their crooks. Prosecutors need to be prohibited from or prosecuted for allowing double disclaimers.

End Plea Bargaining

Prosecutors can allow plea bargaining if they don't want to proceed to court. Guilt is admitted but to a lesser charge and a lesser penalty is gotten, if it's possible to get a lesser penalty in the captive criminal injustice system. The prosecution sometimes uses the tactic to try and get lower-level accomplices to tattle on higher ups, but the higher ups can then also try get their own plea bargaining. Plea bargaining ought to be disallowed in all cases.

End Non-Criminal Alternatives

A corporate crime by any other name is still a crime unless the name-calling is the hands-off government. While expounding from one side of the mouth that "the primary goals of criminal law are deterrence, punishment, and rehabilitation," our top law (non) enforcement agency leaves open the possibility of applying "non-criminal alternatives" to criminal offenses and offenders.[31] Does that make even an iota of sense? It doesn't to me. To me, it's a "stay-out-of-jail card" and just one more dowry gift from the government and one more travesty of justice. The Department of "Injustice" needs to be pressured to end or prosecuted for providing non-criminal alternatives.

Centralize Prosecution Responsibilities

Prosecuting corporate crime as well as all regulatory violations needs to be made a top priority in the federal government. Currently, prosecutorial authorities are assigned to too many different agencies. The SEC, for instance, can't be relied on to prosecute consistently and firmly financial fraud related to the securities market. All prosecutorial authorities should be centralized in one place and given sufficient funds and a mandate to enforce the laws of the land.

Put Corporate Lawyers on the Hot Seat

Corporate lawyers ought to get the spotlight and the hot seat when they are found to have facilitated corporate crime and/or to have deliberately impeded the course of a criminal investigation. They were among the key gatekeepers who helped open the sluice gates for the Enron fraud to slip through yet were only mildly sanctioned instead of being disbarred and subjected to criminal prosecutions themselves. Obviously they have a professional obligation to their corporate clients, but they have a greater obligation to society of ensuring that justice is upheld.

Stiffen the Penalties

Punishment of corporate crimes, when the government can't avoid giving it and corporate criminals can't get out of it, tends to amount to nothing more than a wrist slap considering the gravity of the crimes and the huge corporate resources that could be tapped. In the 1980s one former prosecutor complained that it was "hardly worth the candle" to bring corporations to trial because the resulting fines were so puny.[32] While it's possible today for fines to be sizeable, they are still easily affordable and thus seen by criminal corporations merely as the price of doing business.[33] It's also more likely than not according to a nationwide study of cases that fines no matter how sizeable will be quietly slashed or allowed to go unpaid and accompanied by the government's lame excuse that compliance, not punishment is the goal.[34]

Imprisonment of convicted senior executives, which would be a "body slap" I guess, rarely happens. While it's true that the Sarbanes/Oaxley Act of 2002, established on the heels of illegal escapades involving Enron and other corporations, does call for up to two years of imprisonment for convicted senior executives, the scope of the law is limited to the reporting of misleading financial statements, and there's always the possibility of a stay-out-of-jail card type of settlement. Even corporate "homicides," which occur daily Mohkiber says, seldom are prosecuted as homicides, and we've seen at least one case where the final outcome was acquittal.[35]

Corporations indicted the first time should have any federal contracts cancelled, be barred from any further contracts, not be allowed to deduct the cost of fines from their taxes, and be chained to on-shore headquarters and operations. Repeat offenders should have their doors shuttered and their assets liquidated. It may never happen, but it's what should happen.

I'm sure the petty thief I cited would have jumped at the chance to be pampered. But that's not the way it works in Corpocracy America. And in the final analysis, corporate criminals who can't avoid punishment can expect to get and usually do get less punishment than they should get. But don't expect them to be soft on people who offend them! Corporate management can be merciless, for instance, in retaliating against whistle blowing employees, sometimes ruining their lives in the process.[36]

Sue the Department of Injustice

The nation's top law "non" enforcement agency should be sued for flagrant malfeasance whenever its pampering is especially egregious, as would be the case, for example, when a corporation's wrongdoing causes people substantial physical injury, death, or insurmountable debt. In order to circumvent a controversial U.S. Supreme Court ruling on what constitutes legal standing in suing federal agencies, plaintiffs would need to have been among those who suffered corporate harm.[37] But a way to circumvent the ruling would be to establish something like a "Citizens Bounty Act" proposed by the NGO, Center for Corporate Policy, as a way "to empower citizens to enforce the law, especially when the government won't."[38]

No More Hands Off Corporate Crooks: End Reckless Deregulation

Federal regulations are meant to guide federal agencies in implementing the laws passed by the legislature. Executive nullification of the rules by eliminating them or ignoring them as in lap dogging allows corporations to skirt the laws and thus operate lawlessly in conducting their business.

Although President Jimmy Carter started the trend toward deregulation, it was President Ronald Reagan who accelerated it with gusto. He shrunk the Federal Register, the repository of regulations, for the first time since 1960. Antitrust regulations were eased, allowing big corporations to get bigger through mergers. An antitrust official under Reagan scoffed at the notion that bigger means more powerful.[39] Reagan declared that he intended to "take government off our backs," the backs of big business he should have said since he actually added substantially more government to the taxpayers' backs.[40]

Echoing Reagan, President Clinton declared that "the era of big government is over" and promptly began deregulating the energy, telecommunications, and financial services industry. Much of the Economic Katrina financial crisis can be attributed to Clinton and the Republicans in Congress who agreed to deregulate the U.S. financial system. Then there is President Bush, unparalleled when it comes to catering to the corpocracy. His anti-regulatory actions even outdid Reagan's record.[41] To ensure that the expectations of the corpocracy were being met on the regulatory front, he ordered that each federal agency's regulatory office be run by a political hack.[42]

One industry after another has been deregulated while the public is told in each instance how competition and efficiency would be boosted, resulting in lower prices and better products and services. It's the hollow free-enterprise promise that never fails to leave the public holding the bag and worse, as when the deregulated energy industry creates blackouts to jack up energy prices; when deregulated toy makers make toys that can kill; when deregulated tires explode on the highway; when the deregulated agricultural industry lets mad cow disease happen; when deregulated drugs and medical devices kill patients, etc., etc.[43]

Anti-trust regulation is especially weak and toothless and needs to be strengthened. No more "mega-mergers" should be allowed that make corporations even more powerful both economically and politically.[44] No corporation or bank should be allowed to get so big that when they are on the brink of failing they are bailed out by the government (i.e., the taxpayers) simply because they are deemed "too big too fail." Free-market ideologues claim that antitrust regulation limits competition. But huge corporations and monopolies are what limit if not kill competition. Moreover, corporate size encourages corporate lawlessness.[45] That is, the bigger the corporation the more likely it will have the opportunity, the incentive, the swagger, the clout, and the impunity from going criminal when it's the surest way to fatter profits.

Huge corporations also represent "inhuman scale" enterprises, the opposite of the "human-scale marketplace" Dr. Korten advocates (see the Appendix C). So do Cavanagh and Mander. They advocate "human scale enterprises in which people know each other, are dedicated to a common purpose, and share rewards more equitably."[46] Besides stricter anti-trust rules, these two authors advocate tax policies favoring such enterprises, participative ownership, and the breaking up large corporations into component businesses that are then sold to workers, customers, suppliers, and community members.[47] To their proposals I would add using corporate chartering as a means to delimit corporate size and showing corporations how to flatten their autocratic organizational hierarchies into more democratic "lowerarchies."[48]

There are several other initiatives aimed at regulatory reform that could be or are currently underway by various NGOs. These initiatives include seeking to nullify all deregulations; adequately staffing the regulatory function and giving regulators the mandate to oversee and enforce their regulations; prosecuting regulators when they fail to write or enforce regulations even when ordered to do so by the judiciary; making the rule making process democratic by ensuring participation of all relevant public interest groups in hearings and outcomes; conducting follow-up evaluations of and setting expiration dates for any deregulations; establishing an independent or quasi-government agency to arbitrate regulatory disputes; and monitoring and contesting court decisions preventing deregulation .

As part of the strategy of educating the American people, the history needs to be told of how regulatory agencies were created to protect public interests from irresponsible industries and then how each agency slowly got captured and corrupted by the corpocracy.[49] For each industry the harm it has caused since being deregulated needs recounted. And the American people need to know what responsible regulation means. What it means to me is that I don't want to fly in a plane, drive a car, eat food, or do anything else where I have to use or be around products and services from recklessly deregulated industries. What about you? Would you be comfortable flying in a plane if you knew its maintenance inspections and repairs were being done offshore by poorly trained and underpaid mechanics? [50]

Some Closing Memory Ticklers and One Liners

3 strikes and you're out? Not if a corporation is at bat.

Unleash the watch dogs and seal the escape hatches!

Who opens the corporate escape hatches?

The U.S. Department of Injustice

The U.S. Corporate Court

The Loophole Bar. Where Houdini lawyers gather.

Criminal intent is a game for psychics.

A criminal corporation with a low culpability score?

Double disclaimer ought to baffle even meager IQs.

"Psst, want a stay-out-of-jail card?"

Stop pampering, start punishing!

Want to fly in an unregulated jet liner?

Know what's in the meat you eat? Meat inspectors don't."

Chapter 9. Ending Hand-Outs to the Corporate Welfare Queen

The Corporate Hypocrisy
Government, Keep Your Hands Off
But
Don't Stop the Hand Outs

"Corpocracy." "Hypocrisy." That they sound alike is immaterial. That the second characterizes the first is very material. There are actually three hypocrisies at work. Corporations want: 1. their huge dowry of hand outs from government to keep growing, 2. government to keep its hands off their business, and 3. social welfare severely curtailed.

Government, meanwhile, is two-faced about the whole matter. Ronald Reagan complained on the campaign stump about the "welfare queen driving the welfare Cadillac" while promising a roll back of the government's social welfare program. Reagan, interested only in the welfare of his corporate patrons and the upper crust, gave them a "massive tax cut," warned that Medicare would destroy America's freedom, raised the Social Security tax on the middle class to shore up that entitlement program, and then started raiding it in a futile attempt to pay for the resulting huge deficits in the federal budget.[1] Bill Clinton, when it was his turn to campaign, pledged to "end welfare as we know it," and once in office gutted welfare for the poor and subsequently recommended a 10 percent increase in corporate welfare spending.[2] Both political parties clearly dance to the same tune under the same tent, and I imagine corporations do more expecting than begging to keep their dowry overflowing.

A Monumental and Mostly Veiled Dowry

The government's dowry to its corporate partner is overflowing with bailouts for "companies too big to let fail;" debt forgiveness; discounted insurance; excessive government payments for contract work; giveaways of public resources; loan guarantees; privatization; price support loans; quotas; subsidies; supply restrictions; tariff protections; tax breaks, and "warfare welfare."

The dowry is mostly veiled, undoubtedly to avoid public outrage. Never in all my years of researching facts and figures have I been so frustrated in trying to pin down the total cost to our treasury in revenue and indebted borrowing from corporate welfare. I came up empty-handed after browsing the Office of Management and Budget in the White House. At the other end of Pennsylvania Avenue the Congressional Budget Office at least acknowledged that it won't even touch the subject, saying in a 1995 tally of the federal government's financial support to business that its "tally has no such purpose [as accounting for corporate welfare]."[3] I should have known that a government that doesn't track corporate crime won't track corporate welfare. Not only does it not track it, it will try to hide it. That was the opinion of the editor of *The New York Times* when its reporters were trying to get data on the cost of the bank bailouts in the wake of Economic Katrina.[4] It was at least "more than zero" the editor facetiously concluded, no doubt in exasperation. The various estimates I found from scattered sources outside the government are mostly ballpark estimates I would suspect.

Although mostly veiled, the dowry's relative size isn't a mystery nor is its disastrous effects on the general welfare of Americans. We know, for instance, that the warfare welfare industry (aka the defense industry) gets a huge chunk of the federal pie, about 50% overall, and that's not counting what I can't see, the off-the-record budget. The U.S. defense budget, more aptly called the military, budget is "greater than the military expenditures of all other nations combined."[5] If we define welfare for the defense industry as any money not absolutely necessary for defending our shores from foreign invasion, then most of the military budget spent on off-shore militarism is a warfare/welfare budget. There is nothing defensive and everything offensive, needless, and senseless about the Iraq War and the Afghanistan War.

We know that "spending for corporate welfare programs exceeds spending for low-income programs by more than three to one;" a miniscule portion "of total federal outlays goes to programs that solely benefit poor people;" and that "welfare programs for corporations do not play by the same [strict] rules as welfare for people."[6]

We know that corporate welfare prevents millions of jobs from being created by small businesses, the well spring of new jobs; hurts consumers because, unlike a truly free market, consumers have no leverage over prices; corrupts the political system; and sacrifices morality by taking from the poor and giving to the rich.[7]

We know that corporate welfare is criminal not just immoral when corporations repeatedly defraud the government and still stay on the dole.[8]

We know that corporate tax breaks cost Americans more than corporations pay in taxes.[9] Without corporate welfare the ordinary citizen would pay less in taxes (listen up cons).

We know from the foregoing that corporate welfare subtracts from rather than adds to the real wealth of our country.

Cut "Ordinary" Corporate Welfare

"Ordinary" corporate welfare is only ordinary in that it excludes the extraordinary warfare welfare. The latter is extraordinary because it's monstrous, deadly, and if left alone will by itself ruin America. I have much to say about it shortly. Meanwhile, I will rely on two experts to tell us how to cut ordinary corporate welfare.

In 1999 Stephen Moore, then the director of fiscal policy studies for the Cato Institute, testified about corporate subsidies in the federal budget before the Budget Committee, U.S. House of Representatives.[10] Ordinarily, I wouldn't turn to Cato, which lists nearly 20 large corporations as sponsors, but its dedicated advocacy of the free market does allow for tempered criticism of corporate welfare. Another set of proposals was made a year later by Ralph Nader in his book, Cutting Welfare.[11] As for Mr. Nader, we all know he's not a pawn of corporations.

Mr. Moore's proposals abbreviated here are to: a). Cut (an unspecified amount of) corporate welfare and use the money saved to "pay for" the costs of halving capital gains taxes on the wealthy. b). Create a Congressional commission of citizens to approve or disapprove a package of corporate welfare spending cuts. c). Put a time limit on corporate handouts as done with social welfare grants. d). Track corporate welfare by requiring recipients to report to Congress. e). Tell companies "you may lobby or you may take federal hand-outs, but you may not do both." f). Eliminate double-dipping. Allow one welfare grant per year. g). Pass a law denying any federal subsidy to any person or company with income of more than $1 million.

Mr. Nader's proposals abbreviated here (and just the most significant ones in my opinion out of his many proposals) are to: a). Sunset corporate handouts by automatically phasing them out in four years and every five years thereafter if renewed at all, and proponents would have to mobilize support for "re-commencement of their favored subsidies." b). Empower citizens to "mount judicial challenges to runaway agencies." c). Require every federal agency to publish on the Internet a list of its hand-outs. d). Ban hand-outs to criminal corporations. e). Require quid-pro-quos such as requiring corporations that get rights to government land to abide by environmental restrictions. f). Prohibit government give-aways by instead selling government property on the auction block. g). Stop funding R & D for fossil fuel and nuclear power. h). Eliminate all corporate tax expenditures, but allow the beneficiaries and their Congressional allies to justify anew these tax supports. i). Require federally bailed out corporations to pay back loans and full bail-outs with interest. j). End discount insurance and loans. k). Stop government-run advertising and marketing schemes for corporations. l). End export assistance programs. m). Fund town meetings on corporate welfare to educate the public.

Considering the two sets of proposals along with other ideas (e.g., plug loopholes in the law banning earmarks or pork barrel spending; heavily publicize the costs of corporate welfare; and expose the self-serving guilt gifts and diversionary practices of corporate philanthropy and social responsibility programs) ought to keep crusaders trying to get the welfare spigot turned off very busy. Yet, all in all I feel somewhat let down by the proposals. Given their hedging and limitations, ordinary corporate welfare would still exist, just not as extravagant as before if all of the proposals were implemented tomorrow. I had expected more of Mr. Nader particularly (although he's probably more realistic than I am). Yet he was the only presidential candidate that put the issue prominently on his 2008 presidential campaign agenda. Moreover, I have found no NGO that has made corporate welfare (aside from anti-war groups) an issue or a project initiative.

End Warfare Welfare and War

I'm also disappointed that neither Moor nor Nader's proposals touched the subject of warfare welfare. Maybe it was because the distaste of the Vietnam War was fading and the Iraqi war was yet to come when they presented their proposals. Touching the subject of warfare welfare, however, doesn't go far enough anyway. We have got to end war, not just the welfare spending for it.

I don't foresee anything hopeful on the issue under President Obama. He may be winding down in Iraq, but he is winding up elsewhere. What has he learned from recent history, particularly from our experiences in Vietnam, Cambodia, and Iraq? What did he learn about the Soviet Union's ten-year failure to control Afghanistan? Thomas Friedman wonders if "Mr. Obama understands how much he's bet his presidency on making Afghanistan a stable country?" "Too late now." Mr. Friedman adds.[12] Mr. Friedman, I wonder if Mr. Obama is betting our country's future on his military gambles and trying to protect his chances for reelection.

War makers, seemingly strategically and morally imbecilic and arrogant have made America the most war-prone nation since WWII.[13] If I had to pick one feature of the corpocracy that would be the most likely to cause the downfall of America it would be war making by a class of power drunk imbeciles in the corpocracy. Top priority ought to be given to ending it before it ends America. Nothing less than a full-scale "waging war on war" is necessary. Listed in Table 9 are some initiatives for starting or continuing a "waging war on war." I'm going to spend the rest of this chapter on some of them.

Table 9

Waging War on War

Establish the Citizen's Assembly for Peace.
Establish the Department of Peace Keeping and National Security.
Establish a Peace Keeping and National Security Council.
Nationalize and reorient the defense industry.
Join the International Criminal Court.
Create a dual draft.
End the propagandizing of the military and militarism.
Determine the lost opportunity costs of warfare welfare.

Impeach or prosecute officials who commit the U.S. to war on false pretenses.

Permanently ban and prosecute defense contractors who defraud the government.

Publish a detailed "name and shame" annual warfare welfare report.

Stop budget overruns in military spending.

Stop emergency and off-the-book defense budgeting and funding.

Include supplemental funding and nuclear weapon funding in the military budget.

Require open and competitive bidding on all contract bids.

Purge the GNP index of defense costs.

Prevent war profiteering.

Stop the manufacture and purchase of useless weaponry.

Stop the sale anywhere abroad of arms from U.S. manufacturers.

Eliminate privatization of the military.

Forbid military recruiting at public schools and colleges.

Eliminate college ROTC programs.

Suspend the U.S. Peace Corps while the U.S. is at war.

Pursue peace through commerce.

Establish the Citizen's Assembly for Peace

There are over 40 anti-war organizations in the U.S. and a smattering of them throughout the rest of the world.[14] The oldest in the U.S. reportedly is the War Resistors League, founded in 1923. The largest in the U.S. reportedly is Peace Action, with over 100,000 members, a national network of 27 state affiliates, and over 100 chapters nationwide.[15] Wars continue unfazed by these fragmented, anti-war organizations. They need, says Lawrence S. Wittner, a professor of history and once a member of Peace Action's Board, "a powerful national peace organization, with a mass membership."[16]

It's Chapters 3 and 4, déjà vu! So you would expect me to propose now "a powerful national peace organization, with a mass membership" and I'll do just that. Let's call it the "Citizen's Assembly for Peace." It would be a virtual network of all existing anti-war groups and unaffiliated activists that volunteer to join without losing their own autonomy or funding. It would include organized religious groups from the various faiths whose sacred scriptures profess peace (peace among religions may be more elusive than peace among nations). It would seek funding from the nearly 20 foundations that fund Peace Action plus what must surely be a large number of other funding sources that exist. Within the Assembly the many groups would organize themselves into various alliances on some rational basis such as their commonalities and special strengths. The Assembly would develop an overall strategic plan to carry out initiatives such as the ones listed in Table 9. An initial priority of the Assembly would be to build a massive protest movement of millions of Americans tired of war to provide the political pressure behind each strategic initiative as it is pursued. This pressure would need to be applied relentlessly on the regime. The regime must be made to understand that it is under a siege that won't let up, that a monumental "war" is being waged on its war making.

Establish the Department of Peace Keeping and National Security

A bill HR 808, The Department of Peace and Non Violence Act, was introduced in the House of Representatives in 2007. The bill is languishing if not dead, and I understand that a similar bill has been introduced almost yearly since the early 1970s.

I suppose a new Department of Peace could become a genuinely "proper peace establishment," but I know for certain that it would add immeasurably to the government bureaucracy and cost. I would propose an entirely different restructuring of the government. The Departments of Defense and Homeland Security should be merged and redefined as the Department of Peace Keeping and National Security and assigned two main roles, national defense of our sovereignty from foreign attack and internal peace keeping outside the jurisdiction of local and State police and the National Guard. The bloated, laughable, and useless Department of Homeland Security needs to be abolished. The Department of State would be retained but its capacity for genuine statecraft needs to be enhanced.[17]

The agenda of the former Department of Defense would be reoriented toward broader uses of a nationalized defense industry. It is a tremendous resource of talent and technology that need not and should not be limited to the art and act of war. For example, two famous weapons labs are already helping corporations and 'spinning off start ups.[18] My guess is that if the talent and technology were inventoried and all their possible applications brainstormed every facet of American life might benefit positively from a redirected talent and technology within the Department of Defense.

Establish a Peace Keeping and National Security Council

The Peace Keeping and National Security Department and the State Department would be overseen and coordinated by a newly established Peace Keeping and National Security Council that would replace the existing National Security Council. The council's chair would be the president's advisor on all matters of peacekeeping and national security. The machinating and war-dependent Defense Policy Board, on which political cronies with defense industry ties sit, would be abolished.[19] In its place would be a new policy board to advise the new council. This board would be made up of a cross representation of expertise drawn from the citizenry, with more representation by nonmilitary interests. It would do intensive foreign policy reviews regularly and make recommendations on policy changes. It would increase public oversight of the defense industry and military and foreign policy.

In its advice to the council the board ought to propose diplomatic alternatives to unilateral military interventions; multilateral military interventions only as a last resort and only under the auspices of the United Nations, not NATO; national self sufficiency free of diminishing global resources such as oil; disavowal and disablement of all U.S. nuclear warfare capabilities in tandem with other countries possessing or desiring such capabilities; responsible funding and constructive participation in the UN; a resolution of the controversial Second Amendment on the right to bear arms; and a balanced policy in the volatile Middle East that helps to stabilize if not defuse its powder keg.

Nationalize and Reorient the Defense Industry

The idea of nationalization may have originated with the late and renowned economist John Kenneth Galbraith when he proposed it in a 1969 article for the *New York Times*.[20] His basic reasoning was that the defense industry essentially had only one customer, the U.S. government. Several decades' later two well-known authors and activists, Charlie Cray and Lee Drutman, revived Galbraith's proposal and expanded it into a compelling argument for converting defense contractors into non-profit public corporations with their nature and operations specified in a federal charter.[21] Taking the profit motive away would mean that corporations would be serving the public interest and not shareholders looking for increases in the quarterly earnings of the corporations. FDR reportedly said at the outset of WWII that he didn't "want to see a single war millionaire created in the United States as a result of this world disaster."[22] A federal charter would also enable Congress if it has enough political will left to exercise more direct control over these corporations, including the shrinking of the defense industry and the defense budget.

Join the International Criminal Court

The killing of a person, the killings of war, or the killings of genocide are abhorred and condemned universally enough to confirm the universal value of the sanctity of human life. Honoring and seeking to protect it is the premise for the embarrassingly belated creation in 2002 of the International Criminal Court. Over 100 countries belong. The U.S. does not. The outgoing president, Bill Clinton, signed the treaty establishing the court. But it wasn't ratified and President Bush cancelled the signature. Had the U.S. ratified the treaty before the incoming Bush administration it is still likely that Bush would have invaded Iraq. The court is basically toothless and timid, going after war criminals only when they live in powerless states, and even in those cases, I don't think any genocidal leader, for example, has yet to be brought to court.

Political pressure needs to be applied on the Congress and the administration to sign and ratify the treaty. The U.S. has lost considerable face among signatory countries that see our intransigence as just another sign of our indifference to human rights. Ratification would at least be a symbolic act that might restore some international respect for us. Certain U.S. Presidents in recent memory dead and alive would escape indictment as being international war criminals by this court but surely not by the International Court of Humanity.

Create a Dual Draft

Class Warfare
It is wrong that America's most privileged
families have abandoned military service.[23]

Had there been a military draft as there was during the Vietnam War, it is very unlikely the Bush administration would have started the Iraqi War. So I propose creation of a dual conscription system with two forms of service and both women and men of eligible age and condition would be required to serve in one or the other. One would be a two-year induction into military service. The other would be some form of non-military service for three years, such as in a new Made in America campaign that I'll propose and explain in the next chapter. The initial selection would be by a coin toss. When the coin turns up the military draft, draftees should have the opportunity to make a good case for opting for the other form of service. The rationale for it lasting one year longer is that there would be a much smaller chance of inductees being "put into harm's way," euphemistically speaking. Inductees into either service should be given some form of subsidized post service educational opportunities along the lines of the GI Bill for returning WWII veterans.

The dual draft would eliminate the multibillion dollar annual cost for recruiting and the need to recruit felons to meet recruit quotas.[24] It would also eliminate the sometimes thuggish behavior of military recruiters at high schools.[25]

End the Propagandizing of the Military and Militarism

A critical eye and a knife need to be taken to the content and the multibillion dollar annual budget for the regime's hyping of national security along with the military's propaganda and self-promotional programs such as televised sponsorships of sports events, flyovers by streams of fighter jets, honor guards at public events, and polished advertising followed up by hard-core recruiting.

Let's start with the hype that a strong military keeps us secure. We built bomb shelters during the Cold War; that's how secure the military made Americans feel! The largest, most expensive, and most sophisticated defense establishment in the world along with a very lax immigration policy and the bungling intelligence community, failed to heed warning signals and to head off the infamous terrorist attack of September 11, 2001.

The American people need to see the claim that "military solutions are the only effective national security solutions" for what it is, a sheer myth that has been perpetuated by the regime.[26] Obama's authorization of more drone strikes on countries not even at war with the U.S., strikes that invariably kill innocent as well as suspected terrorists, fuels more hatred and terrorism directed at the U.S., not less.[27] Having a military capability for national defense against foreign enemies is obviously essential, but it alone can't begin to cope with the other threats to our national security, such as degradation of our environment, internal terrorism, economic decline, an overall national apathy, and all the rest of the toll being exacted on America and Americans by the corpocracy.[28]

The American people also need to understand that if the military were so indispensible it wouldn't need to promote itself so unabashedly and expensively with its media advertising and public relations programs. When people look up in awe at a military aircraft fly-over they ought to look down to see their pockets being picked by the defense industry.

The American people also need to understand the true meaning of patriotism, which is always trotted out to squelch dissention against U.S. militarism. Being patriotic as I have said does not mean "my country right or wrong," a jingoistic, Nazis type of pronouncement, but instead "my country, do right and no wrong."

Determine the Lost Opportunity Costs of Warfare Welfare

The military budget year in and year out is a sinkhole into which more and more money, more and more blood, and more and more American goodwill abroad are poured. And it is getting deeper because of all the bad debt (see next chapter) that is mounting from having to pay for all the military spending (our overall national debt now exceeds 13 trillion dollars). Over 20 trillion dollars reportedly has been spent since 1948 on the military budget.[29] Let's assume for the sake of argument that one-half of that amount is sheer warfare welfare, the other half reflecting a realistic defense budget limited to the costs of responding to attacks on our shores by foreign states and terrorist groups. That means 10 trillion dollars worth of lost opportunities that in a corpocracy-free America would not also have been poured down that sinkhole, money that could have been constructively spent over more than a 60-year period on meeting pressing domestic and global needs in employment, education, nutrition, health care, sanitation, you name it. We would be a very different America today, a solidly secure America, an educated America, an employed America, a healthy America, a happy America, and an America at peace with the world.

But that money can never be recovered. It's gone for good down the sinkhole. So let's look ahead at possibilities, starting with my very rough estimate of what a realistic defense budget would be for FY 2011, $311 billion, excluding the costs of ongoing wars. I arrived at that figure by adding 2 percent annual inflation to what Mr. Lawrence Korb had estimated to be a realistic budget for FY 2002.[30] He was an assistant secretary for defense during the Reagan administration, so I imagine his estimate errors on the side of military gravy, but I started with it. The Obama administration's FY 2011 defense budget calls for $548.9 billion excluding war costs, which is about $238 billion more than my extrapolated figure for a realistic defense budget.

Now, let's suppose we could somehow force the administration and Congress to accept a realistic defense budget beginning with FY 2012 and to end the existing wars, which as of early 2010 had already cost $1 trillion dollars and could eventually accumulate to $3 trillion.[31] If, on the other hand, the corpocracy stays its course throughout FY 2012, the lost opportunity costs from now to then will add up roughly to around $240 billion plus some portion of a trillion dollars for continued warring.

If the Citizen's Assembly for Peace were actually to materialize one of its high priority tasks ought to be to do a much better job than I have done in estimating a realistic defense budget. It should then itemize the lost opportunity costs of not meeting pressing social needs item by item because of military profligacy, and then go on to broadcast their findings and warnings loudly, clearly, and repeatedly to the American people. I'm going to hazard a guess that a corpocracy-free America in FY 2012 could easily afford with the savings from a reduced but realistic defense budget to have at a minimum universal health care, quality education, affordable housing, living wages, and an acceptable level of unemployment for all citizens (see the next chapter).

Pursue Peace through Commerce?

> We are capable of shutting off
> the sun and the stars because
> they do not pay dividends.
> ---John Maynard Keynes

I'm jumping now to the last item in Table 9. It's not my idea. I'm definitely opposed to it, but I ask you to see what you think about it.

In a recent book, Peace through Commerce, a few corporate executives in public relations type functions along with some academicians wrote that the road to peace is through global commerce as practiced by multinational corporations, corporate collaboration with NGOs, and adherence to a global code of ethics.[32] It is an incredibly naïve viewpoint on the part of the academicians and probably a duplicitous one on the part of the executives. The corporate balance sheet is remarkably insensitive to what matters most in life, life itself. War is too profitable for business and too career sustaining for corporatized politicians to ever be ended by them voluntarily. Certain U.S. corporations, for instance, collaborated with Germany before and during WWII.[33] Moreover, the corpocracy will never give up voluntarily its blatant global exploitation of the poor by the powerful and wealthy (see next chapter).

Corporate Philanthropy Programs
Don't be Fooled

Does corporate philanthropy make up for opportunities lost for the general welfare because of corporate welfare? Corporate welfare apologists would have us think so. Don't be fooled. This argument needs to be unmasked for what it is, a diversion, a dissimilitude, and a devious exploitation.

The roots of corporate philanthropy in America, I think, can be traced to the "guilt gifts" from the robber barons of the Gilded Age. Corporations today continue to give billions of dollars annually to charities often with self-serving motives as when, for instance, the gifts are aimed at benefiting board members.[34] Some charities are fakes set up to funnel donations to political patrons. Aside from some outstanding museums and performing arts centers that owe their existence to corporate philanthropists, most do more harm than good. This was the opinion of Andrew Carnegie, one of the original philanthropists, and it was recently reinforced in interviews with grantees.[35] The interviewer found a "huge gap" between giver intentions and the effects of the process and the grants. Grantees were typically treated disrespectfully, were hamstrung by red tape, and questioned both the "priorities and strategies "of the grantors.

The "billionaires bankrolling the Tea Party" are a "rich" example of mixing philanthropy and politics.[36] Two of the billionaires are industrialist brothers, David and Charles Koch, reportedly the third wealthiest Americans. David Koch is a well-known philanthropist of cultural affairs. He was the vice presidential candidate on the 1980 Libertarian ticket and wanted to abolish most of the federal government (Social Security, the regulatory agencies, social welfare, the F.B.I., and the C.I.A), and also public schools. He is now bankrolling the Tea Party, and I would imagine heavily influences its agenda. Let's hope it never prevails because reclaiming democracy will have just been made far more difficult.

Some of the Devil's Charity programs are hatched up on Corporate (i.e., Captital) Hill. Journalist Eric Lipton reports that "charities set up by a score of lawmakers from both parties have become an important — and completely unregulated — way for corporations and lobbyists to get their voices heard and to curry favor on Capitol Hill."[37] Utah's Republican senior senator, Orin Hatch, for example, helped establish the Utah Families Foundation. Nine drug companies forked over big bucks, got invited to one of the charity's benefit events to schmooze with Hatch, and got the senator's support to reduce pressure for low-cost generics. Senator Hatch is quoted as saying that "Organizations choosing to donate to the Utah Families Foundation are giving resources to help Utah's families in need from all corners of our state and that is very admirable."[38] Maybe so, Senator, but I couldn't find anything out on the Internet about the foundation's good works for Utah's needy families, and I imagine that making it easier not harder for them to get low-cost generic drugs would be a very admirable thing to do. Sham charities are nothing more than political charities for the vote peddlers and lifers helping them skirt regulations limiting campaign finance donations and shovel in mounds of corporate money. It's just part and parcel of the pay to play political culture of America's corpocracy that makes public servants look like public serpents (with apology to all snakes). Needless to say for those who find that culture so despicable and undemocratic, a new "public service or else" political culture needs to be established and sooner, not later.

Corporate Social Responsibility Programs Don't be Fooled

Some time ago Novo Nordisk, the Danish global pharmaceutical company, adopted "triple bottom line" accounting to its business activities.[39] The approach has since become a familiar term that is also commonly known as corporate social responsibility, or CSR for short. It refers to a firm's accountability for its financial, social, and environmental performance. Public backlash and activism by NGO's to corporate wrongdoing in no small measure furthered the CSR movement.

CSR is mostly a façade. Corporations set up and trumpet their CSR programs to divert the public's eye from corporate misdeeds and corporate welfare. Corporations give CSR little more than lip service, seeing it as nothing more than an inexpensive propagandizing opportunity to divert attention from their still doing business as usual.[40] CSR, moreover, is a superfluous concept in light of what should be the corporate bottom line of ethics below which a corporation should refrain from going. A firm cannot spoil the environment ethically any more than it can harm society ethically. A firm that is ethically responsible is socially responsible, ipso facto.

CSR can also be counterproductive if the corporation gets distracted from what it should be doing in responding to CSR advocates; if the corporation undertakes sham or misleading CSR initiatives to mask wrongdoing; or if CSR advocates go too far and pressure the corporation to undertake initiatives that risk causing shareholder lawsuits for fiduciary irresponsibility. Corporations simply need to act ethically, but their ethics programs are as much window dressing as are their philanthropy and CSR programs.

The typical ethics program includes training sessions, codes of ethics, hotlines, and provisions for penalties. They are all of dubious value. We don't need to be taught ethics, Socrates would remind us; we just need to live it. Codes of ethics are usually highly legalistic, often quickly "out-of-sight-out-of mind," and essentially worthless in that companies with codes do not do business any more or less ethically than companies without them.[41] The deterrence and corrective capability of hotlines is limited if they are seen as inconsequential or as a set up for retaliation when anonymity is not allowed-and allowing it can be criticized as an authorization of illegitimate concealment.[42] As for penalties, we have seen in the previous chapter that they are essentially nonexistent or trivial. A corporate ethics program, moreover, can actually make matters worse when ethics officers and their institutionalization of ethics displace or diminish personal responsibility and accountability for ethical behavior and, like the ill-conceived culpability score, give the corporation a sense of impunity from its wrongdoing.

Corporate Food Stamps

There is nothing veiled about the corporate elites' hypocritical attitude toward corporate welfare although obviously not by that name. They feel "entitled" to it even though their incomes are hardly limited or nonexistent as is the case with "people on the dole" getting cash and non cash benefits like food stamps.

These elitists never shy from opportunities to promote and seek more entitlements. Just boost our R & D tax credit by five percent and lower corporate tax credits and the country will benefit economically argued one of them in an interview recently with Thomas Friedman.[43] The CEO explained that the last factory he built was in China because without tax incentives it was too costly to build in the U.S.

Mr. Friedman swallowed the argument hook, line and sinker. Many of his readers who wrote in comments, however, didn't bite. "I live and work in China. Mr. Friedman, we (the U.S.) are not going to hell in a hand basket in spite of the efforts of Intel and their ilk, we are headed in that direction precisely because of them. Once the technology these companies bring to China can be perfected by local Chinese companies, I predict the multinationals will be politely asked to leave by the government." "If Intel gets its tax break, will it bring back manufacturing? Not as long as they have their serfs in China." "Mr. Otellini, pay your taxes like everybody else! Try taking home only $30 million instead of $100 million!" "Innovation is not building new factories. Innovation is building new ideas. Let's educate our people rather than give tax breaks for factories."

The arguments can sometimes get downright nasty. A wealthy banker recently compared Obama's proposal to hike hedge fund managers' tax rate to Hitlerism.[44] Mr. Hedge fund manager, there are people far more responsible than Mr. Obama for taking America down the road to Fascism. The proposed tax hike would simply and justly help make taxation a bit fairer in America.

If only the silent majority were revolted by corporate beggars in fine suits, mansions, limousines, and private jets lining up for their food stamps that, if anyone has been adding it up, has cost tax payers trillions of dollars over time and forever counting. The corpocracy's hypocrisy and free loading need to be exposed and shamed, perhaps by giving out on a regular basis "Golden Fleece" awards (similar mostly in name only to the late Senator William Proxmire's award) to the corporate welfare queens and the politicians who let the public be fleeced. Since the corpocracy seems to have not an iota of shame, however, more aggressive and strategic means will obviously be necessary to eliminate all of the corpocracy's badvantages. Whatever means are chosen they must be legitimate and peaceful. Violent uprisings would be dealt with swiftly and forcefully by the corpocracy. Don't ever doubt where loyalties lie in the Devil's Marriage.

Some Closing Memory Ticklers and One Liners

The real welfare queen is driven in corporate limousines and flown in corporate jets.

A government that doesn't track corporate crime won't track corporate welfare.

The government's dowry to its corporate partners is mostly veiled.

Warfare welfare: Begging for war.

The most war-prone nation since WWII? A no-brainer question.

Tolerate for how long the corpocracy's imbecilic, arrogant war makers?

Can't meet enlistment quota? Enlist more felons, intimidate more high school kids.

Let's nationalize and reorient the defense industry.

Military security? Americans built bomb shelters during the Cold War.

Military security? 9/11.

Today's warring begets tomorrow's terrorists.

Don't just give peace making a chance, demand it!

The corporate balance sheet is insensitive to what matters most: life.

Corporate philanthropy or corporate guilt gifts?

The Devil's Charity programs.

Public servants or public serpents?

Corporate responsibility or irresponsibility programs?

The United States of Corporate America?

Corporate entitlements? Think corporate food stamps.

Let's give out Golden Fleece awards to the corpocracy.

Don't ever forget where the loyalties lie in the Devil's Marriage.

Chapter 10. Ending Undemocratic Capitalism

Dialogue from the Netherworld

Democracy requires unfettered capitalism.
> ---Milton Friedman (1912-2006)

No, it's your corpocracy that requires it.
> ---Adam Smith (1723–1790)

I begin this chapter by imagining a dialogue "overheard" from somewhere between the putative father of capitalism, Adam Smith, and the Nobel laureate in economics and guru of free-market capitalism, Milton Friedman. The views of the two gentlemen have little in common, and I can imagine a lively debate.

Adam Smith's espousal of a free market has been far overblown. He made only a passing reference to "the invisible hand" in his <u>Wealth of Nations</u> and never once in it used the term "capitalism."[1] A moral philosopher, he understood the importance of morality, which he believed was manifested in a person's sympathy for others. He would have recoiled at the very idea of the corpocracy and its capitalism, for Smith thought the emerging corporations of his time posed threats emanating from their unlimited life span; unlimited size; unlimited power; and unlimited license.[2] Look familiar don't they?

While Lewis Powell issued his battle plan that led to a new regime, Milton Friedman was later to hand it a blueprint for its new economic system grounded in his free-market ideology.[3] It easily won over President Reagan, dovetailing perfectly with his biases. Reagan then proceeded to let laissez-faire capitalism run amok, which is why I choose to call it "undemocratic capitalism" (and sometimes "corpocratic capitalism").

The previous corpocracies had their own versions of undemocratic capitalism, but the current version is vastly larger, more powerful, wealthier, more hegemonic, more harmful, and seemingly invincible. It's very good for the corpocracy and its allies, but very bad for everyone else at home and away. Let's look at two pieces of recent evidence at home, "Hurricane Katrina of 2005" and the "Economic Katrina of 2008" (and still continuing) and then at some evidence away from home, the borderless exploitation of both real and paper economies.

Undemocratic Capitalism at Home
Hurricane Katrina of 2005

In her book about "disaster capitalism," Naomi Klein quotes Friedman as saying that "only a crisis-actual or perceived-produces real change."[4] A disaster, in other words, was an opportunity for Friedman to apply what he called "shock treatment" to let the free market work.

A perfect "shock lab" was provided by the Katrina hurricane disaster that devastated New Orleans in 2005 and that fell on deaf ears in the Bush administration before it gave woefully delayed and totally inadequate aid. Right-wing think tanks, however, acted more swiftly, descending like vultures onto the city bringing with them Friedman's proposal to "radically reform the educational system" in the shocked New Orleans[5] The Bush administration dutifully followed suit, spending millions of dollars to take public schools away from the public and give it to for-profit organizations to operate private and charter schools. The 123 public schools existing before Katrina were slashed to just four and all of the 4700 unionized teachers were fired, adding further trauma and hardship to the city and its residents. For them the idea of a "free-market" suddenly became the reality of a "fired market." And all this to what end, a better education for school children? It's not likely. The performance of privatized schools around the nation has been rather dismal.[6] Privatization of public schools is just one instance of what has been called "the fox in the henhouse."[7] We shall return to the cancerous growth of privatization later on in this chapter.

Undemocratic Capitalism at Home
Economic Katrina of 2008

The economic meltdown that began in 2008 has been the greatest financial and economic disaster in the U.S. since the Great Depression. The latter doomed the regime of that era. The current regime is still thriving, however. Main Street and the overall economy, on the other hand, have been devastated. It may take years for the country to recover from this "shock-in-reverse" and even longer to assess the final toll. Drawing on countless news reports, analyses, and commentaries I have posted in Table 10 and in no particular order a premature, incomplete, and very general run down on the toll so far from Economic Katrina.

Table 10

The Ongoing Toll from Economic Katrina

Trillions of dollars lost from retirement accounts.
Huge government bailouts of the financial industry.
Government bailouts of auto industry.
Collapse of a major Wall Street investment firm.
Partial nationalization of seven major banks crippled by the meltdown.
Fannie May and Freddy Mac put into a conservatorship.
Further decline in take-home pay.
Staggering amount of jobs lost.
Social welfare and other social service budget cutting.
Beleaguered public libraries become aid shelters.
Adjustable rate mortgages bumping up monthly payments.
Rising number of homeless.
Soaring personal bankruptcies.
Falling home prices.
Soaring home foreclosures.
Rise of swindling debt relief companies.
Frozen credit markets.
Record drop in consumer confidence in the economy.
Plummeting retail sales.
Collapse of major retain chains.
Federal purchase of unpaid and unsecured commercial paper.

Plunging stock market.

Small businesses struggling to get short-term loans.

More debt-ridden companies going bankrupt.

Surging withdrawals of investments from mutual funds.

More cities and government agencies are in an economic crunch.

Growing national debt.

FDIC falls into the red for first time since the 1900s.

Economies of other countries melt down.

World-wide anxiety.

Hurricane Katrina had been brewing for a few days or so. Economic Katrina had been brewing for two decades or so. Very few people, including some astute economists, saw it coming and those who did were ignored. And most everyone who's analyzed the mess has offered a different explanation for it. A year later, having had more time for further analysis and reflection, *The New York Times* concluded that "Pretty much everyone agrees on the causes for the country's desperate financial mess: predatory lenders, weak regulations, even weaker regulators, and risky nigh unto incomprehensible financial instruments."[8] The latter were like bets in a high-stakes game no one truly understood and that could never have been played had the Clinton administration and Congress not repealed the law prohibiting banks from becoming casinos. One of the best accounts I've read, incidentally, on how that repeal turned banks into casinos is to be found in one of my favorite periodicals, *The American Scholar*, and was written by a law professor, William J. Quirk.[9] There's nothing "quirky" about his analysis.

I pretty much agree with the *Times* overall postmortem except some factors were overlooked. My own postmortem tells me the meltdown was caused by a conflation of factors that included: casino banks, Friedman's free-market ideology; a hands-off government; predatory lenders; gullible borrowers; the repackaging and selling of shaky loans as securities; the heady times of easy money and overspending; and incredible booty (astronomical salaries/bonuses) for the masterminds and deal makers on Wall Street even as Main Street was going broke.

Exploitative Globalization

Globalization is very controversial, meaning different things to different people and affecting them differently. In its simplest sense, globalization means the economic presence of and financial imprint on other countries by another country's policies and agents. Globalization is controversial because of its imprints. Some claim their net effect is positive, some say negative. But it is all negatively exploitative when the corpocracy extends its hegemony offshore.

America's corpocracy respects no borders and never has, starting with the first regime and the Banana Wars. Since then the globe has become a giant badvantage, an oversized opportunity for commercial exploitation. With the entrance of Reagan, his pal the Brit Margaret Thatcher, and with Friedman in tow, exploitative globalization by the U.S. corpocracy spread like an epidemic.

The "Unholy Trinity"

This well-deserved nickname refers to the International Monetary Fund (IMF), the World Bank (WB), and the World Trade Organization (WTO).[10] They became the primary enabler of the corpocracy's global hegemony and in effect have made "American firms de facto agents of foreign policy."[11]

The trios' purpose ostensibly from the beginning has been to reduce poverty and to develop the economies of Third World countries. In reality the aim of its work has been totally different, very "unholy." Huge amounts of money masquerading as developmental loans and contingent on the currency devaluation and paring of the borrowing country's social programs are siphoned off to huge, transnational corporations, many of which are U.S. firms, and the pockets of the governing and power elite of the country. The country goes further into debt and becomes even more vulnerable to being further exploited, including being subjected to sham debt relief programs.

No matter where on the globe the exploitation takes place there is a similar pattern of corporate behavior involved that includes such despicable, inhumane practices as relying on militaries and militias to purchase commodities made by forced labor; using armed groups to protect corporate assets; supplying arms to rebel and government forces; actually participating in military actions; engaging in smuggling, money laundering, and illegal currency transactions; and sweat-shop production of goods.

Needless to say, no transnational corporation, no totalitarian regime, no quasigovernmental agency inside or outside the Unholy Trinity will own up to such practices. They "can't admit," says a very knowledgeable authority on the subject, that "it is human rights violations that make ... countries attractive to business -- so history has to be fudged, including denial of our support of regimes of terror and the practices that provide favorable climates of investment, and our destabilization of democracies that [don't] meet [the] standard of service to the transnational corporation...."[12] I liken exploitative globalization by the U.S. corporacy as taking economically impoverished and starving countries on a death march.

Global Exploitation of Paper Economies

Borderless transactions in paper, or currency, have now vastly overshadowed borderless transactions in goods, services, and commodities. With today's electronic technology, trading in foreign currencies can and do occur around the clock. This size and speed create a golden opportunity for currency speculation.

Currency speculators are domestic or foreign depending on their origin. They can throw their own or another country already struggling economically into an even deeper crisis from the resulting currency devaluation. I don't know if speculators who cause their own country's economy to collapse have ever been called "economic traitors," equivalent to "economic hit men" who exploit foreign countries, but the analogy seems to fit.[13]

The influence of Milton Friedman and the Unholy Trinity can also be seen in foreign currency speculation. He had argued against government efforts to stop currency speculation, contending that speculators ultimately help stabilize the economy and to allow people to hedge their bets in the trading of currencies.[14] Consistent with Freidman's free-market philosophy, the IMF opposes government intervention in response to currency devaluation from speculation. The theory and advice, however, fly in the face of a globe full of evidence to the contrary.

Most if not all Asian countries, Brazil, England, Indonesia, Mexico, Scandinavia, South Korea and South Africa have each suffered devastating financial crises from currency speculation. Take Malaysia in 1997, for instance. Its prime minister at the time, Dr. Mahathir Mohammed, was so outraged that he wanted "currency trading to be made illegal!"[15] One country at least, China, has done just that and with finality by making currency speculation a capital offense punishable by death (at the same time, though, she is acting like a rogue state when she deliberately exports undervalued goods).

Setting the Stage for True Economic Reform

We are not Malaysia or China. Neither the Wall Street bankers who were the primary instigators of Economic Katrina nor the politicians who enabled it were executed or held accountable at all. Bankers, moreover, have been getting multi-billion dollar bail outs from the politicians and taking part of the hand-out as bonuses to themselves.

Until the regime is ended there can be no true economic reform, only band aid patching, and another economic crisis even worse is sure to be just around the corner.[16] Lobbyists have been swarming all over legislative deliberations on financial reform, and we can expect only cosmetic changes at best by the current administration's economic team. Its members mostly came through the revolving doors from Wall Street, were very cozy with it, and had a hand in shaping the very policies that enabled the crisis. The legendary Paul Volcker, economist, former Chairman of the Federal Reserve under Presidents Carter and Reagan, and Chairman of President Obama's Economic Advisory Board, gives legislative reforms a B- grade and observes that "There is a certain circularity in all this business. You have a crisis, followed by some kind of reform, for better or worse, and things go well for a while, and then you have another crisis."[17] In other words Chairman Volcker, we will be revisited by a third great depression on down the decade some day. Is that essentially what you are telling us?

If progress were being made in unleashing democracy power in some form or other against other elements of the corpocracy, it would be a good time to set the stage for achieving true economic reform. Let's assume there has been a taskforce commissioned by some nongovernmental group and charged with polling the opinions of middle class Americans, the socioeconomic group absolutely essential to any true democracy and viable economy, and then melding the solicited public opinion with the taskforce's a) consideration of new ways of thinking about capitalism; b) enunciation of a proposed new national economic policy; c) design of a new form of capitalism that I'll call simply "democratic capitalism," d) proposed objectives and initiatives to implement the design, and e) report on the findings and recommendations to the administration, to the Congress, and to the American people.

There should be no economists on the taskforce who were blindsided by Economic Katrina, who nourished it with their free-market ideology, or who are still in the dark and disagreement. As recently as late Summer 2010 economist Thomas Friedman was saying that after talking to senior economic policy makers he came away concluding that "things are getting better, except where they aren't. The bailouts are working, except where they're not. Things will slowly get better, unless they slowly get worse. We should know soon, unless we don't.[18] Who needs their advice? Instead, members should include some prominent and innovative thinkers about the reform of capitalism but who aren't economists. I have identified some who, based on their writings, ought to be invited (Aristotle in absentia).

In Appendix C I have abstracted some of their writings and will be drawing upon them in presenting nine broad objectives and a host of more specific initiatives to create a democratic capitalism. The nine are these.

> End free market ballyhoo.
> End fear mongering over national debt.
> End privatization.
> End economic disparities and poverty.
> End shut-out capitalists.
> End financial speculation.
> End exploitative globalization.
> End unsustainable development.
> End elitist pay without performance.

End Free Market Ballyhoo

> Tea Party Patriots, Inc. ("TPP") is a non-partisan, non-profit social welfare organization dedicated to furthering the common good and general welfare of the people of the United States. TPP furthers this goal by educating the public and promoting the principles of fiscal responsibility, constitutionally limited government and **free markets.**
>
> ---www.teapartypatriots.org.

The proof is already in the flattened pudding that free-market theory is utterly unworkable, destructive, and a hypocritical ploy by the regime. As author Thom Hartmann has noted, "one of the most pernicious claims the 'coporatocracy' (his term) makes is that business flourishes best in a perfectly 'free' market---so all of society does better."[19] Proponents of a free market theory have for decades pointed to productivity gains and wage increases as confirmation of their arguments for deregulation and a swift transition from the manufacturing to the service sector, yet the productivity gains are "grossly overstated" because of the unmeasured effect of outsourcing, wages have been falling, not rising, and a resurgence of manufacturing would help, not hurt the economy.[20] Their arguments, moreover, have been further if not totally repudiated by Economic Katrina.

The so-called Chicago School of Economics, where Friedman once held forth, is hugely responsible for extolling the virtues of the free-market. And it is especially noteworthy and satisfying to learn that another influential member of that camp, lawyer and economics writer Judge Richard A. Posner, has since turned heretic and is now debunking the free-market ideology.[21] He should be the honorary chair of the task force, and it should include in its proposed national economic policy a denouncement of free-market theory! The policy also needs to delineate government's proper obligations and role both in society and in its market place so as to strike a balance between total government rule on the one hand and total market rule on the other (recall Abraham Lincoln's view of the proper goal of government mentioned in the first chapter).

Notice
to
Tea Party and other Free Marketeers
What you really should want
is a
Corpocracy-Free Market

End Fear Mongering Over the National Debt

In one of his many insightful columns Paul Krugman writes that fear mongering over the national debt may prove to be as destructive as was fear mongering over weapons of mass destruction (WMD) the Bush Administration relied on to justify bombing Bagdad and starting the war against the relatively defenseless Iraqi government and its military. Just as the WMD were never found so too says Krugman has no evidence been found that proves the fearful claim by politicians, cons, and others that the national debt destabilizes our economy as well as jeopardizes its recovery and weakens our influence internationally. The reason the unfounded claims could prove destructive in the short term is that they create a pressure for reductions in federal spending that would actually worsen the current socioeconomic situation.[22]

As I see it there is good national debt and there is bad national debt. Good debt means enough federal spending on programs to help meet real economic and social needs such as more employment, better education, and better and affordable health care that once better met will require far less government spending in the future, by then only maintenance spending in contrast to remedial spending. Bad debt means going into the red from unreasonably and unfairly low taxing of the wealthy; from more rather than less corporate welfare, especially warfare welfare; and federal spending on initiatives our society doesn't really need, actually suffers from it, and shouldn't be burdened by them.

National debt is a political and socioeconomic phenomenon. When President Clinton left office there had been no federal deficit for three years and surpluses were expected to continue for a decade longer. President Bush's policies, on the other hand, created massive bad debt. His policies were to overspend on the wrong initiatives and charge the wealthy even less for expenses.[23] Both presidents in their policies contributed in no small measure to Economic Katrina, and attempts to recover from it simply inflated the debt (not all of the economic stimulus spending in my opinion was bad debt). Today, the national debt seems to be around $13 trillion. Meanwhile, the social needs of the country have been festering from underfunding of education, health care, and employment programs, the very needs that had they been attended to would have, as I said, resulted in good and shorter term debt.

The task force needs to examine federal spending levels under varying political, economic, and social conditions and propose some kind of a gauge for determining what would be the appropriate deficit levels in the short and long term under the various conditions, including a good estimate of what would be a realistic defense budget (see previous chapter). It should also spell out the implications of its proposals for the rest of the strategic objectives and initiatives to end the corpocracy.

End Privatization

Rabid government haters and corporate purveyors of privatization argue that business can do much better than government in providing public services and meeting public needs in general. Not so! Michael

Edwards, activist and author, explains in his book <u>Small Change</u> that the inherent nature of business with its profit-seeking motive and its short-term perspective and demands makes business unable to come even close to solving hardcore problems like poverty, epidemics, war, social discord, and the like.[24] I would simply add this question: How many business firms, large or small, can you name that are making significant inroads on such problems?

Yet the public sector is increasingly being taken over by the private sector. Privatization, argue Si Kahn and Elizabeth Minnich, co-authors of <u>The Fox in the Henhouse</u> is the private sector's way to "undercut, limit, shrink, or outright take over any government and any part of the public sector that stands in the way of corporate pursuit of ever larger profits and could be run for profit."[25] I've already cited the example of public schools being privatized in New Orleans (the cons want all public schools to fail). Consider another example beginning as a riddle: What a) sorts mail but is not the USPS, b) cuts Social Security checks but is not the SSA, c) counts the census but is not the Bureau of the Census, d) monitors air traffic but is not the FAA, and e) runs space flights but is not NASA? Give up? It is Lockheed Martin, the largest military contractor in the U.S. This company is just one of several examples the two writers give of privatization.[26] Or consider the privatization of airport security by the government allowing the airlines to provide it and on the cheap. Paul Krugman has controversially speculated that the cheaper security made the terrorists' catastrophic September 11, 2001 high jacking of the passenger jets easier.[27]

Take any industry and any common property, such as airwaves for example, and they have been privatized, usually more so than less. Corporations with exceptions don't actually steal public property. It's usually gifts in the dowry from government. Taking these gifts back, needless to say, won't be child's play, but it ought to be a high priority of any broad-scale offensive to reclaim our democracy and regain fuller control over our common goods and how we chose to satisfy our common needs.

Taking them back totally, as in the nationalization of industries, would be a draconian and politically suicidal step. Nevertheless the task force should strongly advocate nationalizing certain public-sensitive industries such as the defense industry, the energy industry, the financial services industry, and the health care industry.

Regarding this last industry, Thom Hartman makes some cogent points. If health care is a privilege, then privatization by the health care industry is not a national and human offense. But if it is a right, as it is in most developed countries, then letting profit takers takeover is a blatant denial of a right to which each citizen is entitled upon birth. Hartman notes that even communist China provides health care for its people.[28] But the corpocracy easily thwarted the single-payer or national health insurance option during the rancorous and seemingly interminable health care reform debate of 2009 and into early 2010. This option would have barred the health care insurance industry from the trough. As it now stands, the new reform law will be a big boon to this industry and the pharmaceutical industry. "Anything less than national health insurance is voodoo" says an NGO advocating for national health insurance.[29]

Keeping or taking back public sector services only partially does not seem to work well. Profit seeking thwarts rendering better and cheaper services to the public. The federal partnership with the insurance industry in proving flood insurance is a case in point. Government bears all the risk and the insurance companies get all the revenue.[30] The insured get flooded with debt.

The task force should explore all proposals for reversing privatization. These include: Barne's proposal (see Appendix C) that the government assign common property rights to institutions, distinct from government and from corporations, and that would be set up as trusts to manage the common property; Hartmann's mostly politically oriented initiatives (see Appendix C); Terry's proposal for a "Nation of Owners," (see Appendix C); litigation such as relying on the Commerce Clause of the U.S. Constitution to rebuff in court further privatization efforts; and educating and mobilizing the public against privatization.

End Economic Disparities and Poverty

The late Justice Louis Brandeis said, "We can have a democracy or we can have great wealth in the hands of the few. We cannot have both." And we don't. We don't have a genuine democracy but we do have great and sometimes vulgar (i.e., ill begotten) wealth in the hands of one percent of Americans who possess nearly forty percent of all wealth in the nation.[31] And at the opposite end of the socioeconomic spectrum, in 2007 there were 37.3 million people living in poverty, or 12.5 percent of the U.S. population, and a bleak prospect of most Americans at some point in their life falling into poverty.[32] More poverty-stricken people live in America than in any other developed country.

The glaring and inexcusable gap between our own haves and have not's is sensed by the silent majority, as silent, submissive, and inattentive to all the other telltale signs as they may be. In a 2009 poll nearly one-half of them reported being disturbed over the gap between the rich and the poor in the U.S.[33] That slightly more than one-half aren't conscience-stricken must be good news to the dividing and conquering regime.

The mighty U.S. has spent trillions to develop the most sophisticated weapons but not for the decades-old war on poverty. When it comes to this war the U.S. is an undeveloped nation that has made mostly minimal, token, and begrudging efforts toward meeting Article 25 of the 1948 United Nation's Declaration of Universal Human Rights in which everyone on earth is declared to have the right to an adequate standard of living.

A granted but unfulfilled right may be worse than no right at all. It certainly is a breech of universal values and an overflowing wrong. Article 25 ought to be made an economic policy goal that should also seek the end of poverty and a start toward a shared prosperity and property ownership for all Americans as Jeff Gates has proposed (see Appendix C). It's a lofty goal even without the current economic crisis, but a goal that may be reachable if the current crisis ever subsides. As President Obama said in his inaugural address, "We remain the most prosperous, powerful nation on Earth." But, Mr. President, the prosperity has been monopolized and the power has been abused.

Along with this policy goal the task force ought to propose a national definition and declaration of the meaning of wealth in a true democracy. The definition might be along the lines of Peter Barnes' "common wealth," Rianne Eisler's "the real wealth of a nation," or Dana Zohar and Ian Marshall's "wealth we can live by" (see Appendix C). Accompanying the policy goal ought to be at least seven objectives for reducing economic disparities and ending poverty: end rationalizations for the status quo; the fair sharing of democracy's cost; reducing joblessness to the greatest extent feasible; increasing wages; reducing the costs of daily living; the upgrading of American education, and the creation of a Made-in-America Campaign.

End Rationalizations for the Status Quo

Two tiresome rationalizations of economic disparity and poverty need to be put to rest. One is the argument of trickle-down economics. The second is the mean-spirited argument that the poor get what they deserve. In the face of enormous economic inequities and social injustice these knee-jerk responses of the regime and its allies are pathetic and immoral.

To rationalize its own excesses, including its hand outs from the government, corpocratic capitalism spouts the theory of trickle down economics. In reality, the excesses gush upwards. What small residual trickles down stops at the back door of the middle class, never going down farther to "the projects," a euphemism for public housing where the poorest of poor who aren't homeless live in dangerous and fetid conditions.

The other argument is that poverty is self-imposed by overspending and sloth. It's true we have a consumptive society stoked by corporate interests (some seventy percent of our economy is consumptive), but most Americans living below the poverty line don't fall there because of their own failings. Recall my reference in the first chapter to the findings of Mark Rank, the professor of social welfare, who contends persuasively I think that economic and political factors, not any personal shortcomings of individuals account for the appalling level of poverty in America (Professor Rank in his book makes numerous proposals for ways to reduce the poverty level).[34] I have concluded from my own research of the literature that people in poverty are there because of one or more of four mostly circumstantial factors: joblessness, "dead wages" (those that don't qualify as "living wages"); the expensive cost of daily living; and poor education. All four are recipes for snuffed drive and sloth. All four are situational factors, not personal factors, and belie the belief held by many Americans, especially the cons, that being poor is the result of personal irresponsibility.[35]

Share Democracy's Cost Fairly

Justice Oliver Wendell Holmes once said something very wise, very humane, very patriotic, and very practical. He said, "I like paying taxes. With them I buy civilization." Democracy is precious and worth the cost, yet many wealthy individuals and many corporations don't pay their fare share of it.

The task force needs to consider any and all good ideas on how to achieve fair-share taxation, including Barnes' proposals for common tax credits (see Appendix C). Just as importantly. the task force needs to peer through the regime's veil and do a "tax-escape" audit" of all forms of corporate welfare, including tax havens, tax cuts for the filthy rich, etc.[36] While this exercise is being done, a poll needs to be taken of middle-class Americans asking them what they think would need to be done to protect and promote the general welfare of all Americans (e.g., taxing everyone fairly, providing all Americans with affordable housing, a job paying no less than a living wage or guaranteed unemployment insurance at the same level until a job is gotten, security from an America at peace with the world, etc, etc). Next, an analysis would be made to estimate how much it would cost to meet each of these needs and how they could be met if there were fair taxation; that is, without any corporate welfare. Finally, another poll would be conducted, telling people about the findings and asking them if they would be willing to apply their democracy power to end corporate welfare for the sake of the general welfare.

Move toward "Full" Employment

Over 40 years ago the Full Employment and Balanced Growth Act was passed. It was an abject failure.[37] The Great Society's "War on Poverty" clashed with the country's real war at the time and never recovered. The Act could never have achieved full employment in any case and was more a symbolic gesture. Full employment of employable people, of course, is an unreachable goal. People will always outnumber available jobs, and continuing technological "progress" means more outputs with still fewer people inputs. So there will always be the need for a strong social welfare program, including possibly some kind of more or less open-ended unemployment benefits, which will never happen with the current regime that deliberately allows benefits for hundreds of thousands of the unemployed to expire because offsetting spending cuts aren't made.

While full employment is unrealistic, economist Paul Schiller nevertheless asserted, unbelievably right in the midst of Economic Katrina, that such a goal, with interim lesser targets and supported by new fiscal and monetary policies might at least shore up public confidence in the economy and lead to more employment.[38] I would suggest instead a different goal, that of an "acceptable unemployment level," and define it as that level reached only after all conceivable and realistically possible employment measures have been effectively applied to create new jobs and to save existing ones.

The most fertile source for creating new jobs is the small business sector. It has far more firms and is far more innovative than behemoth corporations. Unfortunately, only a miniscule portion of the administration's stimulus plan of 2009 was allocated to reinvigorating this sector.[39] Whatever the allocation, larger or smaller, it should not be funneled through the federal Small Business Administration. It ought to be abolished or totally reformed. Only a tiny slice of the small business sector ever gets loans from this agency.[40] Instead, the two NGOs, American Independent Business Alliance (AMIBA), and Business Alliance for Local Living Economics (BALLE), are the ideal NGOs to spearhead, with support from other NGOs and through prodding of the administration, the creation of new jobs in the small business sector. As part of this overall initiative, there ought to be a program for creating paid apprenticeships with small businesses.

Another fertile source for creating new jobs is government itself. Serious consideration ought to be given to resurrecting the public work relief programs of the Works Progress Administration and the Civilian Conservation Corps established in response to the first Great Depression in the 1930s. Millions of Americans were employed not on make-work projects but in much needed work such as highway and building construction, slum clearance, reforestation, and rural rehabilitation. Some 70 plus years later there is just as great a need for similar public works projects. There surely ought to be a job in Obama's "most prosperous" America for any able-bodied person.

There are other initiatives the task force ought to consider for lowering unemployment to an acceptable level. They include forbidding job outsourcing and company relocations to other countries; employment tax credits and job-sharing incentives (two positive forms of corporate subsidy); and compensation for household care givers and volunteer workers that would probably pay many times over in a more educated work force, in reduced health care costs, and in reduced social welfare costs. This last initiative is drawn from the ideas of Aristotle and Eisler (see Appendix C). If Aristotle's view of the economy as household management and Eisler's notion of the household economy and its productive value were to be explicitly and officially recognized as a contributor to the GDP, then millions of otherwise officially "unemployed" would need to be treated as gainfully employed and ought to be compensated in some way by the government.

One conclusion is crystal clear. Even a more modest employment goal is doomed to fail unless the regime is upended and its allies quieted. They will block every employment initiative the government may get the nerve to muster. They will trot out their tiresome and thoroughly repudiated dual arguments that by letting the free market work the economy will grow and create new jobs and secondly that spending more federal dollars on employment programs will raise the federal deficit. I can't repeat enough times. The free market theory is just that, theory, and it's all bunkum. The GDP and stock market are up from the depths of Economic Katrina and yet the unemployment rate has soared. As for all the shortsighted and mean-spirited fear mongering over the federal deficit, there are far worse deficits in our social fabric and they have been caused in no small part by an unacceptable unemployment level. They are the deficits of increased poverty; increased crime; increased illnesses; broken families; loss of self-esteem; and increased social restlessness and unease.

Increase Wages

In the opinion of the Clinton administration's labor chief, "the only way to keep the economy going over the long run is to increase the wages of the bottom two-thirds of Americans."[41] He said that, by the way, after having been in the administration whose signing of the NAFTA and GATT trade agreements for the benefit of the corpocracy caused Americans' wages to go into a "free fall."[42]

The national minimum wage law is based on a minimum level of consumption, has been on the books since the late 30"s, and has become a farce. It falls short of a wage a middle class family actually needs to live not luxuriously, just worry-free of being able to meet reasonable needs. Many states' laws consequently have set a higher minimum, and several jurisdictions have established local policies requiring still higher so-called living wages. But they are "just a starting point," claims Thom Hartmann, because "even people making a 'living' wage often must work two jobs."[43]

The argument that raising wages raises unemployment is false, Hartmann claims, and notes that "every time the minimum wage gets raised, employment goes up."[44] Corporations don't want to concede that raising wages lower profits, not employment.

Corpocractic capitalism offers "dead" wages, not living wages, mostly by emasculating the bargaining power of labor unions. For any wage earner nowadays to keep up with inflation isn't like running on a treadmill, it's like running on two of them at once. Moreover, many low-wage earners aren't paid even the minimum wage to which they are entitled, are denied overtime pay, and are dissuaded from filing worker compensation claims.[45]

Anyone who needs work ought to get work and be fairly compensated for it. The task force should consult with jurisdictions about what lessons were learned in requiring a living wage. Consideration could also be given to proposing a nationwide living wage and offsetting the costs to employers possibly through tax credits adjusted by the financial health of the employers.

Reduce the Costs of Daily Living

So much personal wealth owned by so few helps to drive up the cost of daily living simply because the wealthy can afford to pay more for goods and services. A major cause of indebtedness, Professor Howard Karger contends in his book, Shortchanged, is due to "the high cost of living in a privatized society," not to "over consumption." He notes that the rising cost of necessities now amounts to 75% of a family's two-person income, leaving little left for luxuries for the "functionally poor."[46]

One of life's necessities is getting affordable preventive and therapeutic health care, the latter especially for acute and chronic medical conditions. When these conditions afflict the functionally poor and the uninsured in general more misery is simply heaped on misery. While the new health care reform law of 2010 (written by lobbyists) will extend insurance coverage it does not provide universal coverage and traps many people already covered in costly state-run high-risk plans. Moreover, there will probably be endless legal battles contesting the new law's implementation.

Ralph Nader, in his July 16, 2010 Nader Alert e-mail to me pointed out that Iran has a much better health care system than in the impoverished parts of our own country. This sad state of affairs is morally repulsive. It is also economically insane. A healthy people in the long run help, not hurt the national economy, and trying to stay or get healthy can overwhelm ordinary household budgets. I recently read a letter to the editor of *The New Yorker* in which the writer raised a very insightful question that had never occurred to me. "Could it be," the writer asked, "that unaffordable health care is the ultimate cause of the recession" (i.e., Economic Katrina)?[47] That is, earning power may have shrunk at least partly because health care costs spiraled, leaving wage earners to turn to mortgaging their homes far beyond their value once the bubble burst.

Affordable and decent housing is one of life's necessities and is becoming increasingly less available, especially, Professor Rank notes, among low-income households. To reverse that trend he proposes establishing a national housing trust fund with budgetary sensitive ways to pay for it (e.g., end federal subsidies of mortgages on million dollar and up homes), expanding and using more effectively the government's housing voucher program, providing refundable housing tax credits for low-income homeowners and renters, and enforcing fair-housing laws.[48]

The last two necessities I'll mention briefly here are the need among low-income families and single-parent households for affordable and decent child care and child support. All children, not just those in affluent households, are America's future for better or worse. It behooves America on economic and moral grounds to ensure that the general welfare of needy children is not neglected. America is failing that obligation miserably. Many day care centers are of poor quality, even good centers may offer only partial-day care, and many single custodial parents do not get the child support payments ordered by the courts. I will refer the reader to Professor Rank's book where he addresses these problems and proposes a number of solutions.[49]

Move toward a Quality American Education

Yet another factor linked to poverty is poor education. America is currently producing high school drop-outs "at an average of one every 26 seconds."[50] Nearly one-third of America's youth entering high school never graduate. A blue-ribbon commission's searing indictment of America's educational system more than 25 years ago spawned a flurry of educational reforms, yet the same report, says a prominent educator, could be written today because our educational system still is "in turmoil."[51] Getting a poor education hits hardest those who need quality education the most, children from families in the lowest socioeconomic ranks. A recent study of the academic performance of children across the entire socioeconomic and minority group spectrum found a gap in the quality of education these children are getting so gaping that it will take more than a century to close if ever.[52] And remember those civic clueless high school students.

It's beyond the scope here to propose an array of new educational reform initiatives. Even so, education can't be disconnected from our economy or our current economic system. One shouldn't be reformed without reforming the other also. A good starting point for thinking about interconnected reforms I think is to remember Riane Eisler's views on what the real wealth of nations really is all about, on the basic purpose of an economic system, and on the need for massive investment in child care and human development (see Appendix C).

Create a Made-in-America Campaign

I proposed this idea without explaining it in the previous chapter. I will explain it now. Suppose that we lived in a corpocracy-free America. All non-military corporate welfare would thus have been eliminated. There would also be no warfare welfare, only a realistic defense budget and no more warring. What could we do with all of the billions or trillions of dollars saved? Besides spending directly on the objectives already mentioned for ending economic disparity and poverty, we could create a Made-in-American Campaign to reduce America's humongous trade deficit by making in America the products and services we are now buying from other countries. The task force would need to identify what all of those items are and what would be needed in the way of capital, labor, and material to make those items here at home. The resources and production would be funded from the money no longer misspent by the former corpocracy. This kind of business subsidy would be truly beneficial. The dual draft system would supply some of the labor needed and the available, unemployed labor pool would supply the rest. I know the idea sounds fanciful, but as I like to say, anything conceivable may be possible.

End Shut-Out Capitalists

So much capitalism, so few capitalists! Democratic capitalism would put an end to that. Gates (see Appendix C) has proposed many specific initiatives besides his six strategic proposals for infusing more capitalists into capitalism. They include government contracts to encourage employee stock ownership plans (ESOPs); strategic government purchases from firms with certifiably broad-based ownership; strategic government licensing; converting private access to public access of natural resources; employee ownership of public services such as snail mail; the favoring of more inclusively owned firms that seek trade assistance; government loans to business firms contingent on their more inclusive ownership; orienting development banks to businesses with more participatory ownership; a robust antitrust policy; strategic public pension plan investments; exploiting a variety of government subsidies (the good kind of subsidies that don't constitute corporate welfare); and changing a variety of tax policies to create more capitalists.

Gate's proposed initiative to further ESOPs ought to be debated before any decision to move forward on it is made. They have been an upside-down incentive for management and might turn out to be so for employees. They are often merely a means for employers to benefit from extra tax credits. And usually they are not accompanied by empowerment of workers to become more involved in important business decisions. On the other hand, the one major advantage of ESOPs, if the disadvantages can be eliminated, is that if employees own a majority of the stock they are the company's primary owners with controlling power over the business.

Yet another path to shared capitalism would be to pursue policies that extend the whole range of stakeholder ownership in enterprises. As Korten explains, "stakeholder ownership involves placing the rights and powers of ownership of productive assets in the hands of people who have more than just a financial interest or stake in their long-term viability."[53] These people include, besides workers, suppliers, customers, and residents of the communities where the enterprises are located.

Majority employee-owned U.S. companies are probably the most prevalent of non-traditional ownership. They number in the thousands, have "at least 50% of their stock owned by an ESOP, a stock purchase plan in which most full-time employees can participate, a profit sharing plan or other trust, or some combination of such plans."[54] Other stakeholder ownership patterns include a variety of cooperatives such as consumer co-ops.

The major drawback to stakeholder ownership of publicly held corporations is that only stakeholders who own shares in the firm have the power, as weak as it often is, to influence their representatives, the members of the board of directors. This may seem appropriate on the surface since shareholders invest their money in the firm, but they don't directly affect the success of the firm, unlike workers who do its work, unlike suppliers who supply it, unlike customers who buy from it, and unlike communities that provide public services necessary for it to exist.[55]

End Financial Speculation at Home and Away

Aristotle (see Appendix C) had a disparaging view of making money from money, the pure and simple aim of financial speculation, financial manipulation, and outright financial fraud. It creates, to paraphrase him, an "unnatural" wealth. To quote me, it creates all too often vulgar wealth. Financial speculation, including commodities speculation needs to be outlawed.

If I understand Roger Terry correctly (see Appendix C), he would eliminate the very need of Wall Street. Not a bad idea if only we could get away with it. But we would have to go beyond Wall Street in New York City. Its dominance is being eroded not only by foreign currency speculation but also by the sprouting of private marketplaces here and there, some so clandestine as to be "all but invisible, even to regulators."[56]

A strategy that makes sense to me would be to phase out over time the stock market wherever it operates while somehow protecting long-term investors until the process is completed. My reasoning is this. First, much of the stock market is a cesspool of investments in socially irresponsible corporations. Second, there just aren't that many socially responsible corporations beyond their window dressing in which to invest. Third, those corporations that invest only for making money rather than for product and service improvements are no longer truly useful or necessary for the real marketplace of goods and services. Fourth, start-ups can go to banks rather than through initial public offerings.

David Korten (see Appendix C) would severely curtail Wall Street's scope. He starts with this observation, "money is a useful medium of exchange except in the hands of speculators where it becomes an anti-democratic, anti-market instrument of instability and unjust extraction."[57] He then goes on to propose these particular initiatives for neutering Wall Street: prohibit banks from financing speculators; substantially tax short-term capital gains (why not heavily tax gains from all stock market investments?); encourage use of local currencies; make creating new money a public function, not one of bank loaning; charge fees for holding any financial assets; reinvigorate community banking; prohibit the use of financial assets as collateral for borrowing; and prohibit foreign currency speculation.[58]

A big tail, the banks, in America, is wagging a bigger dog, the financial industry and Washington. The tail needs to be cut into smaller pieces. Or they need to be nationalized, putting Washington in control of them. This, the *New York Times* editorialized would be "the least bad solution to a truly desperate situation."[59] Such a proposal would meet an avalanche of protests. Among them would be the argument that government doesn't know how to run banks. That argument doesn't wash. Government runs the nation's central banking system (i.e., Federal Reserve), FDIC, and much more. Some 100 private banks, in contrast, have recently run themselves into the ground, and another 400 and counting are on the brink of nose diving.[60]

Needless to say it might be easier to move a mountain than to create a democratic capitalism without financial speculation or with a diminished and regulated version of it. Wall Street owns a big chunk of Washington, not the other way around despite the huge taxpayer funded bailouts. An exasperated Senator Dick Durbin, perhaps I should call him a misfit in the circus, complained that the banks "are still the most powerful lobby on Capitol Hill. And they frankly own the place."[61] And that ownership seems to be inhibiting any bold Wall Street reforms President Obama might otherwise implement. His proposal to overhaul the financial regulatory system, says one commentator, "is little more than an attempt to stick some new regulatory fingers into a very leaky financial dam rather than rebuild the dam itself," and the new rules that finally emerged validate the commentator's assessment; the rules were given as I said a B- grade by Paul Volcker, and have been found wanting by numerous other knowledgeable authorities.[62] Paul Krugman, who has been tracking the progress of the rulemaking, adds that the Obama administration "still seems to operate on the principle that what's good for Wall Street is good for America."[63] Since lobbyists haven't been banned and the revolving doors and archways haven't been blocked yet, why should we expect anything differently?

Despite the seeming implausibility of any meaningful reform, the task force should propose that America go after Wall Street for the sake of Main Street by considering ideas such as those of Korten and Terry and maybe suggesting an outlier like Durbin to lead the charge. A capitalism that allows financial investments is one thing, a capitalism that allows financial speculation amounting to reckless gambling and "rational irrationality" is quite another.[64]

End Exploitative Globalization

The task force should consider several specific initiatives to end exploitative globalization: abolishing the Unholy Trinity; repealing international trade agreements; ganging up on the globalizers; starting anew globally; and pursuing greater localization.

Abolish the Unholy Trinity

Anti-globalization activists and authors John Cavanagh and Jerry Mander argue that reforming the WTO, the WBO and the IMF rather than abolishing them is not a good option. They are, the authors say, "so fundamentally at odds with the human interest."[65] Whether these institutions are ended through whatever a decommissioning process might entail or by the U.S. officially announcing its withdrawal of membership and funding will be immaterial as long as they are ended.

Litigation against the WTO is another course of action, although the WTO prevails whenever trade disputes filed by the U.S. are settled in court.[66] As far as I know there has yet to be brought before the highest court a constitutional challenge to the WTO's overruling of the U.S.

Repeal Existing Trade Agreements

Getting rid of the WTO won't get rid of existing international trade agreements. Other than ruling on disputes that arise, it's unlikely the judiciary will entertain legal attacks on the legitimacy of the agreements as legally binding contracts, although I suppose it's possible the International Trade Commission, a quasi-judicial Federal agency, could be sued for yielding to the WTO. Another option is legislative action. U.S. trade agreements are ratified by Congress and will have to be repealed by Congress. To that end a few petitions have been written but are languishing, probably because the petitioners are individuals acting alone or are members of small NGOs. What are needed are petitions with tens of thousands of signatures.

What are needed also are enforceable rules for a just and sustainable international trade and finance system. Cavanagh and Mander propose four essential rules: 1. All people in any country must have the right to determine their country's economic priorities and policies while at the same time not infringing on the rights of people in other countries. 2. There must be "balanced trade" among trading countries. 3. There must be "fair commodity prices," no domestic subsidies, price supports, no "dumping" with lower prices. 4. There must be no restrictions on intellectual property rights other than those that would stimulate innovation and creativity.[67]

Gang Up on the Globalizers!

There are many NGOs in the U.S. fighting exploitative globalization. But there aren't 10,000 of them. Representatives of 10,000 NGOs from 82 countries organized an international coalition calling for the European Union to ensure effective participation of the poorest countries in considering reforms of international financial institutions such as the WBO and the IMF.[68] Let me repeat that number, 10,000 NGOs! Visualize representatives from over 10,000 NGOs protesting in front of the U.S. Capital, at 1600 Pennsylvania Avenue, at the CIA, at the Pentagon, at the USCC, at corporations, especially ones in the defense industry, and on Wall Street. If that mobilization were to materialize en force as something like an International Democracy Power Force, what do you think might happen? The corpocracy might bloody some of the protestors but it might also be the beginning of the breakup of the Devil's Marriage.

Start Anew Globally

One or more institutions will be needed to replace the ones abolished. The most logical start is an institution that already exists, the United Nations. For over half a century it has had numerous international mandates. Three of its organizational components are most relevant here, the Economic and Social Council (ECOSOC), the International Court of Justice (ICJ), also called the World Court, and the UN Conference on Trade and Development (UNCTAD). Until it was shunted aside by the Unholy Trinity, UNCTAD had been a means for poor countries to reorient their economies toward constructive developmental efforts.

Cavanagh and Mandy have proposed that UNCTAD first successfully challenge the longstanding premise that the only way for developing countries to achieve prosperity is to become fully integrated into the international system, meaning the Unholy Trinity's system, and then secondly to go on to become the rule-making body for international trade. The authors also propose adding six more global institutions to assume the functions of the Unholy Trinity plus some more functions.[69] I would only add here that rather than just "dampen" currency speculation, as the authors suggest, the UN with the concurrence of financial markets in each country should work toward outright banning of such speculation. China, the country that treats it as a capital offense would surely go along with such an international ban!

The UN's full potential for global governance has been curtailed partly because its domain is so large and heterogeneous and partly because it has invariably been criticized and marginalized by Republican administrations in the U.S. Incredibly, the acting U.S. envoy to the UN in 2005 had remarked a decade or so earlier that "There is no such thing as the United Nations. There is only the international community, which can only be led by the only remaining superpower, which is the United States."[70] Reforming the UN and giving it even more responsibilities will thus be an uphill battle. It has never been an effective institution in representing and advancing the interests of the Third World. It has never had any countervailing impact on the Unholy Trinity. It favors multinational corporations at the expense of developing localized companies and markets. Yet the prospect for reform may be a bit brighter now that President Obama has replaced Bush's representative at the UN.

Localize More, Globalize Less

It's conceivable that, quite apart from any anti-globalization strategies, the same end may some day be achieved at least to some degree by various trends we see today, a few probably irreversible. They are, Cavanagh and Mander say: proportionately greater distribution costs domestically and internationally; the related trend of oil reserves dwindling; niche marketing; the shift from goods to services; more businesses operated from homes using computers; terrorist threats; and growing disdain for the work places of large corporations.[71]

Cavanagh and Mander clearly aren't recommending that we suspend anti-globalization strategies and wait for these trends to grow, but they do view them as making inevitable the application of their concept of "subsidiarity." They refer to it as "an operating principle favoring the local whenever a choice exists, which means in practice that all decisions should be made at the lowest level of governing authority competent to deal with them."[72] Moreover, most decisions they say that involve the public can be made at some geographical level within the country, not outside it. The coauthors propose numerous initiatives for localizing more and globalizing less (e.g., establish government policies to support local enterprises).

Additionally, there ought to be a national policy stipulating that wealth earned in America stay in America. As Robert Reich, the former Labor Secretary in the Clinton administration has pointed out, "the rich don't necessarily invest their earnings and savings in the American economy;

they send them anywhere around the globe where they'll summon the highest returns."[73] Money reinvested in America yields a qualitatively different and valuable return, a boost in the American economy, including employment.

End Unsustainable Development

Economic growth that helps us to climb out of a recession is one thing. But endless economic growth, the Holy Grail of corpocratic capitalists, their economists, and the cultists of growth is like the Greek poet Ovid's ancient tale of a greedy timber merchant, Erisychthon, who cuts down a sacred tree, angering Ceres, the Goddess of Plenty. She condemns him to eat everything in sight including himself after all else had been consumed. The authors who retell the tale believe he symbolizes the essence of materialistic capitalism, an insatiable "monster devouring itself."[74] If it weren't so hard to pronounce, the economic meltdown of 2008 could be nicknamed the Erisychthon hangover.

Vaclav Havel, whom I mentioned earlier, is a modern day Ovid of sorts, having told the world that nature is warning us about our immoral footprint on her and that we must end the debt accumulated from constant economic growth and start paying back.[75] It's this immoral footprint that prompted the UN as long ago as 1983 to convene what became known as the Brundtland Commission to assess the extent of that impact and the damages it had inflicted. Besides giving its assessment, the Commission in its report introduced what has become a widely accepted definition of sustainability; development that "meets the needs of the present generation without compromising the ability of future generations to meet their needs."[76] Ralph Nader, who was instrumental in getting the Environmental Protection Agency established has just as simple a definition: "That you take out of the Earth no more than you put into it. That you put into the Earth no more than you take out."[77]

Note that the Commission defined sustainability in terms of development, not growth. The two are very different. The concept of growth carried to its logical extreme is classical Ovidian. growth. Cut and sell more trees. Get bigger. Cut and sell still more trees. Get bigger still. Bigger becomes biggest and then grows beyond its adjectives. Go find and deforest another forest. And bigger than biggest is simply still more growth. At some point in the growth spiral growth becomes unsustainable. There are no more forests.

The concept of development, in contrast, connotes improvement in quality, not increments in quantity. Get better, not bigger. Get from better to best. And the concept of best is synonymous with excellence, the epitome of quality. Unlike endless growth, excellent quality is not endless. There's nothing beyond the eight criteria of excellence (e.g., reliability), and none of which involves unlimited growth.[78] Once all eight are met, excellence has been achieved. Sustaining excellence requires only continually satisfying the criteria (e.g., no unreliability).

Stop Ovidian Growth

Nature will inevitably have the Last Laugh over our dumb growth, but His/Her laugh could be delayed by ending the corpocracy once and for all. And we can't wait until it eventually devours itself for at some point America would also be devoured.

Four positive ways to slow if not stop unbridled growth have already been discussed: the tightening of antitrust regulations; the ending of corporate welfare; the ending of exploitative globalization; and more reliance on localized commerce. Other strategies involve fighting in court "big-box" stores that seek to enter yet more communities and displace yet smaller stores; and cultivating "smart" growth, not "no growth."

Make Commerce Greener

At best pollution permits are a temporary and partial solution to curbing pollution. They may slow its rate, but they will not make commerce much greener. At worst, they tell us all that we have the "right" to pollute as long as we pay for the permits. What legitimate authority gave us that right we should ask? The only legitimate authority would be Nature. If it/she/he could talk to us, what we would hear would be cries of anguish and pain, not "here's your permit."

One positive outcome emerging from Economic Katrina is the blossoming of usually small business firms working to create new products that will make smaller footprints on Nature. Additionally, there are a few goliaths, perhaps outliers in or outsiders of the corpocracy that have sensed the environmental crisis we are in and singlehandedly or together in small consortiums are trying to come up with greener innovations.

Making products and services greener will lighten our polluting footprint. But much more needs to be done beyond ending corpocratic capitalism. One promising course of action would be to carry out the four strategies proposed by the authors of the book on natural capitalism summarized in Appendix C.

End Elitist Pay without Performance

> For capitalism to work executive pay
> must be linked to performance.
> ---Ben Bernanke
> Chairman of the Federal Reserve

Mr. Bernanke, who should have known better, misjudged the causes and the severity of Economic Katrina, but he's absolutely right about executive pay.[79] One reason capitalism isn't working is because there is typically little connection between the pay of corporate executives and how well and honestly their companies meet stakeholder expectations in a capitalistic market. In essence, executive pay without (the right kind of) performance is just one more badvantage corrupting capitalism. To make matters much worse, two related badvantages are that executive pay is unconscionably high and that while CEOs are fattening their own pay they are simultaneously laying off workers by the thousands.

A prime and revolting example of these badvantages in play during Economic Katrina is the bailout bonuses for Wall Street executives. But pay without performance pervades all of corporate America, not just Wall Street. Long before Economic Katrina happened, for example, eleven companies with high risk ratings and a composite loss of $640 billion in shareholder value paid their CEOs a total of $865 million.[80] That's nearly $80 million for each of the eleven failing CEOs and about two thousands times more than the average worker in their companies who probably was paid an annual wage of around $40 thousand. In his time, two millennia ago, Plato suggested a 9-to-1 ratio between the highest and lowest paid citizen. In his time, the late management guru Peter Drucker suggested between 20-to-1 and 25-to-1 ratio between CEOs and the workforce. Rick Wartzman, executive director of the Drucker Institute, said Drucker contended that excessively paid CEO's alienated "people on the plant floor who were convinced their bosses are crooks," were "morally unforgivable when laying off workers," and "tore at the fabric of society as a whole."[81]

The public outrage over executives of federally bailed out Wall Street firms giving themselves lavish bonuses prompted President Obama to set a pay cap of $500 thousand on senior executives of these firms. The public ought to be insulted by his timid measure. Bailed out executives ought to be fired, not bailed out and then capped. But the same pay cap ought to be imposed on CEOs of all corporations that receive handouts from the government.

The public ought to be equally outraged over the contempt fat cat CEOs have for ordinary workers not just in the CEOs' demanding and getting unconscionable and unearned compensation but also in their simultaneously laying off thousands of workers. The NGO, Institute for Policy Studies (IPS), reports that CEOs of the 50 corporations laying off 3,000 or more workers since the onset of Economic Katrina "took home 42 percent more pay ($12 million on average) in 2009 than their peers at S&P 500 firms."[82] On its website the NGO lists the 50 CEOs and urges readers of the site to "Find a layoff-leading CEO below: you can write a post on your Facebook wall, send a tweet to your followers, and tell your friends that you won't stand for injustice. Together we can shame these companies and stop executive excess."[83]

When you think about it for a split second, the phenomena of pay without public service is happening in the other part of the Devil's Marriage as well. Although their pay can't compare with CEO pay, politicians are given six figure salaries, generous health care and retirement benefits, plush offices, and bloated staffs. And for what? Public service? No, corporate service.

The IPS entreaty is well intentioned to be sure, but I seriously doubt that shameless, overpaid CEOs (and politicians, too) can be shamed into pay cuts by face book messages, tweeting, bill boarding or by any other means of publicity about their notorious pay and contempt for workers. The only way to ensure pay with (the right kind of) performance is to end undemocratic capitalism and close down the circus. Needless to say, though, achieving those goals is easier said than done and shaming is at least a first step.

Is Any Capitalism Fit for a Real Democracy?

We have gone through many ideas for a democratic capitalism, but is it possible that capitalism and democracy don't mix at all, ever? I raise the question because some people would answer "yes." One of them in a round-about way is Lester Thurow, a former dean of the MIT Sloan School of Management, professor of management and economics, and author of numerous bestsellers on economic topics. In one of his books he flat out says that "capitalism is perfectly compatible with slavery [and] democracy is not compatible with slavery."[84]

Well, Professor, I agree with you only if you are referring to corpocratic or undemocratic capitalism. And I think it is now more imperative than ever to rid ourselves of it and envision and build a new and much better kind of capitalism. I know of no other acceptable alternatives to democratic capitalism. Communism? Definitely not! Unlike his teacher Plato, who advocated communistic guardianship of property, Aristotle did not, thinking it to be unnatural. Socialism? I suppose the kneejerk reaction of the cons, for whom the idea of social justice is synonymous with socialism, would be to call my version of democratic capitalism, "socialism" because it seeks to make capitalism more egalitarian and economically just.

Charles Derber tells me he thinks "many of my preferred forms of capitalism are not really capitalism in any orthodox sense" and goes on to advise me either to "nuance my view that there is no alternative to capitalism" or to "simply reframe the argument, indicating the "good capitalisms" that I explore are not truly capitalist in the hegemonic model and that more clear alternatives are growing in the periphery of the developing world, as well as in U.S. local economies." Contending that there is no alternative, he says, "seems a false and dangerous argument, [because those clear alternatives do in fact exist]." He tells me he "is working on a new book about alternative systems that we see seeds of around the world - and in the U.S."[85] I look forward very much to reading that book because I have for the time being exhausted my self and my ideas on the matter.

A democratic capitalism is a necessary but not totally sufficient condition (because there's still, e.g., the circus to close down) for giving an affirmative answer to columnist Bob Herbert's question at the end of the quote in one of his columns:

> Let's try investing in America and its people
> for a change, rather than just hurling our billions
> into the abyss. We can find trillions for a foolish
> war and for pompous, self-righteous high-rollers
> who wrecked their companies and the economy.
> But what about the working poor and the young
> people who are being clobbered in this downturn,
> battered so badly that they're all but destitute?
> Can we find any way to help them?
>
> ---Bob Herbert[86]

Some Closing Memory Ticklers and One Liners

What did Adam Smith tell Milton Friedman?

Economic Katrina: The hurricane that blew away Main Street.

The globe is a giant gift basket for corpocratic capitalism.

The Unholy Trinity.

Are "economic hit men" at home the same as "economic traitors?"

Rethink capitalism from A to Z minus E for economists.

A granted but unfulfilled right may be worse than no right.

Justice Holmes: I like paying taxes. It buys me civilization.

Let's do a tax escape audit.

Fairly share democracy's costs.

Do you know of any honest wealth, honestly?

Wall Street's financial services or disservices?

Cesspool of investments? Wall Street.

Gang up on the globalizers!

Localize more, globalize less.

Shrink the goliaths!

Farming socioeconomic/ecological weeds with dumb growth.

Can't get pollution permits from Mother Nature.

Chapter Eleven. Unleashing
Your Democracy Power

I don't mean to be presumptuous or impertinent, but this chapter is about you and what you might do now that you have read this book. Do you think the Devil's Marriage exists and is a menace to America and her democracy? If you are not sure yet you could do a reality check to help you decide.

Reality Check

Look again at the list of telltale signs of the corpocracy's influence if not outright domination in our lives, our society, our government, our environment. Go down the list of those signs and for each or some of them ask yourself what incidents you experienced in the last few weeks show that you had less control or influence over them in the various spheres of your life than you would have preferred. From what this exercise reveals you could gauge your own "liberty quotient" to see how much or how little influence you have over your own health, happiness, and prosperity. Think about the liberty quotients and the general welfare of other Americans, particularly Americans without jobs, without health insurance, without a decent standard of living. Visualize what the general welfare of Americans would be like in a corpocracy-free America. Think about the first Declaration of Independence and why it was written and signed and then think about whether a Second Declaration of Independence might be in order at least figuratively speaking. Should you want to do some more reading as part of your reality check do some of the reading I did (see the references in the Notes).

How Willing and Ready are You?

If you think the corpocracy is more real than imagined, how willing are you to help oppose it? If you decide you aren't willing and would just as soon sit on the sidelines and let others do it for you, could you look Thomas Paine, George Washington and his Revolutionaries, Thomas Jefferson, Abraham Lincoln, Teddy Roosevelt, and FDR in the face if they were to return for just a minute to see what you were doing to help reclaim democracy? Or think about your legacy that you leave behind.

You may be willing to volunteer some of your time, but how much of it can you spare? If, like me, you are retired, you have relatively more time on your hands. If you aren't retired, it may seem you don't have enough hands or time. If that is so, then you could limit your democracy power for the time being by selecting and working on initiatives taking the least amount of your time.

Review your strengths so you make the most of them. If you have a career you probably have a clear idea of what they are. If, for instance, you are a lawyer, but probably not a corporate lawyer, and you have gotten to this step, you could be a strong opponent of the regime. The same goes if you are in fields such as education, communications, or any other field that matches well with one or more of the strategies and initiatives discussed in this book. Regardless of whether you have a career, if you associate yourself with one of more of the potential allies of democracy that need to be recruited and cultivated then you ought to be a strong candidate for being recruited and cultivated. Better still, cultivate yourself! If you are already a social activist and/or a member of one or more NGOs opposed to the regime then you are already primed and activated!

Prime Your Democracy Power

What you might consider doing now is ask yourself which strategic objectives described in this book do you think should be given the higher priorities and resources? Which ones interest you more and match your capabilities, including any experience you may already have with them?

Organize the opposition.
Tell the people.
Close the corpocracy's political/judicial circus.
Dig up the corpocracy's legal roots.
End hands-off corporate criminals.
End hand-outs to the corporate welfare queen.
End undemocratic capitalism.

Unleash Your Democracy Power

There are three ways to unleash your democracy power if you haven't been doing so already. You can do it unilaterally through "Me" Power. You can leverage your own democracy power by unleashing it together with others through "We/Me" Power. And you can do both.

Unleash Your "Me" Power

It is sometimes much easier or only makes sense to act alone (one wouldn't, for example, petition others to co-sign a complaint about a personal gripe with a particular corporation). Moreover, it is an outlet for a civil conscience, builds up a repertoire of experience, and just may have the effect wanted.

Acting alone can involve confronting particular corporations (e.g., write them a complaint), withdrawing support from particular corporations (e.g., stop buying their products or services and telling them why), sending messages about and against the regime and its allies (e.g., letters to the media and to politicians and voting against the worst vote peddlers), and maybe talking about this book with your social and other circles, perhaps sprinkling your conversations with some one-liners.

Take me as a good or bad example of "me" power. So far I have exercised it mostly through writing, writing and writing: to the administration, to members of Congress, to editors, to newspaper columnists, and to you (this book).

Unleash Your "We/Me" Power

But let's be realistic. "Me" Power against the regime is like David or Danielle without a slingshot against Goliath. Acting alone typically amounts I think to pestering the regime. It ignores or swats away pests. Pestering can't end the regime. Although he wrote it as one individual and thus demonstrated that acting alone can sometimes be a strong catalyst to action, Powell's "battle plan" to resurrect the corpocracy was absolutely not an action plan for individuals

Neither is the POW! plan an action plan for individuals acting alone. It calls for an organized, strategic, and amply funded challenge to the regime and I hope you join together with others in doing the challenging. The best way to do that I think is for you to promote and get involved with others in the organizing, priming, and unleashing of democracy power. You could as I did web browse NGOs (e.g., those in Appendix A) and tentatively pick one or more whose missions dovetail the most with your own interests, concerns, and capabilities; join one or more; and get actively involved with and through them. Or you could join a movement and maybe even launch the People's Reignbow Coalition!

Some Closing Memory Ticklers and One Liners

Need to take another look at the telltale signs?

What's your liberty quotient?

What's the liberty quotient of the have-nots?

Unleash your "Me" Pow!er.

Pepper your conversations with one-liners.

Unleash your "We/Me" Pow!er.

AFTERWORD

I started doing the research for and the writing of this book a very long time ago. I was immersed in the details of every one of quite a few drafts. I followed current events and new literature and added them when they were spot on (as you can see from the newest footnotes). Now it is time for me to reflect on what I have written and to add some afterthoughts.

Imagining an "Alter America"

I have done much imagining in this book, most particularly about the U.S. Chamber of Democracy, the People's Reignbow Coalition, the Second Declaration of Independence, the Citizen's Assembly for Peace, and several commissions and taskforces. I could hardly do more serious imagining where the stakes for not imagining and not acting constructively are so high.

After the book's chapters had been finished I was reading about a person whose imagination had soared above mine, Aristophanes, the ancient Greek playwright. Critical of war and war profiteering of his day he wrote a comedy about an Athenian housewife, Lysistrata. Weary of the real Peloponnesian war between the men of Athens and the men of Sparta, she persuades women from both cities into going on a sex strike until the war ends. The war ends.

What makes this tale timeless is not the fictional sex strike but the reality that with a very few exceptions (e.g., Cleopatra, Margaret Thatcher) wars throughout history have been started and conducted by males. A good example of their juvenile-like foolishness, macho exhibitionism, testosterone-fueled aggressiveness, and male bonding is the Spanish-

American War of 1898. Teddy Roosevelt called his men the "Rough Riders." They sang "Rough, rough, we're the stuff. We want to fight and we can't get enough." The Riders left behind because the troop ships were too crowded reportedly wept over being left behind. The ones who made the trip were on a mission not to save America but to build her an empire.[1] They all impress me as having been a bunch of bullies and a bit loony. I must acknowledge, though, that the Rough Rider was the first American to win the peace prize for negotiating the end of the Russo-Japanese war. Go figure!

Societies throughout history with few exceptions have been dominated through and through by males. Besides loving war, they occupy positions of power in government, business, religion, and households. The "dominator society," says Riane Eisler, who has studied this prevailing mode of social and economic structures and cultures throughout the history of the world, "has four core elements: rigid top-down control; intense abuse and violence" manifested (my pun intended) in "child and wife beating and chronic warfare;" "the rigid ranking" of men over women; and a culture of stories, beliefs, and the like that "justify domination and violence as inevitable, even moral."[2] In contrast, Eisler calls the ideal model the "partnership" society. Few societies, one of them being Finland she says, come close to this model, that of a democratic, egalitarian, and non-violent family and social structure.

Why would any intelligent woman or any intelligent and non-violent man if they had a choice choose to live in a society where violence is inevitable and morally justified? Short of sex strikes, involuntary castrations, or becoming a second Finland, how does the U.S. ever get close to choosing and building a kind of partnership society? In her book, The Real Wealth of Nations, Eisler proposes a "caring revolution" with an emphasis on fundamentally restructuring our economic system (recall Chapter 10 and Appendix A).[3]

Peace, of course, is more than economics, as Eisler well knows. It's also a matter of politics. Since wars can't destroy ideas or imagination I'm going to imagine a new political configuration, Alter America, sort of analogous to the alter ego of a person's personality. It would be a model of a democratic, egalitarian society. It would have two primary goals. One would be to pursue and achieve the initiatives proposed throughout this book by "housing" the U.S. Chamber of Democracy, the People's Reignbow Coalition, and the Citizen's Assembly for Peace. The other would be to show Americans what a democratic, egalitarian, partnership society would look like by contrasting what the real regime of Real America is doing with what Alter America would do. For example if the corpocracy escalated a war, Alter America would denounce it loudly and widely and would tell the American people what it would do instead.

Alter America would be founded, let's say, by the Citizen's Assembly for Peace. The model economic system would be democratic capitalism like that proposed in Chapter 10. There would be an alter Constitution that reflects some of the initiatives proposed in this book. For example, the document would explicitly prevent corporate personhood and require federal chartering of corporations. It would also require a national referendum on whether to start a preemptive war or to escalate markedly an existing one. There would be an alter government, a mirror image of our real, present-day one. For example, it would not be a model of a hands-off or hand-outs government. Alter America's president, a miniature legislator and Supreme Court would be chosen by the Citizen's Assembly for Peace or by a real poll of Americans who believe in the idea of an Alter America. My ideal for the presidency would be someone like Riane Eisler, a board member of the Women's International League for Peace and Freedom, or a mother or wife of a loved one lost in battle who has become an anti-war activist.[4] There would be an alter agency for each real federal agency. A primary responsibility of certain alter agencies would be to promote non violence and to curb and penalize violence. For example, the alter "Department of [Quality and Universal] Education" would put a premium on early education on non-violence; the "Product Safety [and Toy] Commission" would provide restrictions on and disincentives for making and selling warrior toys and games; the Bureau of Alcohol, Tobacco, and [Limited] Firearms would convince Americas of the Constitutional requirement for limited use of guns; and the "Federal [Truthful and Pacific] Communications Commission" would substantially curb the programming of violence into the mass media and would eliminate the advertising and propagandizing of the military.

Every objective, every initiative in this book and then some perhaps would have to succeed in turning Alter America into a new Real America. For now, Alter America can only serve as an inspiring model.

Where is the Real America Headed?

> The nation ceased to exist.
> ---Alexis De Tocqueville,
> Democracy in America, Vol.I, 1835

De Tocqueville, of course, was referring to the nation of Native Americans. But will some French political thinker and historian say that about America in the future?

After lengthy research on how mighty institutions fall, best-selling author Jim Collins has concluded that there are five sequential stages of their decline: "1. hubris born of success, 2. undisciplined pursuit of more, 3. denial of risk and peril, 4. grasping for salvation, and 5. capitulation to irrelevance or death."[5] Where would you peg America? I would peg her somewhere in the third stage, with a relatively small number of activist citizens and NGOs not being in denial and doing what they can to reclaim democracy for America. There is still time left if we don't waste it to reverse America's course to ruiNation.

The Road to Peace?

Is the road to peace a dead end? Let's not let it be so, for if it were to be, it would be the road to a dead America. As I have said the one single feature of the corpocracy most likely to end America in my opinion is the corpocracy's warfare welfare and warring. We Americans absolutely must shed our culture of war, a "madness for war" that the corpocracy depends on and that Americans have come to accept, even expect.[6] Our madness for war is why I spent so much work and time writing about this issue in Chapter 9. I now want to add some additional thoughts.

The road to peace for America will have to go through the Middle East. Although there are reportedly "30 wars and violent conflicts being waged around the globe," the Middle East endures as America's flashpoint.[7] An editorial in *The New York Times* raised the question of "where do we go from here" in that region?[8] My answer was published as "an all editors' selection" for being among the "most interesting and thoughtful comments that represent a range of views." Here was my answer: "The question needs to be broadened and five answers courageously debated. How can the U.S. stop alienating the Middle East and thereby provoking unnecessary threats not only to us but also to that region? This question should constantly be on the table for serious diplomatic discussion. The first answer, persuade Israel through incentives and appeals to international harmony to return the land acquired in the 1967 war. Second, tell the Palestinians we will help them build their new state if they ask us. Three, renounce our dependence on oil and feverishly develop alternative sources of energy. Four, stop subsidizing our defense industry. Five, stop acting aggressively and unilaterally and start acting peacefully, diplomatically, and multilaterally through a strengthened UN and a reoriented and revitalized State Department wholeheartedly supported by the president and Congress. Ever happen? Let's hope so. Future generations blameless for our inactions and bad actions today deserve a world we ought to be rebuilding for their arrival into whatever faith, culture, and nationality they may be born. Peace, Shalom, Salam."

I had hoped that when President, Barack Obama took office he would not be just the next nominal leader of the corpocracy. I had hoped that he would be a leader and statesmen in tough times like FDR was. I had hoped he would take some very bold initiatives and not be concerned about whether he was risking reelection for a second term. I had hoped he would start us on a road to peace by making a pronouncement along these lines to every head of state and leader of a terrorist group: "As members of the international community neither we nor you should continue along the hurtful paths of our past. The world is smaller, making its problems bigger. When any one of us oversteps the boundaries of helpful international behavior our hurtful footprints are felt world-wide. It is in all of our interests and for generations yet born to enter a new dawn of international friendship, cooperation, and peace. To that end I am inviting you to join with me in creating a Global Goodwill Network under the auspices of the UN to seek ways to make our smaller world a more peaceful and habitable one for all its inhabitants. I am going to ensure that America abides by the rule of law and will sign and get ratified America's membership on the International Criminal Court. A world in which countries trade fairly among themselves will be a world more at peace than at war, so I intend to ensure that America's business transactions with the rest of the world will be fair ones and that exploitative globalization by multinational corporations headquartered in the U.S. ceases. I intend with the help of Congress to rethink and alter our approach to economic, foreign, and military policy and will accelerate withdrawal of our combat forces and military bases on foreign soil. I will insist that in return for continued U.S. support of both sides there absolutely must be a two-state solution to the Israeli-Palestinian conflict. I will shore up our obligations and support for a reformed and reinvigorated UN that encourages localized markets, not globalized ones. I will also propose creation of a new UN entity, The Councils of the Continents, with each having the primary responsibility for restoring goodwill in their own territories. For those who join us we shall establish cooperative partnerships. For those who choose not to do so, we shall keep inviting you."

To expect such an overture from President Obama at the outset was probably incredibly naïve on my part. He did start off his new job with a conciliatory message that contrasted markedly with the "do it my way or highway" Bush-Cheney team. He has said that "a two-state solution in the Middle East is vital to defusing Muslim anger at the West (and anger that reportedly motivated Osama Bin Laden to concoct and direct the terrorist attack in the U.S.) and he is brokering yet more peace talks between Israel and the Palestenians.[9] But he has escalated the American war in Afghanistan, a fractious country of warring tribes and corrupt government that the Soviet Union couldn't control after ten years of occupation there (just as France gave up after ten years of occupying Vietnam before the Johnson and Nixon administrations sent thousands of Americans and many more Vietnamese to their deaths in their land). I have read that he "was open to negotiating a peace settlement with the Taliban."[10] How serious he really is about doing so is questionable. His diplomatic efforts have been "all style, no substance" says Amitai Etzioni, a professor of international relations at George Washington University, just a few stone throws from the White House.[11] He has not cut all his strings to the self interests of powerful corporations and their industries even though they seem to hate him with a passion. They hated FDR, too, who said he "welcomed their hatred." "It's time," says Paul Krugman, for President Obama to find his inner FDR and do the same."[12] I very much doubt that he will, Mr. Krugman, and, regardless, it's high time "we the people" recognized the need for and the ways to exercise the power of the powerless!

Going Beyond These Pages

Writing this book has let me exercise my "me" power. It has let me add my voice to other modern day Paul Reveres (like some of the writers I acknowledge in the preface) warning people about the Devil's Marriage. Now it is time for me to go beyond these pages and see what I can do to help build "we" power into democracy power strong enough, united enough, purposeful enough, to break up that marriage. It's a tall, tall order.

I will be "pestering" the anti-corpocracy NGOs long after this afterword to unify their forces into something like the U.S. Chamber of Democracy, or at least to do more collaborative work toward achieving the strategic objectives like those described in the POW plan. It is, I think a solid one, and the almost countless initiatives discussed seem nearly exhaustive.

As for the possibility of mobilizing a People's Reignbow Coalition, nothing, it's said, unites disparate or even in-fighting groups like having a common adversary. The groups I identified in Chapter 4 as prospective members of a unified and broad coalition have a common adversary, the corpocracy, whether they recognize all of its telltale signs or not. I will be reaching out to those groups looking for one or more that might be willing to spearhead efforts to fuse as many of the groups as possible into a democracy power movement. I will also be consulting with experts who have experience in fusing and growing grass roots movements.

But I want to emphasize that the need to end the corpocracy is so critical that the end justifies my being open-minded, flexible, and ethically responsible about the means to that end. I will not stubbornly cling to the idea of a USCD and a People's Reignbow Coalition if other acceptable means of reclaiming democracy can be developed. I will explore whatever alternatives may be promising.

A New Think Tank?

Lewis Powell's "battle plan" sprouted numerous think tanks for rationalizing the build up of the current regime. Eventually think tanks, outnumbered as they are sprouted with counter arguments to those rationalizations. At the moment I'm running near empty on imagination and more concrete ideas for how to how to end the corpocracy before it ruins America. I could use a think tank made up of readers of this book. May I "pick your brain?" Please e-mail me (democracypower@bellsouth. net).

In Closing

No society with enough sense of what is happening, with enough moral conscience to be outraged, and with enough backbone to stop it would tolerate the Devil's Marriage. It is dangerous for our own economic well being, health, safety, and security and for the world. Our descendants some time in the future will be living in an age where international cooperation will be absolutely necessary because of the scarcity of the sources of life, air and water. If the warring corpocracy has not been ended by then it may be forever too late. Will we sharpen our senses, speak our conscience, and stiffen our backbone before it's too late? Will we take back our country for the sake of democracy's self rule, the general welfare of us all, and brighter prospects for our descendants? Will we end the corpocracy or let it end us?

Thank you for reading this book. I hope you see the telltale signs of the Devil's Marriage in America and that in one or more ways you will personify democracy power if you haven't been doing it before now in helping to break up that marriage once and for all.

Appendix A

Some NGOs and their Missions Selected from the Author's Original List*

The Alliance for Democracy. www.thealliancefordemocracy.org. To end the domination of our economy, our government, our culture, our media and the environment by large corporations, to promote true democracy in our country, and to help achieve a just society with a sustainable, equitable economy.

The Alliance for Justice. www.allianceforjustice.org. To advance the cause of justice for all Americans, strengthen the public interest community's ability to influence public policy, and foster the next generation of advocates.

The Alliance for Responsible Trade. www.art-us.org. To promote equitable and sustainable trade and development.

American Independent Business Alliance. www.amiba.net. To support home town businesses in a community or geographic region.

Ballot Initiative Strategy Center. www.ballot.org. To help progressives participate in launching ballot initiatives and democratic action.

Business Alliance for Local Living Economics (BALLE). www.

livingeconomies.org. To catalyze, strengthen, and connect local business networks dedicated to building strong local living economies.

Campaign for America's Future. www.ourfuture.org. To challenge the big money corporate agenda by encouraging Americans to speak up—to discuss and debate a new vision of an economy and a future that works for all of us.

Campaign Legal Center. www.campaignlegalcenter.org. To represent the public interest on matters of campaign finance and elections, political communication and government ethics.

Center for Constitutional Rights. www.ccr-ny.org. To protect and advance the rights guaranteed by the U.S. Constitution and the Universal Declaration of Human Rights.

Center for Corporate Policy. www.corporatepolicy.org. To curb corporate abuses and make corporations publicly accountable.

Center for Democracy and the Constitution. www.constitution411. org. To end corporate rights that destroy the environment, our future, and democracy.

Center for Democracy and Technology. www.cdt.org. To promote democratic values and constitutional liberties in the digital age.

Center for Economic Research and Change. www.cersc.org. To better understand today's world and to help put forward the vision of a better future.

Center for Justice & Democracy. www.centerjd.org To fight on behalf of consumer interests the civil tort reform movement and to protect our civil justice system.

Center for Partnership Studies. www.partnershipway.org. To create a more peaceful, equitable and sustainable world through cultural transformation.

Center for Policy Alternatives. www.stateaction.org. To strengthen the capacity of state legislators for progressive change.

Center for Progressive Leadership. www.progressleaders.org. To develop diverse leaders who can effectively advance progressive political and policy change.

Center for Political Accountability. www.politicalaccountability.net. To bring transparency and accountability to corporate political spending.

Center for Responsive Politics. www.opensecrets.org. To create a more educated voter, an involved citizenry, and a more responsive government.

Center for Voting and Democracy. www.fairvote.org. To transform our elections to achieve unfettered, fraud-free access to participation, a full spectrum of meaningful choices and majority rule with fair representation and a voice for all.

Citizen Advocacy Center. www.citizenadvocacycenter.org. To build democracy for the 21st century.

Center for Partnership Studies. www.partnershipway.org. To create a more peaceful, equitable, and sustainable world through cultural transformation.

Citizens for Tax Justice. www.ctj.org. To give ordinary people a greater voice in the development of tax laws.

Citizens Trade Campaign. www.citizenstrade.org. To achieve through international trade and investment economic justice, human rights, healthy communities, and a sound environment.

Citizen Works. www.citizenworks.org. To advance justice by strengthening citizen participation in power.

Common Cause, www.commoncause.org. To strengthen public participation and faith in our institutions of self-government; to ensure that government and political processes serve the general interest, rather than special interests; to curb the excessive influence of money on government decisions and elections; to promote fair elections and high ethical standards for government officials; and to protect the civil rights and civil liberties of all Americans.

Corporate Accountability International. www.stopcorporateabuse.org. To challenge irresponsible and dangerous corporate actions around the world.

Demos. www.demos.org. To achieve a more equitable economy; a vibrant and inclusive democracy; an empowered public sector that works for the common good; and responsible U.S. engagement in an interdependent world.

The Equal Justice Society. www.equaljusticesociety.org. To reshape jurisprudence to ensure that the rights of all are expanded, rather than diminished, by our courts and policy makers.

50 Years Is Enough. www.50years.org. To transform the international financial institutions' policies and practices, to end the outside imposition of neo-liberal economic programs, and to make the development process democratic and accountable.

Foundation for Taxpayer and Consumer Rights. cwd.grassroots.com. To save Americans billions of dollars by fighting corrupt corporations and crooked politicians.

Institute for Local Self Reliance. www.ilsr.org. To provide innovative strategies, working models and timely information to support environmentally sound and equitable community development.

Interfaith Alliance. www.interfaithalliance.org. To protect the integrity of both religion and democracy in America.

Jobs with Justice. www.jwj.org. To win justice in workplaces and in communities where working families live.

Moveon.org. www.moveon.org. To help concerned citizens find their voice in a system dominated by big money and big media.

National Consumer's League. www.nclnet.org. To represent consumers on marketplace and workplace issues.

National Initiative for Democracy, www. ni4d.us. To make or change laws at all levels of government, including at the federal level by the initiative of the people.

New Democracy Project. www.newdemocracyproject.org. To provide policymakers and the public with thoughtful solutions that promote democratic participation, economic fairness and social justice.

Open Democracy. www.opendemocracy.net. To provide stimulating, critical analysis, promoting dialogue and debate on issues of global importance and linking citizens from around the world.

Our Future. www.ourfuture.org. To challenge the big money corporate agenda.

Oxfam. www.oxfamamerica.org. To help people gain the hope, skills, and direction to create a new future.

People for the American Way. www.pfaw.org. To reduce social tension and polarizations, encourage community participation, foster understanding among different segments of our society, and increase the level and quality of public dialogue.

Persons, Inc. www.personsinc.org. To campaign for an amendment to the U.S. Constitution stating clearly that the Bill of Rights is only for individual human beings.

Program on Corporations, Law, and Democracy (POCLAD). www. poclad.org. To launch democratic insurgencies that put corporations once again subordinate to "We the People;" and to rethink organizing strategies, exercise democratic authority at the local level, and strip fundamental powers-such as free speech and due process-from corporations.

Progressive Government. www.progressivegovernment.org. To propel the progressive movement toward running the country by identifying and promoting leaders who articulate and champion a progressive agenda.

Progressive Majority. www.progressivemajority.com. To elect progressive champions.

Public Campaign. www.publiccampaign.org. To dramatically reduce the role of big special interest money in American politics.

Public Citizen. www.tradewatch.org. To promote government and corporate accountability in the globalization and trade arena.

Public Citizen Litigation Group. www.citizen.org/litigation. To represent consumer interests in Congress, the executive branch and the courts.

Reclaim Democracy. www.reclaimdemocracy.org. To restore democratic authority over corporations, revive grassroots democracy, and revoke the power of money and corporations to control government and civic society.

Revolving Door Work Group. www.revolvingdoor.info. To promote ethics in public service and an arm's length relationship between the federal government and the private sector.

Strategic Corporate Initiative. www.corporateethics.org. To design, inspire, and direct a movement to transform the role of corporations in our society.

True Majority. www.truemajority.org. To compound the power of all those who believe in social justice, giving children a decent start in life, protecting the environment, and America working in cooperation with the world community.

United for a Fair Economy. www.faireconomy.org. To raise awareness that concentrated wealth and power undermine the economy, corrupt democracy, deepen the racial divide, and tear communities apart.

Some Think Tanks

Center for American Progress. www.americanprogress.org. To improve the lives of Americans through ideas and action.

Center on Corporations, Law & Society. www.law.seattleu.edu. To promote interdisciplinary scholarship and dialogue on issues related to the roles and obligations of corporations in an increasingly privatized and interdependent global society.

Center for Economic and Policy Research. www.cepr.net. To promote democratic debate on the most important economic and social issues that affect people's lives.

Center for International Development and Conflict Management. www.cidcm.umd.edu. Through research and development, to understand conflict and to helpsocieties create sustainable futures for themselves.

Institute for Policy Studies. www.ips-dc.org. As a hybrid think tank and social activist NGO working with social movements to promote true democracy and challenge concentrated wealth, corporate influence, and military power.

Progressive Policy Institute. www.ppionline.org. To define and promote a new progressive politics for America in the 21st century.

Political Research Associates. www.publiceye.org. To expose and challenge the right and larger oppressive movements, institutions, and forces.

Redefining Progress. www.rprogress.org. Working with government and advocacy groups, Redefining Progress develops innovative policies that balance economic well-being, environmental preservation, and social justice.

World Citizens' Foundation. www.worldcitizen.org. To design solutions to international problems based on the fundamental principles of equal human dignity, liberty, democracy and constitutionally protected basic rights of all.

*I selected these NGOs from my original list of some 150 NGOs. After finishing the writing of this book I was too exhausted to check back to see if the mission statements in this appendix are current. I apologetically leave that determination up to the book's readers.

Appendix B

Some Alternative Outlets for Truth Telling and Monitoring Lies

AlterNet. www.alternet.org
Alternative Radio. www.alternativeradio.org
Brave New Films. www.robertgreenwald.org
Center for Digital Democracy. www.democraticmedia.org
Center for Media and Democracy. www.prwatch.org
Democracy Now. www.democracynow.org
Fairness and Accuracy in Reporting. www.fair.org
Free Press. www.freepress.net
Free Speech TV www.freespeech.org
Independent Media Center www.indymedia.org
Independent Press Association. www.indypressny.org
Internet outlets
Local progressive newsprints
Media Access Project. www.mediaaccess.org
Media Matters for America. www.mediamatters.org
The Nation. www.thenation.com
New Dimensions Radio. www.newdimensions.org
Open Democracy. www.opendemocracy.net
Positive Futures Network. www.yesmagazine.org
The Progressive. www.progressive.org
Project Censored: www.projectcensored.org

Public Broadcasting System. www.pbs.org
Public Information Network. www.endgame.org
Tom Paine.com. www.tompaine.com
True Majority. www.truemajority.org

Appendix C

Creative Economic Thinking from A TO Z Minus E for Economists

> You cannot solve today's problems with the same thinking that caused the problems.
> ---Albert Einstein

> The greatest danger in times of turbulence is not the turbulence; it is to act with yesterday's logic.
> --- Peter Drucker

Nearly the entire economics profession was blindsided by Economic Katrina. You will find in this synopsis some creative thinking about economics from no one in the economics profession.

Aristotle[1]

Since ancient Greece influenced the design of American democracy, I thought it would be instructive to know what Aristotle thought about economics. In his day the Greek word for economy meant "household management" within the context of the community.

Economic activity in his view consisted of individuals doing things necessary for survival and also for the good life, which to him meant a moral life of virtue that leads to happiness. He criticized money-making as a way of gaining wealth, thought it was unnatural for people to use money to make more money-the essence of capitalism-and considered usury, or predatory lending, to be the most immoral form of economic activity. Seeking wealth is justifiable, Aristotle thought, as long as the wealth amounted to no more than an accumulation of material goods sufficiently useful for the household.

While there were banks in his day, there is a running debate by scholars over whether or the extent to which lending was done productively, that is, with the intent of making money off of the loans. I can't imagine, though, any banking business done then as sleazily as we see done today.

It's interesting to note that a totally free market was not the custom in ancient Greece. For instance, public officials monitored measurements, levied taxes on various transactions, and even fixed retail prices! Ancient democracy survived without a free market. American democracy can't survive with it!

Peter Barnes on "Capitalism 3.0"[2]

Peter Barnes co-founder, president, or a director of various socially responsible businesses, wants "capitalism 3.0" to replace "capitalism 2.0," the existing economic "operating system." He complains that corporations, with no resistance from our government, are privatizing the commons, profiting from it and externalizing the costs.

He defines "the commons" as assets we all share by inheriting or creating them together and subdivides them into three sectors, nature, community, and culture. Together they represent our "common wealth" (a most insightful concept), in contrast to our "private wealth," the latter representing all the property we inherit or accumulate individually. Private wealth collectively in the U.S. was estimated to be around $48.5 trillion in 2005. What do you think our total American common wealth is? Economists can't begin to estimate it in its entirety, but what they can estimate, Barnes tells us, comes to about $70 trillion. Is it any wonder then why, as Barnes asks, corporations on the one hand take valuable stuff "worth trillions of dollars" from the commons for short-term profit and on the other hand dump bad stuff into nature's commons and pay nothing?

His proposal relies heavily on the idea of property rights because our U.S. Constitution guarantees them, they shape economies, they produce value or wealth, and, most importantly, there's no requirement that they be concentrated in profit-maximizing hands, thus opening up the possibility of "propertizing" the commons without privatizing it (another very insightful idea). He proposes that the government assign common property rights to institutions, distinct from government and corporations that would be set up as trusts to manage the common property. A few such trusts already exist in the U.S, such as a trust in Marin County, California where ranchers can sell easements to it. For natural assets with their limited sources, the institutions would need to be capable of limiting their use. For the other two sectors with their endless potential, public access would need to be maximized and public usage fees minimized.

He introduces the idea of "commons tax credits" as a means for funneling more money into trusts by raising taxes in the uppermost tax bracket and giving its wealthy taxpayers the choice either to pay the extra tax to the government or to one or more qualified trust funds.

Barnes adapts the economist's concept of rent, or money paid because of scarcity, to his proposed trusts for nature. The trusts would sell pollution rights to polluters and get the rent in return. The trusts would limit the number of rights sold so as to increase the cost of their rent. For corporate polluters the cost would be high enough to create an incentive to pollute less. Some of the rent would be converted into per-capita dividends for consumer citizens. Consumers of pollution-laden products would pay more in rent (via higher prices) than they get back in dividends, while consumers of less-polluting products would get back more in dividends than they pay in rent. It is in this way that rent gets recycled from over-users, who tend to be the wealthier ones to under-users, who tend to be the poorer ones. This shifting of income would help alleviate what Barnes calls a pathological flaw of capitalism 2.0, the wide income gap between high and low income groups.

Barnes also shows how there could be per-capita dividends from trusts created for the commons' other two sectors. For example, treating the capital market as common property, a trust could charge a usage fee to publicly traded corporations for selling stocks and for having been given various rights such as limited liability, perpetual life, copyrights, patents, and the like.

Over time the propertizing of the commons would amass a portfolio worth trillions of dollars that could be used to fund three "universal birthrights;" a regular dividend to everyone, an opportunity endowment for each new child, and health insurance for everyone. Clearly, Barnes' proposal is a very expansive one and, superficially at least, a seductive one. Barnes appeals to capitalists, wage earners, lawyers, economists, commons entrepreneurs, and others to help build the commons sector into a full-fledged capitalism 3.0 and shows how it can benefit each of these diverse groups.

His proposals are among the most unique I've ever read on capitalism. His advocacy of pollution rights, though, really troubled me though until I got a further explanation from him. I was troubled because to me every human being has a sacred obligation to nature and a moral obligation to generations yet unborn to respect nature.

When I mentioned to Barnes my concern he explained that his proposal is a market-based one that doesn't imply moral approval of pollution.[3] In contrast, giving rights away free would imply some moral or social approval. But the rights would not be free with his approach. They would have to be paid for, and the money paid (i.e., rent) would benefit everyone. Furthermore, the rights would not be permanent, but would be for one time only. He also reminded me of his assertion in his book that "It is more disrespectful of the sky to pollute it without limit or payment than to turn it into a common property held in trust for future generations."[4] Moreover, he continued, every human being is a polluter and pollution can't be stopped overnight. So the best we can do, he says, is to steadily reduce our polluting. And to do that requires, as he has pointed out, a declining quantity of pollution rights with rising prices and per capita dividends. This internalizes the external costs of pollution and creates the virtuous recycling from over-users to under-users.

Riane Eisler on the Real Wealth of Nations[5]

Riane Eisler, trained in sociology, anthropology, and law, wrote a book about the "real wealth of nations." Unlike Adam Smith's classic work, "the wealth of nations," which monetizes wealth and focuses on the market, Eisler argues that the real wealth of a nation ultimately depends not on the market but on the quality of its human and natural capital. Yet it is this very capital that the corpocracy exploits for its own self interests to the detriment of what she believes ought to be the primary purpose of any economic system, the promotion of human welfare and happiness. The economy, in other words, should not exist solely for corporations or even for the marketplace.

From her perspective, neither corporations nor the marketplace are at the center of any viable economic system. The center, she says, is the household economy because it is there that the socially and economically essential work of caring for people and the development of future contributors to economic productivity start. This household economy, therefore, needs to be given the most attention in economic reforms. They would include, for instance, recognizing the household as the core economy, placing a monetary value on the work of care giving, accounting for its positive contribution to productivity in economic indicators such as the GDP, fairly compensating care givers, and making massive investments in child care and human development programs.

Her perspective is so broad that she adds five more economic sectors to that of the core, household sector. They are the unpaid economy made up mostly of volunteers; the conventional market economy; the illegal economy like illegal arms trade; the government economy that includes not just the large population of government workers but also the laws, rules, and policies that (should) govern the market economy; and the natural economy, a sector as basic as the first in that our environment produces natural resources used and misused by the market economy. I think the six could be put conveniently into two distinct categories, a monetized economy and a non-monetized economy, and then, with a nod to Daly, wrap the ecosystem around the two.

A functional economic system along with its larger context would be one she posits that depends on what she calls the partnership model of mutually respectful and caring relations as opposed to the traditional and current domination model. She shows how the Nordic countries, the only ones coming close to her partnership model, are faring well economically and socially. Having a national capacity and resources for providing optimal human development is clearly necessary for having a healthy economy, and she persuasively links the domination form of child rearing and thus suboptimal human development to adverse consequences later in life that show up in the kinds of leaders and followers our society has, in our belligerent relationships with other countries, and in our diminished capacity for a functional and healthy economy. She also argues convincingly how disastrous it could be if the domination model is played out with new and risky technological developments on the horizon.

Since she is a social activist, her book is much more than just being theoretically significant. She makes a number of practical suggestions about what needs to be done on Wall Street (e.g. stiff taxes on short-term speculations), in government (e.g., massive investment in child care and human development), by business leaders (e.g., changing from top-down to empowering corporations), and among social activist citizens (e.g., mounting a global movement to change laws and customs-she describes how she wrote an amicus brief that helped women legally gain equal rights).

Jeffrey Gates on Shared Capitalism[6]

Jeffrey Gates wrote a book jam packed with ideas about what he calls "shared capitalism for the twenty-first century." His is a decidedly populist view, not surprising since he was counsel to the U.S. Senate Finance Committee (1980-87), working with Senator Russell Long of Louisiana, son of populist governor and U.S. Senator Huey P. Long. In this role, Gates crafted federal law on employee stock ownership plans (ESOPs) and pension plans.

Capitalism creates financial capital, not capitalists, he notes. Moreover, most financial capital is held by institutional investors, the absentee owners of public corporations. This, he says, creates a "detached and disconnected capitalism largely on automatic" with investment decisions devoid of longer-term concerns, including the costs of externalization.

Unshared capitalism, while made to order by the corpocracy, is totally unfit for a democracy. His solution is to make widespread ownership a specific goal of national economic policy. His opinion that people take responsibility for what they own resonates with me, having watched for two decades party-going renters misbehave and scar property in an ocean-side condominium where my wife and I owned and never rented a unit.

Achieving inclusive ownership on a national scale will take, he believes, a political era like the progressives and populists of the 1930s and a leader like FDR. Gates identifies six strategic initiatives: a public opinion poll that asks the right questions about inclusive ownership and informs politicians about the public will, which he believes would support populist capitalism; a government declaration of widespread ownership as a national economic goal; a bipartisan commission on economic empowerment, which he believes will conclude the desirability of widespread prosperity; a government office of asset ownership; a regular assessment of what the impact of inclusive ownership has been; and an annual ownership survey to determine who owns what.

Thom Hartmann on the Middle Class, Democracy, and Economics[7]

Hartman argues convincingly that the "corporatocracy," his term for the corporate aristocracy that seeks to control all aspects of our lives, is "screwing," his term again, the middle class through such means as demonizing labor unions and shrinking them by shifting more and more jobs overseas, lowering wages through government sponsored free-trade, getting the government to shift more and more wealth upwards, and to deregulate everything in sight having to do with commerce.

The corporatocracy's "declaring war on the middle class," spells doom for democracy. He points out through good examples that a political democracy and an economically viable middle class are the natural state of the entire animal kingdom. Ancient Greeks were smart enough to understand the connection and know without a democracy and its middle class they would have been subjugated by the aristocracy. For America to reclaim her democracy and for the middle class to revitalize it self Hartmann suggests a variety of indirectly related initiatives that could eventually reverse privatization and revitalize the middle class such as; educating the public about the corpocracy's designs on Social Security, enacting a nation-wide instant run-off voting system, establishing progressive taxation, ensuring a living wage, invigorating the labor movement, ending the military's constant draining of revenue, and creating an alternative-energy industry.

Hawkins, Lovins, & Lovins on Natural Capitalism[8]

These authors of a book of the same title warn that if we continue to ignore the value of natural capital, i.e., nature's life-support systems for humankind, there will come a time when there won't be any more life support. Doomsday may be a century or two away, but the quality of life up to that point will have deteriorated at an increasing pace.

Pursuing four central strategies of natural capitalism, these authors say, will enable commercial enterprises and communities to operate as if all forms of capital were important. The core strategy is that of radically increasing resource productivity by being more efficient, less wasteful in how natural resources are extracted and used.

The second they call "biomimicry" that involves eliminating waste in the making of things by imitating biological processes in the manufacturing process. The third is to change the relationship between producer and consumer from one based on goods and purchases to one based on a "flow of economic services" that will in turn deemphasize possession as a measure of affluence and emphasize that well-being depends on the "continuous receipt of quality, utility, and performance." The fourth involves "reinvesting in sustaining, restoring, and expanding stocks of natural capital."

Howard Karger on the Fringe Economy[9]

Howard Karger, a professor of social policy, and author of the book, Shortchanged, defines the fringe economy as comprising "corporations and business practices that pray on the poor by charging excessive interest rates or fees, or exorbitant prices for goods and services."

He divides the fringe economy into seven sectors; storefront loan businesses (e.g., pawnshops), the credit card industry, alternative financial services (e.g., check cashing and rent-to-own), fringe housing, real estate speculation and foreclosure, the fringe auto industry, and the "getting-out-of-debt" industry (e.g., the multibillion dollar debt management business). All of these sectors seek to sink already indebted people further into debt by escalating and profiting from the interest fees levied on them.

When I asked him if he foresaw Economic Katrina coming since I didn't see a hint of it in his book, he answered that he had foreseen only the tip of the iceberg, the meltdown of the subprime mortgage market, but failed to see how interwoven that market was in other forms of dodgy financial instruments or how the mortgages were packaged and sold internationally.[10] Howard, at least you foresaw a part of it. Most who should have didn't.

The solution to the problems of the fringe economy, Karger thinks, is not to eliminate it because compared to fringe services the mainstream ones are not as accessible physically or as culturally compatible to poor neighborhoods. Instead, he suggests numerous solutions that might accommodate the realities of these neighborhoods while also eliminating some of the abusive and fraudulent practices of doing business with the people who live in those neighborhoods.

David Korten on a Post-Corporate World[11]

Dr. Korten, an author and activist, believes that our images of the world help shape our behavior, so changing the world must include changing our image to that of a post-corporate world without the corpocracy and its capitalism. What does he tell us this world would look like first generally and then specifically in the economics sphere?

Our own American way of life would resemble what some parts of the world, including a small proportion of Americans already seem to be voluntarily doing; namely choosing a simpler, less materialistic lifestyle, including curbing excessive consumption of the non-necessities. Human values and behavior would shift toward having and enjoying the "essentials of life" such as a sufficient and secure means of livelihood. Life, he says, would be the measure of our well-being, not how much money we have.

We would have in place of the capitalism as we know it today an economic democracy, which Korten says would have the broadest possible ownership of productive assets that are located in the communities where the owners live. There would be, Korten says cleverly, markets that are "human scale on a large scale." He explains what he means by this with a hypothetical example of a corporation that's already organized around self-managing units, a configuration I've been preaching for years. Korten's idea here is that each unit could be bought out by its stakeholders-employees, suppliers, customers, and others in the locale of the unit. That idea in my opinion is far better than pushing for ESOPs and needs to be taken as far and as fast as it can be taken.

His overall strategy is two-fold and simple conceptually but much less so pragmatically: 1. "Withhold resources from the institutions of capitalism" (e.g., don't invest in the stock market) and 2. "Build sustainable community-based alternatives for meeting our needs." He recommends several specific initiatives, some of which I covered in Chapter Ten.

Roger Terry on Economy Insanity[12]

Roger Terry wrote a book in 1995 on "economic insanity" (no, it isn't a "mis"fortune telling of the insane meltdown of 2008 thirteen years later). He's co-founder of a small business firm, the "fun company."

Terry contends the growth-driven capitalism of big, authoritarian, and unaccountable organizations is devouring the American dream. As proof he points to the erosion of the good life of being happy; how we have become a nation not of citizens but of consumers of "life-style enhancing" things, yet in actuality we produce more (in waste) than we consume in products and services; how seeking limitless economic progress is both illusory and self-destructive; how we live in a capitalistic society, but most of us are dependent wage earners, not independent capitalists; and how the rich are getting richer and the poor are getting poorer-an inevitable result of capitalism.

Terry questions three underlying assumptions of our current capitalistic system that he contends are so inherently wrong that the system can't be fixed; 1) limitless, perpetual economic growth is an imperative good, 2) increasing productivity is a cure-all for an ailing economy, and 3) maintaining a good life depends on continuous technological advances.

The growth imperative, he argues, is illogical, immoral, misguiding, and destructive. It's illogical because we consumers buy products we don't really need (e.g., personal computer upgrades) from companies that are fearful of not making and selling new products lest their competitors do so and grab more of the market share. It's immoral because it lets companies rationalize wrongdoing for the sake of survival. It's misguiding because companies are diverted from what should be their true purpose, to serve society in useful ways. It's destructive because our planet and our pocketbooks are being irretrievably depleted by a growth-driven, consumer-oriented economy.

He argues that productivity increases, contrary to the prevailing assumption, don't make the economy grow and thereby don't improve our standard of living. He observes that while productivity has gone up over the last 25 years, real wages haven't. Productivity increases, instead, are siphoned into the pockets of the rich, into pay for support people (e.g., consultants) who don't produce anything, and into payments on un-forgivingly huge debts fueled by the growth imperative.

Technological advances, he claims, are "inherently self-destructive" because they are "quickly bankrupting us." Only a few select companies and the more affluent among us can afford the technology race. The rest go out of business or into deeper debt.

He goes on to outline the features of a new economic system. It would be a structurally different capitalism, one we've never seen before. It would be a "Nation of Owners," in which there are three levels of ownership: (a) small enterprises, like his own, with the founders and a few partners who share ownership commensurate with their seniority and other factors like start-up funding; (b) larger enterprises, the corporations of today, would be owned collectively by their members, who would elect managers for limited terms of office; and (c) public enterprises, such as utilities, education, defense, and the like, would be created and managed by public boards or local governments.

Here is a sketch of what he says life would be like under this different capitalism. It would be a "truer form" of capitalism because anyone able-bodied and "even minimally motivated would own capital and in reasonably equal portions," thus guaranteeing freedom of opportunity and markedly reducing inequality of income. There would no longer be a Wall Street since absentee owners, i.e., shareholders, would gradually be replaced by working owners, which in turn would eliminate the motive of short-term profits and its immoral consequences. Our government would be much different-it wouldn't be controlled by a corpocracy. Our economy would be developing better rather than growing bigger. Businesses would be motivated to serve society instead of serving themselves. There would be no more drudgery at work, exploitation of workers, cutthroat competition, takeovers, downsizings, wholesale firings, ballooning personal and collective debt, frivolous products, superfluous support structures, or any other ills you might associate with the present system. Sounds like utopia, doesn't it?—unless you're a fat-cat CEO or you can't wait for the next computer upgrade

Danah Zohar and Ian Marshall on Spiritual Capital[13]

Zohar is broadly trained and experienced in law, classical literature, physics, religion, anthropology, and psychology. Marshall is a Jungian-oriented psychiatrist and psychotherapist. Married to each other, the authors would make, I think, engaging conversationalists at any dinner party without the snarling corpocrats and cons at the table.

The co-authors argue that material capitalism is unsustainable, depleting our natural resources, creating political and social instability, eroding our moral standards, and degrading the very meaning of life in terms of its deepest values and aspirations. Material capitalism, fostered and perpetuated by the corpocracy, needs to be replaced, the authors say, by "spiritual capitalism" that produces "wealth we can live by." Their spiritual capitalism has no religious connotations. It is the amount of knowledge and expertise available about "meaning, values, and fundamental purposes." It produces not material wealth that ultimately consumes itself but a self-sustaining wealth "that enriches the deeper aspects of our lives."

Notes

Preface Note

1. You Tube. Bill Clinton Loses his Temper and Lashes Out at Amy Goodman. November 8, 2000. www.youtube.com.

Chapter 1 Notes

1. Over 10 years ago I reviewed a book in which the author, Professor Ralph Estes, introduced the term, "corpocracy." But he didn't define it! He simply suggested that "whatever it is called," it represents the "great and growing business influence over our government, our society, and our lives." See Estes, R. <u>Tyranny of the Bottom Line: Why Corporations Make Good People do Bad Things</u>. San Francisco: Berrett-Koehler, 1996, p. 105. The only other book I know of that has "corpocracy" in its title is one by Robert A.G. Monks, <u>Corpocracy: How CEOs and the Business Roundtable Hijacked the World's Greatest Wealth Machine -- And How to Get It Back</u>. NY: Wiley, 2007. To Monks, imperial, rapacious CEO's and derelict boards of directors carry much of the blame for corporate excesses and it is the reform of corporate governance that he believes is necessary to restore corporate accountability and responsibility.

2. Derber, C. <u>Regime Change Begins at Home: Freeing America from Corporate Rule</u>. San Francisco: Berrett-Koehler, 2004, p. 38, 172.

3. Ibid., p. 7.

4. Hartmann, T. Screwed: The Undeclared War Against the Middle Class-And What We Can Do About It. San Francisco: Berrett-Koehler, 2006.

5. Rank, MR. One Nation, Underprivileged: Why American Poverty Affects Us All. NY: Oxford University Press, 2005, p. 64.

6. Ibid, p. 6, 51.

7. U.S. Supreme Court ruling, Citizens United v. Federal Election Commission, No. 08-205, January 21, 2010.

8. Eisler, R. The Real Wealth of Nations: Creating a Caring Economics. San Francisco: Berrett-Koehler, 2007. See pages 193-195 for her analysis of child rearing in "dominator" families.

9. Krugman, P. Health Care Realities. *The New York Times Online*, July 30, 2009.

10. Hertz, N. The Silent Takeover: Global Capitalism and the Death of Democracy. NY: The Free Press, 2001.

11. Hartmann, op cit., p. 14.

12. Duhigg, C. Pollution Grows with Little Fear of Punishment. *The New York Times Online*, September 12, 2009.

13. These five examples are drawn from the following sources respectively: Nace, T. Gangs of America: The Rise of Corporate Power and the Disabling of Democracy. San Francisco: Berrett-Koehler, 2003, p. 186; Abramowitz, M. & Mufson, S. Papers Detail Industry's Role in Cheney's Energy Report. *The Washington Post*, July 18, 2007, p. A01; Strassel, KA. Corporate America Takes on Spitzerism. *The Wall Street JournalOnline*, September 25, 2006. See also, Lenzer, L. & Miller, M. Buying Justice. *Forbes.*,July 21, 2003, 64-72; and, Greenhouse, S. Bill Easing Unionizing Is Under Heavy Attack. *The New York Times Online*, January 8, 2009 (See also, Greenhouse, S. Fierce Lobbying Greets Bill to Help Workers Unionize. *The New York Times Online*, March 10, 2009.

14. The FDR quote is taken from Corporate Law: A History. Part 2: Supreme Court Cases. www.spiritone.com.

15. Shirer, WL. The Rise and Fall of the Third Reich. NY: Simon and Schuster, 1960.

16. Wolf, N. The End of America: A Letter to a Young Patriot. White River Jct: VT, Chelsea Green Publishing, 2007 (1st Edition).

17. Kirkpatrick, DD. Rulings Against Spending Caps May Start Flood of Election Ads. *The New York Times Online*, January 8, 2010.

18. See www.opensecrets.org.

19. Barnes, R. & Eggen, D. Supreme Court Rejects Limits on Corporate Spending in Electoral Campaigns. *The Washington Post Online*, January 21, 2010.

20. Surowiecki, J. Exit through Lobby. *The New Yorker*, October 19, 2009, p. 32.

21. Ibid.

22. Orey, M. The Supreme Court: Open for Business. *Business Week*, July 9 and 16, 2007, p. 30-31.

23. Hamburger, T. Archive for Tuesday. *Los Angeles Times Online*, January 08, 2008. www.articles.latimes.com.

24. Lichtblau, E. Chamber of Commerce Accused of Tax Fraud. *The New York Times Online*, September 10, 2010.

25. Megalli, M. & Friedman, A. Masks of Deception: Corporate Front Groups in America. Washington, DC: Essential Information, December, 1991, p. 181-182.

26. See e.g., Nader, R. & Smith, WJ. No Contest: Corporate Lawyers and the Perversion of Justice. NY: Random House, 1996.

27. See www.clubforgrowth.org.

28. Mitchell, LE. The Speculation Economy: How Finance Triumphed over Industry. San Francisco: Berrett-Koehler, 2007. See also, Terry, R. Economic Insanity: How Growth-Driven Capitalism is Devouring the American Dream. San Francisco: Berrett-Koehler, 1995.

29. Herbert, B. Out of Touch. *The New York Times Online*, May 1, 2009.

30. Krugman, P. The Politics of Spite. *The New York Times Online*, October 4, 2009.

31. Cohen, A. Larry Craig's Great Adventure: Suddenly, He's a Civil Libertarian. *The New York Times Online*, September 24, 2007.

32. Brody, JE. Frank Talk About Care at Life's End. *The New York Times Online*, August 23, 2010.

33. Adcox, S. SC Politician's Welfare Comments Called 'Immoral'. *Associated Press, Yahoo News Online*. Jan 25, 2010.

34. Fiuhy, B. Carl Paladino Backs Welfare Prison Dorms, Hygiene Classes. *Huffington Post Online*, August 21, 2010.
35. Vedantam, S. Study Ties Political Leanings to Hidden Biases. The Washington Post, January 30, 2006, p. A05. See also, Maclay, K. Researchers Help Define what Makes a Political Conservative. UC Berkley News Online, July 22, 2003. www.berkeley.edu.

36. Derber, op cit., p. 100.

37. See, e.g., Blum, W. Killing Hope: U.S. Military and CIA Interventions Since World War II. Monroe, ME: Common Courage Press, 2003 (revised edition 2004); Blum, W. Freeing the World to Death: Essays on the American Empire, Monroe, ME, Common Courage Press, 2004; Blum, W. Rogue State: A Guide to the World's Only Superpower. London: Zed Books, 2006 (Updated Edition); and Higham, C. Trading with the Enemy: The Nazi - American Money Plot 1933-1949. NY: Delacorte Press, 1983.

38. Shane, S., Mazzetti, M., & Worth, RF. Secret Assault on Terrorism Widens on Two Continents. *The New York Times Online*, August 14, 2010.

39. Terkel, A. Pence: Baghdad Bazaar Is Like 'Any Open-Air Market In Indiana In The Summertime. April 4, 2007. www.thinkprogress.org.

40. Lucas, F. Members of Congress Invest in Businesses in Terror-Sponsor States. *CNS News Online*, August 2, 2007.

41. Mayer, LR. Some Members of Congress Profit from Iraq War Contractor Stocks: No Wonder We Can't End the War! April, 2008. Ms Mayer's source for this article is the Center for Responsive Politics. www.organicconsumers.org/articles/article_11363.cfm.

42. Rich, F. Will the Real Traitors Please Stand Up? *The New York Times Online*, May 14, 2006.

43. Krugman, P. America Goes Dark. *The New York Times Online*, August 8, 2010.

44. Herbert, B. Wars, Endless Wars. *The New York Times Online*, March 2, 2009; see also, No 'Graceful Exit' *The New York Times* Online, August 16, 2010.

45. Derber, op cit., p. 135.

Chapter 2 Notes

1. Nace, T. <u>Gangs of America: The Rise of Corporate Power and the Disabling of Democracy.</u> San Francisco: Berrett-Koehler, 2003, p. 32.

2. Derber, C. <u>Regime Change Begins at Home: Freeing America from Corporate Rule.</u> San Francisco: Berrett-Koehler, 2004, p. 28.

3. Ibid., p. 28-29.

4. See e.g., Higgs, R. The Cold War: Too Good a Deal to Give Up. *The*

Independent Review Online, May 15, 2002; Higgs, R. The Living Reality of Military-Economic Fascism. Ludwig von Mises Institute Daily, January 1, 2007. www.independent.org; and Rich, F. Obama at the Precipice. *The New York Times Online*, September 26, 2009.

5. Derber, op cit., p. 29.

6. Landay, J. The Powell Manifesto: How a Prominent Lawyer's Attack Memo Changed America. www.mediatransparency.org/story, August 20, 2002. The full text of the memorandum written by Lewis F. Powell, Jr. on August 28, 1971 to the U.S. Chamber of Commerce is at www. reclaimdemocracy.org. All quotations in this chapter of Powell's message are taken from the full text of his memorandum.

7. Nace, op cit., p. 138.

8. See Landay, J. op cit.

Chapter 3 Notes

1. I should mention the NGO, Corporate Ethics International. It is an example of an NGO that does collaborates with a few other NGOs. For example, collaborating with representatives from three other NGOs it has issued a report on a strategic initiative to bring corporations back under control. See, Marx, M. Strategic Corporate Initiative: Toward a Global Citizens' Movement to Bring Corporations Back Under Control. Corporate Ethics International, September 2007. www.CorporateEthics. org.

2. Landay, J. The Powell Manifesto: How a Prominent Lawyer's Attack Memo Changed America. www.mediatransparency.org/story, August 20, 2002. The full text of the memorandum written by Lewis F. Powell, Jr. on August 28, 1971 to the U.S. Chamber of Commerce is at www. reclaimdemocracy.org.

3. See, wikibin.org/articles/list-of-grassroots-organizations.html.

4. McGrath, B. The Movement: The Rise of Tea Party Activism. *The New Yorker*, February 1, 2010, p. 40-49.

5. See, www.teapartypatriots.org.

6. Rogers. J. Toward a Progresssive Strategy in the States. In Heuvel, VK. & Borosage, RL. <u>Taking Back America</u>. NY: Nation Books, 2004, p. 173-189.

7. See, McKinnon, M. & Lessig, L. How to Sober Up Washington. *The Daily Beast Online*, April 4, 2010; also, Johnson, K. States' Rights Is Rallying Cry of Resistance for Lawmakers. *The New York Times Online*, March 16, 2010.

8. Healey, J. It's on! 13 State Attorneys General Challenge Healthcare Reform Law. *Los Angeles Times Online*, March 23, 2010.

9. Collins, G. A Confederacy of Dunces. *The New York Times Online*, April 7, 2010.

10. Lang, B. Texas Governor Floats Possibility of Secession. *CBS News Online*, April 16, 2009.

11. Williams, W. Do States Have a Right of Secession? *Capitalism Magazine Online*, April 19, 2002.

12. Hamm, S. Main Street is Fed Up: A Wide Swath of Investors Feels Duped. *Business Week*, September 3, 2007, p. 42.

13. Gates, J. <u>Democracy at Risk: Rescuing Main Street from Wall Street, A Populist Vision for the Twenty-First Century</u>. Perseus Publishing, Cambridge, MA: 2000.

14. Kelly, M. <u>The Divine Right of Capital: Dethroning the Corporate Aristocracy</u>. San Francisco: Berrett-Koehler, 2001, p. 173.

15. Ibid., p. 178-179.

16. Danaher, K. <u>Insurrection: Citizen Challenges to Corporate Rule</u>. NY: Routledge, 2003, p. 306.

17. Sirota, D. The Uprising: An Unauthorized Tour of the Populist Revolt Scaring Wall Street and Washington. New York: Crown Publishing, 2008.

18. Havel, V. et al. The Power of the Powerless: Citizens Against the State in Central-Eastern Europe. NY: M.E. Sharpe, 1985.

19. Epstein, B. Anarchism and the Anti-Globalization Movement. *Monthly Review Online*, September 2001.

20. Nace, T. Gangs of America: The Rise of Corporate Power and the Disabling of Democracy. San Francisco: Berrett-Koehler, 2003, p. 202-203.

21. Margalit, A. On Compromise and Rotten Compromise. Princeton University Press, Princeton: 2009.

22. See, e.g., Lubbers, E (Ed). Battling Big Business: Countering Greenwash, Infiltration, and Other Forms of Corporate Bullying. Monroe, ME: Common Courage Press, 2002.

Chapter 4 Notes

1. Brumback, GB. Tall Performance From Short Organizations Through We/Me Power. Bloomington, IN: 1st Books Library, 2002.

2. Edwards, L. The Power of Ideas: The Heritage Foundation at 25 Years. Ottawa, IL: Jameson Books, 1998.

3. Covington, S. How Conservative Philanthropies and Think Tanks Transform US Policy. *Covert Action Quarterly*, Winter 1998. www.thirdworldtraveler.com.

4. Ibid.

5. Paget, K. The Big Chill: Foundations and Political Passions. *The American Prospect Online*, May 1, 1999. www.prospect.org.

6. The Alliance for Justice NGO in seeking to reassure foundations that

supporting advocacy groups is "legal, important, and doable," offers a handbook that describes a "full range of advocacy activities that foundations can support," and explains how it can be accomplished. See www.afj.org.

7. Derber, C. <u>Regime Change Begins at Home: Freeing America from Corporate Rule</u>. San Francisco: Berrett-Koehler, 2004, p. 244-265.

8. The bloggers' comments were in response to this news report: Liptak, A. Justices Overturn Key Campaign Limits. *The New York Times Online*, January 21, 2010.

9. Lubbers, E. (Ed.). <u>Battling Big Business: Countering Greenwash, Infiltration, and Other Forms of Corporate Bullying</u>. Monroe, ME: Common Courage Press, 2002.

10. See www. gleitsman.org.

11. Wolf, N. <u>Give me Liberty: A Handbook for American Revolutionaries</u>. NY: Simon & Schuster, 2008 (1st Edition).

12. Kahn, S. & Minnich, E. <u>The Fox in the Henhouse: How Privatization Threatens Democracy</u>. San Francisco: Berrett-Koehler, 2005, p. 145.

13. Gogoi, P. Judge Shoots Down BofA Settlement. *USA Today*, September 15, 2009, p. 1A.

14. See www.wikipedia.com regarding "Efforts to Impeach George W. Bush."

15. See Chapter 9 on the pervasiveness of corporate lawlessness. See Drutman, L. & Cray, C. <u>The People's Business: Controlling Corporations and Restoring Democracy</u>. San Francisco: Berrett-Koehler, 2004 for the authors' argument that "rewiring the corporation---is ultimately a poor substitute for establishing meaningful citizen control over corporations through democratically created laws" (p. 119). Underlying their argument is the premise that "large, publicly traded corporations are---inherently destructive" (p. 131). See also, Bakan, J. <u>The Corporation: The Pathological Pursuit of Profit and Power</u>. NT: The Free Press, 2004. Bakan tells about

a psychologist who matched corporate characteristics to a checklist of psychopathic traits.

16. Court, J. <u>Corporateering: How Corporate Power Steals Your Personal Freedom---and What You Can Do About It</u>. NY: Jeremy P. Tarcher/ Putnam, 2003, p. 38.

17. See, e.g., Moyer, B., et al. <u>Doing Democracy: The MAP Model for Organizing Social Movements</u>. Gabriola Island, BC: New Society Publishers, 2001; Drutman & Cray, op cit. pp. 256-280; and Kahn, S. <u>Organizing: A Guide for Grassroots Leaders</u>. Silver Spring, MD: NASW Press, 1991 (Revised Edition).

18. Personal communication with Charles Derber, August 25, 2010. Quoted verbatim with permission.

19. Editorial. The Wrong Kind of Enthusiasm. *The New York Times Online*, August 25, 2010.

20. Prothero, S. Millennials do faith and politics their way. *USA Today*, March 29, 2010, p. 9A.

21. Kahn & Minnich, op cit., p. 258.

22. Sorkin, AR. To Battle, Armed With Shares. *The New York Times Online*, January 4, 2006.

23. See, Investment Managers Worldwide Predict SRI Will Be Mainstream in 10 Years *BizEthicsBuzz Online*, May 31, 2005.

24. Haberman, C. On 5th Ave., A Grandmothers' Protest as Endless as the Wars. *The New York Times Online*, May 6, 2010.

25. Goss, S. Free Enterprise, A Pipe Dream. *EzineArticles.com*. Undated, Mr. Goss is a small business consultant.

26. See www.amiba.net and www.livingeconomies.org.

27. See www.ashoka.org. See also, Bornstein, D. <u>How to Change the</u>

World: Social Entrepreneurs and the Power of New Ideas. NY: Oxford University Press, 2004.

28. Kelber, H. The Unemployed Now Have Their Own Union, and It's Catching on Quickly. *Alter Net Online*, February 24, 2010.

29. Court, op cit. p.38. For some ideas on corporate self reform, see; Brumback, GB. Toward Becoming a Great Corporation. Part's One-five, *The CEO Refresher Online*, November, Vol. 15, Issue 11.4; December, Vol. 15, Issue 12.6; January, Vol. 16, Issue 1.13; February, Vol. 16, Issue 2.8; and April, Vol. 16, Issue 4.4.

30. Brumback, GB. Democracy Pow!er: The USCD and the Peoples' Reignbow Coalition. *Dissident Voice Online*, April 2, 2010.

31. Personal communication with Doug Page. March 2, 2010.

32. Personal communication with Charles Derber, March 2, 2010.

33. McDonald, C. Green, Inc. An Environmental Insider Reveals How a Good Cause Has Gone Bad. Guilford, DE: The Lyons Press, 2008.

34. See www.majorityagenda.com.

Chapter 5 Notes

1. Landay, J. The Powell Manifesto: How a Prominent Lawyer's Attack Memo Changed America. www.mediatransparency.org/story, August 20, 2002. The full text of the memorandum written by Lewis F. Powell, Jr. on August 28, 1971 to the U.S. Chamber of Commerce is at www. reclaimdemocracy.org. This footnote covers all quotations appearing in this chapter of Powell's text.

2.. Gatto, JT. The Underground History of American Education: A Schoolteacher's Intimate Investigation Into the Problem of Modern Schooling. NY: The Oxford Village Press Oxford, 2000.

3. Chaker, AM. Companies Design, Fund Curricula at Universities. *The Wall Street Journal Online*, September 11, 2006.

4. Draffan, G. The Corporate Consensus: A Guide to the Institutions of Global Power. Part 1: The Dynamics of Power. www.endgame.org, November 2000.

5. Punch, M. <u>Dirty Business</u>. London: Sage, 1996.

6. Gladwell, M. The Talent Myth: Are Smart People Overrated? *The New Yorker*, July 22, 2002.

7. See e.g., Washburn, J. <u>University, Inc.: The Corporate Corruption of American Higher Education. Basic Book</u>s, 2005; also, Kohn, A. The 500-Pound Gorilla: The Corporate Role in the High-stakes Testing Obsession & Other Methods of Turning Education into a Business. October, 2002, Phi Delta Kappan. www.alfiekohn.org.

8. See aynrand.org.

9. Norton, G. 2.8% of Oklahoma High School Students Pass Citizenship Test. *Daily Kos Online*, September 8, 2009. The same abysmal test results are found when students in other states such as Arizona, for example, are tested.

10. Pierce, CP. <u>Idiot America: How Stupidity Became a Virtue in the Land of the Free</u>. NY: Doubleday, 2009.

11. Surowiecki, J. Greater Fools. *The New Yorker*, July 5, 2010, p. 23.

12. See www.allianceforjustice.org.

13. See www.art-us.org.

14. Herrera, JD. How the American Democracy Project is Revolutionizing Campus Civic Engagement. *Public Purpose Online*, February/March, 2008.

15. DiNovella, E. Amy Goodman Interview. *The Progressive Online*, February, 2008.

16. Drutman, L. & Cray, C. <u>The People's Business: Controlling Corporations and Restoring Democracy</u>. San Francisco: Berrett-Koehler, 2004, p. 220.

17. Kull, S. Misperceptions, the Media, and the Iraq War. www. worldpublicopinion.org. Program on International Policy Attitudes and Knowledge Networks. October 2, 2003.

18. McChesney, RW. <u>Rich Media, Poor Democracy: Communication Politics in Dubious Times</u>. Champaign, IL: University of Illinois Press, 1999.

Chapter 6 Notes

1. Landay, J. The Powell Manifesto: How a Prominent Lawyer's Attack Memo Changed America. www.mediatransparency.org/story, August 20, 2002. The full text of the memorandum written by Lewis F. Powell, Jr. on August 28, 1971 to the U.S. Chamber of Commerce is at www. reclaimdemocracy.org. This footnote covers all quotations appearing in this chapter of Powell's text.

2.. Oxman, R. Then We Can Change the World with Fifty People. *Dissident Voice Online*, April 1st, 2010. His website is www.oxtogrind.org.

3. See www.democracyforamerica.com.

4. Bessette, J. "Deliberative Democracy: The Majority Principle in Republican Government," in Goldwin, RA & Schambra, WA. <u>How Democractic is the Constitution?</u> Washington, D.C., AEI Press, 1980, pp. 102–116.

5. Fishkin, JS. <u>When the People Speak: Deliberative Democracy and Public Consultation</u>. NY: Oxford University Press, 2009.

6. Brooks, D. The Bloody Crossroads. *The New York Times Online*, September 7, 2009. See also, Krugman, P. State of Paralysis. *The New York Times Online*, May 24, 2009; and Steinhauer, J. Top Judge Calls Calif. Government 'Dysfunctional.' *The New York Times Online*, October 10, 2009.

7. See www.ni4d.us

8. Amato, T. <u>Grand Illusion: The Myth of Voter Choice in a Two Party Tyranny</u>. NY: The New Press, 2009.

9. U.S. Term Limits, Inc. v. Thorton, decided May 22, 1995. See www.findlaw.com.

10. Polermo, JA. California Needs a New Constitution. *The Huffington Post Online*, May 26, 2009.

11. Rahn, R. The Imperial Congress. *The Washington Times Online*, February 11, 2007.

12. Packer, G. The Empty Chamber: Just how broken is the Senate? *The New Yorker*, August 9, 2010, p. 38-51.

13. Drutman, L. & Cray, C. <u>The People's Business: Controlling Corporations and Restoring Democracy</u>. San Francisco: Berrett-Koehler, 2004, p. 220.

14. DeGroat, B. Corporate Political Donations make Millions for Shareholders. *News Service Online*, January 24, 2007. See www.ur.umich.edu.

15. Dunham, RS. Loopholes a Jet can Fly Through: How Politicians get around Pesky Laws Prohibiting Corporate Contributions. *Business Week*, May 22, 2006, p. 34-36.

16. Editor. Corporate Political Spending: Company Contributions are Becoming Increasingly Transparent. *CRO Magazine*, January/February 2007, p. 12.

17. Surrusco, M., Goldin-Dubois, J., & Davis, E. Designer Districts: Safe Seats Tailor Made for Incumbents. Common Cause Education Fund, April, 2005. www.commoncause.com.

18. Ibid.

19. Ismail, MA. Pushing Prescriptions: Drug Lobby Second to None; How

the Pharmaceutical Industry Gets its Way in Washington. The Center for Public Integrity, www.publicintergrity.org.

20. Editorial. The Drug Industry's Offer. *The New York Times Online*, June 24, 2009.

21. Draffan, G. The Corporate Consensus: A Guide to the Institutions of Global Power. Part 1: The Dynamics of Power. www.endgame.org, November 2000.

22. Birnbaum, JH. The Road to Riches is Called K Street: Lobbying Firms Hire More, Pay More, Charge More to Influence Government. *The Washington Post*, June 22, 2005, p. A01.

23. Alpern, S. It's Time We Took a Look at Corporate Lobbying. Trillium Asset Management. August, 2003. www.trilliuminvest.com. See also, Associated Press. The Influence Game: Lobbyists Prosper in Downturn. *The New York Times Online*, May 3, 2009.

24. I calculated this sum from data available on the website www.opensecrets.com retrieved April 2008.

25. Javers, E. When Pork-Barrel Pols aren't Enough: Now Lobbyists are Helping States and Counties Bring Home More of the Bacon. *Business Week*, June 12, 2006, p. 68-71. See also, Associated Press. The Influence Game: Lobbyists Prosper in Downturn. *The New York Times Online*, May 3, 2009.

26. Kirkpatrick, D. Health Lobby Takes Fight to the States. *The New York Times Online*, December 28, 2009.

27. Murray, D. Corporate Lobbying: 'Line Sitters' Cash in on Quest for Influence. *The Blade Online*, December 7, 2003.

28. Kirkpatrick, DD. Law Meant to Curb Lobbying Sends It Underground. *The New York Times Online*, January 17, 2010.

29. Lipton, E. & Lichtblau, E. Senator's Ties to Real Estate Draw Criticism. *The New York Times Online*, May 9, 2008.

30. Smith, BA. & Hoersting, SM. Let the Grassroots "Lobbying" Grow: Key to cleaning up Washington. *National Review Online*, February 21, 2006.

31. Hightower, J. Thieves in High Places: They've Stolen our Country and it's Time to Take it Back. NY: Viking, 2003, p. xix.

32. Drutman & Cray, op cit., p. 228.

33. Editorial. Lobbying From Within. *The New York Times Online*, June 17, 2005.

34. Lipton, E. Toy Safety: Safety Agency Faces Scrutiny Amid Changes. *The New York Times Online*, September 2, 2007.

35. Krugman, P. A Serious Drug Problem. *The New York Times Online*, May 6, 2005.

36. Klein, N. The Shock Doctrine: The Rise of Disaster Capitalism. NY: Metropolitan Books, 2007, p. 316.

37. Adapted from the report, "A Matter of Trust," dated 2005 by the Revolving Door Work Group. www.revolvingdoor.info.

38. Luo, M. In Banking, Emanuel Made Money and Connections. *The New York Times Online*, December 3, 2008.

39. Brooks, D. The Insider's Crusade. *The New York Times Online*, November 21, 2008.

40. Neas, RG. The New Face of Jim Crow: Voter Suppression in America. A Special Report. People for the American Way Foundation, August, 2006. www.pfaw.org.

41. Neas, ibid.

42. Stout, D. Supreme Court Upholds Voter Identification Law in Indiana. *The New York Times Online*, April 28, 2008.

43. Priest, D. & Arkin, DM. A Hidden World, Growing Beyond Control. *The Washington Post Online*, July 19, 2010.

44. Associated Press. O'Connor Worries About Courts' Autonomy. *The New York Times Online*, November 5, 2006.

45. Drutman & Cray, op cit., p. 47-48.

46. Barnes, R. & Johnson, C. Pro-Business Decision Hews To Pattern of Roberts Court. *The Washington Post*, June 22, 2007, p. D0.1

47. Editorial. Justice Denied. *The New York Times Online*, July 5, 2007.

48. Toobin, J. No More Mr. Nice Guy: The Supreme Court's Stealth Hardliner. *The New Yorker*, May 25, 2009, p. 42-51, p. 44.

49. Liptak, A. & Roberts, J. Campaign Cash Mirrors a High Court's Rulings. *The New York Times Online*, October 1, 2006.

50. Lenzner, R. & Miller, M. Buying Justices. *Forbes*, July 21, 2006, p. 64-72.

51. Liptak & Roberts, op cit.

52. Olsen, B. Oregon Democratic Party Backs US Supreme Court Impeachment. Reuters, July 21, 2001.

53. Mataconis, D. Time for Term Limits for the Supreme Court? www.belowthebeltway.com. February 23, 2009.

54. Smith, JE. Stacking the Court. *The New York Times Online*, July 26, 2007.

55. See Message from the Honorable Ronald A. Cass, Chairman of the Center for the Rule of Law. www.ruleoflaw.org.

Chapter 7 Notes

1. Nace, T. <u>Gangs of America: The Rise of Corporate Power and the Disabling of Democracy.</u> San Francisco: Berrett-Koehler, 2003, p. 74-75.

2. Estes, R. <u>Tyranny of the Bottom Line: Why Corporations Make Good People do Bad Things</u>. San Francisco: Berrett-Koehler, 1996, p. 47.

3. Drutman, L. & Cray, C. <u>The People's Business: Controlling Corporations and Restoring Democracy</u>. San Francisco: Berrett-Koehler, 2004, p. 13-14.

4. Nader, R., Green, M. & Seligman, J. <u>Taming the Giant Corporation: How the Largest Corporations Control Our Lives</u>. NY: W. W. Norton and Company, Inc., 1977.

5. Creswell, J. Protected by Washington, Companies Ballooned. *The New York Times Online*, July 13, 2008.

6. Nace, op cit., p. 204-206.

7. See, Beware of Stealth Attacks on Your State's Constitution. April 17, 2002. www.reclaimdemocracy.org.

8. Anonymous. Developments in the Law—Jobs and Borders: Drawing Lines around Corporate Inversion. *Harvard Law Review Online*, Vol. 118, May 2005.

9. My account of the Waite "caper" is drawn mostly from Chapter Nine, of Mr. Nace's book, op cit., p. 102-109. See also, Meyers, W. The Santa Clara Blues: Corporate Personhood versus Democracy. www.mcn.org, and/or www.iipublishing.com. For the actual court proceedings of the Santa Clara decision see, www.tourolaw.edu/patch/Santa.

10. Yeadon, G. Corporate Law: A History. Part 2: Supreme Court Cases. www.spiritone.com.

11. Myers, op cit.

12. Noyes, E. The Proper Role of Government. October 10, 2008. www.superliberty.com.

13. Nace, op cit., p. 208.

14. Drutman & Cray, op cit., p. 77

15. Starting with constitutional amendments at the state level is the strategy proposed by Jan Edwards, a member of the Women's International League for Peace and Freedom, and co-chair of the Redwood Coast Alliance for Democracy that introduced the first ever successful resolution on corporate personhood to the Point Arena, California City Council in 2000. See Challenging Corporate Personhood: Corporations, the U.S. Constitution, and Democracy: An interview with Jan Edwards. *Multinational Monitor Magazine Online* October/November 2002.

16. Derber, C. <u>Regime Change Begins at Home: Freeing America from Corporate Rule</u>. San Francisco: Berrett-Koehler, 2004, p. 226.

17. Egelko, B. Top Court Turns Down Wal-Mart -- Cities Can Ban Big-Box Stores. *San Francisco Chronicle Online*, July 13, 2006.

18. Shepherding a definitive corporate personhood case with an airtight argument all the way to the U.S. Supreme Court is the option recommended by William Myers, op cit.

19. Nace, op cit., p. 79.

20. Ruger, T. Left to their Own Devices: By Helping to Shield Manufacturers from Lawsuits, the FDA is Pushing Tort Reform by Fiat— and Leaving Potentially Flawed Devices on the Market. *Legal Affairs Online*, September|October, 2005. See also, Greenhouse, L. Justices Shield Medical Devices from Lawsuits. *The New York Times Online*, February 21, 2008.

21. Court, J. <u>Corporateering: How Corporate Power Steals Your Personal Freedom---and What You Can Do About It</u>. NY: Jeremy P. Tarcher/Putnam, 2003, p. 101.

22. Grossman, PZ. The Market for Shares of Companies with Unlimited Liability: The Case of American Express. *The Journal of Legal Studies*, Vol. 24, 1995, p. 63-85. See also, Weinstein, M. Share Price Changes and the Arrival of Limited Liability in California. *The Journal of Legal Studies*, Vol. 32, 2003, p. 1-25.

23. Henriques, DB. Companies are Piling up Cash. *The New York Times Online*, March 4, 2008. See also, Kelley, M. The Divine Right of Capital: Dethroning the Corporate Aristocracy. San Francisco: Berrett-Koehler, 2001.

24. Conley, D. Reward but No Risk. *The New York Times Online*, May 10, 2003.

25. Glater, JD. To the Trenches: The Tort War Is Raging On. *The New York Times Online*, June 22, 2008.

26. Orey, M. The Supreme Court: Open for Business. *Business Week*, July 9-16, 2007, p. 30-31, p. 30.

27. The Case Against Corporate Crime: Judgment Day-An Interview with Miles Lord. *MultiNational Monitor Online*, May 1987.

Chapter 8 Notes

1. National Institute of Law Enforcement and Criminal Justice. Illegal Corporate Behavior. U.S. Department of Justice, Law Enforcement Assistance Administration, October 1979. This agency's report was cited in the website of the NGO, Corporate Accountability International, www.stopcorporateabusenow.org.

2. Nace, T. Gangs of America: The Rise of Corporate Power and the Disabling of Democracy. San Francisco: Berrett-Koehler, 2003.

3. Mokhiber, R. Top 100 Corporate Criminals of the Decade. *Corporate Crime Reporter Online*. www.corporatecrimereporter.com.

4. Martin, J. Nader: Crusader, Spoiler, Icon. *OnTheIssues.Org*, Sep 1, 2002, p. 276.

5. See, e.g., Brumback, GB. Getting the Right People Ethically. *Public Personnel Management*, 1996, Vol. 25, p. 267-276.

6. See, e.g., Brumback, GB. Tall Performance From Short Organizations Through We/Me Power. Bloomington, IN: 1stBooksLibrary, 2002. See also my five-part series, Toward Becoming a Great Corporation, in the *CEO Refresher Online*, November, 2009, Vol. 15, Issue 11.4; December 2009, Vol.15, Issue 12.6; January 2010, Vol. 16, Issue 1.13; February 2010, Vol. 16, Issue 2.8; and April 2010, Vol. 16, Issue 4.4.

7. The overall effectiveness of the Sarbanes-Oxley law is doubtful. See e.g., Borrus, A. & McNamee, M. A Legacy that May Not Last. *Business Week Online*, June 2, 2005; McGhee, T. Jury's Out on Effectiveness of Corporate Ethics Law Sarbanes-Oxley Act. *Denver Post Online*, April 21, 2007; and Watnick, VJ. Whistleblower Protections Under the Sarbanes-Oxley Act: A Primer and a Critique. Bepress legal series, paper 1822, www.law.bepress. com., 2006,

8. Snyder, LB. Is Attorney-Client Confidentiality Necessary? *Georgetown Journal of Legal Ethics Online*, Spring, 2002.

9. See Center for Corp Policy, www.corporatepolicy.org.

10. I thought I was clever in thinking of the analogy to Houdini only to find it later in this article: France, M. Close the Lawyer Loophole: Their Ability to Reduce Legal Liability for Executives is Fueling White-collar Crime. *Business Week Online*, February 2, 2004.

11. Nader, R. & Smith, WJ. No Contest: Corporate Lawyers and the Perversion of Justice. NY: Random House, 1996.

12. France, op cit.

13. France, op. cit

14. Rosenzweig, P. Sentencing of Corporate Fraud and White Collar Crime. March 26, 2003. www.heritage.org/Research/Crime/test032403. cfm.

15. See e.g., Simons, KW. Should the Model Penal Code's Mens Rea Provisions Be Amended? *Ohio State Journal of Criminal La*w, Vol. 1, 2003, p. 179-204.

16. Nace, op cit., p. 79.

17. Nader, R. The Business Judgment Rule, July 18. 2005. www.nader. org.

18. Buttar, S. Subsidizing Corporate Crime and Rewarding Constitutional Abuses. *The Huffington Pos Online*, July 20, 2008.

19. Court, J. Corporateering: How Corporate Power Steals Your Personal Freedom---and What You Can Do About It. NY: Jeremy P. Tarcher/ Putnam, 2003, p. 92-94.

20. Court, op. cit., 92-94.

21 See e.g., Sengupta, S. Decades Later, Toxic Sludge Torments Bhopal. *The New York Times Online*, July 7, 2008.

22. Josephson, M. Holding the Top Man Accountable. *Ethics: Easier Said Than Done*, 1989, Vol. 2, p. 26.

23. Brumback, op cit. (see Note 6 for this chapter).

24. 3-Strikes 1994 to 2004: A Decade of Difference. The case was Bill Lockyer v. Leandro Andrade (2003) 123 S.Ct. 1166. www.threestrikes. org/TenYearReport04.

25. Mokhiber, R. Twenty Things You Should Know About Corporate Crime. Speech delivered by Mr. Mokhiber, editor of *Corporate Crime Reporter*, to the Taming the Giant Corporation conference in Washington, D.C., June 9, 2007. See www.corporatecrimereporter.com/twenty061207. htm.

26. For an account of non-prosecutions and of the Arthur Anderson case, see this report by Russell Mokhiber: The New Conventional Wisdom:

Prosecute Individuals, Not Corporations. *Corporate Crime Reporter*, December 6, 2006.

27. See Mokhiber, op cit., 2007, for an account of "empty closets."

28. Lichtblau, E. In Justice Shift, Corporate Deals Replace Trials. *The New York Times Online*, April 9, 2008.

29. In my files are news clippings and articles about a certain recidivist corporate criminal that was finally banned by the government from further contracts until it established a compliance program. It did and the ban was lifted in three months. I tracked publicity about the contractor for several years after the lifting of the ban. Among the subsequently reported misdeeds were these: low balling bids, violation of safety regulations; a bonus plan for the top 25 managers deemed "just outrageous" by a government official; and, in the last file entry, giving a 10-year employee a layoff notice the very day the employee returned from bereavement leave following the death of the employee's young son!

30. Murphy, DE. 10 Year Anniversary Prompts Look at Compliance by Organizations. November 4, 2003. www.ussc.gov., web site of the U.S. Sentencing Commission.

31. U.S. Department of Justice. Bringing criminal charges against corporations. Memorandum of June 16, 1999 from the Deputy Attorney General. See www.usdoj.gov/criminal/fraud/docs.

32. Etzioni, A. Going Soft on Crime. *The Washington Post Online*, April 1, 1990.

33. In searching the Internet I found the website, www.endgame.org created by George Draffan that gives a compilation of "Multimillion Dollar Fines & Settlements Paid by Corporations."

34. Mendoza, M. & Sullivan, C. Fines for Corporate Crimes Slashed or Go Unpaid: "Tough" Penalties Often Prove Illusory. The Associated Press, March 19, 2006. This revealing article can also be found on the website www.reclaimdemocracy.com.

35 Mokhiber, op cit., 2007.

36. Alford, CF. <u>Whistleblowers: Broken Lives and Organizational Power</u>. Ithaca, NY: Cornell University Press, 2001.

37. The 1992 decision by the Supreme Court was in the case of Lujan v. Defenders of Wildlife. Center for Corporate Policy, op cit.

38. Center for Corporate Policy, ibid.

39. Nace, op. cit., p. 82.

40. Mokhiber, RL & Weissman, R. Tax Cuts for the Rich, Deregulation, Death Squads, Apartheid, Deficits, Busted Unions and Busted S&Ls: Remembering Reagan. June 11, 2004. www.counterpunch.org.

41. Brinkley, J. Out of Spotlight, Bush Overhauls U.S. Regulations. *The New York Times Online*, August 14, 2004.

42. Mills, D. Bush Directive Increases Sway on Regulation. *The New York Times Online*, January 30, 2007.

43. For some descriptions and analyses of deregulation see e.g., Drutman & Cray, op cit., p. 133-150. See also Sherer, R. These Messes are what Deregulation Gets Us. *The Nation Online*, December 26, 2000.

44. Robert Reich, when he was Secretary of Labor in the Clinton administration, wrote in the *LA Times* that mega-mergers threatened democracy. In a press briefing he said that the president disagreed. See William J. Clinton Press Briefing by Mike McCurry May 26, 1998, www.presidency.ucsb.edu/press_briefings. See also, Drutman & Cray, op cit., p. 154.

45. Baucus, MS. & Near, JP. Can Illegal Corporate Behavior be Predicted? An Event History Analysis. *Academy of Management Journal*, 1991, Vol. 34, p. 9-36.

46. Cavanagh, J. & Mander, J. (Eds.). <u>Alternatives to Economic</u>

Globalization: A Better World is Possible. San Francisco: Berrett-Koehler, 2004, p. 289.

47. Ibid., p. 289.

48. Brumback, op. cit.

49. For a very succinct account of regulatory capture by the corpocracy see Barnes, P. Capitalism 3.0: A Guide to Reclaiming the Commons. San Francisco: Berrett-Koehler, 2006, p. 35.

50. Smith, G. & Bachman, J. Flying in for a Tune-Up Overseas. *Business Week*, April 21, 2008, p. 26-27.

Chapter 9 Notes

1. See Krugman, P. The Politics of Spite. *The New York Times Online*, October 4, 2009; see also, Hartmann, T. Screwed: The Undeclared War against the Middle Class. San Francisco: Berrett-Koehler, 2006, p. 163-165.

2. Nader, R. Cutting Corporate Welfare. NY: Seven Stories Press, 2000. See also the testimony of Stephen Moore, Director of Fiscal Policy Studies Cato Institute Washington, D.C. before the Budget Committee U.S. House of Representatives Corporate Subsidies in the Federal Budget. June 30, 1999. www.cato.org/testimony.

3. See Federal Financial Support of Business. The Congress of the United States Congressional Budget Office, July 1995. www.cbo.gov/doc.cfm?index=15&type=0.

4. Editorial. Bailout Hide and Seek. *The New York Times Online*, September 13, 2008.

5. Kennedy, DM. The Best Army We Can Buy. *The New York Times Online*, July 25, 2005.

6. OMB Watch. Facts on Corporate Welfare. www.ombwatch.org, February 25, 2002.

7. Carney, TP. <u>The Big Ripoff: How Big Business and Big Government Steal Your Money</u>. NY: Wiley, 2006.

8. See, e.g., Salinger, LM. Encyclopedia of White-collar & Corporate Crime. Cody, WY: Sage, 2004.

9. Citizens for Tax Justice. www.ctj.org.

10. Testimony of Stephen Moore, op cit.

11. Nader, op cit.

12. Friedman, TL. The Class Too Dumb to Quit. *The New York Times Online*, July 21, 2009.

13. Sherry, M. Our Madness for War. *The American Scholar*, Autumn, 2010, p. 102-104. This is a review by Mr. Sherry, a historian, of a book written by another historian, John W. Dower, entitled <u>Cultures of War: Pearl Harbor/Hiroshima/9/11/Iraq</u>. NY: Norton, 2010.

14. See http://en.wikipedia.org/wiki/List_of_anti-war_organizations.

15. See www.peaceaction.org.

16. Wittner, LS. (Edited by John Feffer). How the Peace Movement Can Win. *Foreign Policy in Focus Online*, April 24, 2007.

17. Ross, D. Remember Statecraft? *The American Scholar*, Summer, 2007, p. 47-57. See also, Etzioni, A. All Style, No Substance. *The American Scholar*, Summer 2010, p. 28-35.

18. Engardio, P. Swords into Diapers. *Business Week*, September 22, 2008, p. 62-64.

19. For a brief but good account of the Defense Policy Board see Rossi, M. <u>What Every American Should Know About Who's Really Running the World: The People, Corporations, and Organizations that Control Our Future</u>. London: Plume, 2005, p. 232.

20. Galbraith, JK. The Big Defense Firms are Really Public Firms and should be Nationalized. *The New York Times Online*, November 16, 1969.

21. Cray, C. & Drutman, L. Corporations and the Public Purpose: Restoring the Balance. *Seattle Journal for Social Justice*, Winter 2005.

22. Cray, C. More Bucks for the Bang Gang. *The Huffington Post Online*, September 17, 2008.

23. Bunting III, J. Class Warfare. *The American Scholar*, Winter, 2005, p. 12-18.

24. Alvarez, L. Army Giving More Waivers in Recruiting. *The New York Times Online*, February 14, 2007.

25. Greenblatt, M. Army recruiters threaten high school students. www. KHOU-TV.com, July 28, 2008.; see also, Dobbs, M. Schools and Military Face Off. Privacy Rights Clash With Required Release of Student Information. *The Washington Post*, June 19, 2005, p. A03.

26. Robinson, S. Debunked: Ten Conservative Myths about National Security. Campaign for America's Future, www.ourfuture.org, September 12, 2008.

27. Wright, R. The Price of Assassination. *The New York Times Online*, April 13, 2010.

28. Daly, HE. & Cobbs, JB.,Jr. <u>For the Common Good: Redirecting the Economy toward Community, the Environment, and a Sustainable Future</u>. Boston: Beacon Press, (2nd Edition), 1994.

29. Thiele, E. Military Spending: Cost of Iraq War is but the Tip of the Iceberg. *Global Research Online*, June 14, 2010, www.globalresearch.ca.

30. Korb, LJ. Ten Myths About the Defense Budget. *In These Times Online*, April 2, 2001.

31. A trillion dollars had reportedly been spent just for the wars in Iraq and Afghanistan as of May, 2010; see, Prashad, V. What Did Our Trillion Dollars Buy? Three Wars Uncompleted, the Price Unpaid. *Counterpunch Online*, June 18, 2010. It has been estimated that the Iraq war alone could cost America $3 trillion; see, Stiglitz, JE & Bilmes, LJ. <u>The Three Trillion Dollar War: The True Cost of the Iraq Conflict</u>. NY: W. W. Norton & Company, 2008.

32. Williams, OF. (Ed.). <u>Peace through Commerce: Responsible Corporate Citizenship and the Ideals of the United Nations Global Compact</u>. South Bend, IN: University of Notre Dame Press, 2008.

33. Higham, C. <u>Trading with the Enemy: The Nazi - American Money Plot 1933-1949</u>. NY: Delacorte Press, 1983.

34. Bebchuk, L. & Fried, J. <u>Pay without Performance: The Unfulfilled Promise of Executive Compensation</u>. Cambridge, MA: Harvard University Press, 2004, p. 28.

35. Damon, W. <u>The Moral Advantage: How to Succeed in Business by Doing the Right Thing</u>. San Francisco: Berrett-Koehler, 2004.

36. Rich, F. The Billionaires Bankrolling the Tea Party. *The New York Times Online*, August 28, 2010.

37. Editorial. Alms for the Rich and Powerful. *The New York Times Online*, September 7, 2010. See also, Lipton, E. Congressional Charities Pulling In Corporate Cash. *The New York Times Online*, September 5, 2010.

38. Byrne, J. GOP Senator Orrin Hatch's Charity Tied to Massive Pharmaceutical Donations. *The Raw Story Online*, March 2, 2009, www.rawstory.com.

39. Saha, PM. Novo Nordisk - Sustainable Leadership. *Ethical Corporation Online*, December 12, 2005.

40. Roner, L. The State of Corporate Citizenship - Words Ahead of the Substance. *Ethical Corporation Online*, January 17, 2006.

41. Mathews, MC. <u>Strategic Interventions in Organizations: Resolving Ethical Dilemmas</u>. New Bury Park: Sage, 1988.

42. Alford, CF. <u>Whistleblowers: Broken Lives and Organizational Power</u>. Ithaca, NY: Cornel University Press, 2001.

43. Friedman, T. A Word From the Wise. *The New York Times Online*, March 2, 2010.

44. Alter, J. A 'Fat Cat' Strikes Back. *Newsweek Online*, August 15, 2010

Chapter 10 Notes

1. Korten, D. <u>The Post-Corporate World: Life after Capitalism</u>. West Hartford, CT and San Francisco: Kumerian Press and Berrett-Koehler, 1999, p. 152-154.

2. Monks, R.A.G. <u>The New Global Investors: How Shareholders can Unlock Sustainable Prosperity Worldwide</u>. Oxford, UK: Capstone Publishing Ltd, 2001.

3. Friedman, M. <u>Capitalism and Freedom</u>. (40th anniversary Ed.). Chicago: University of Chicago Press, 2002.

4. Klein, N. <u>The Shock Doctrine: The Rise of Disaster Capitalism</u>. NY: Metropolitan Books, 2007, p. 6.

5. Ibid., p. 5.

6. See e.g., Kahn, S. & Minnich, E. <u>The Fox in the Henhouse: How Privatization Threatens Democracy</u>. San Francisco: Berrett-Koehler, 2005; also, Schemo, DJ. Study of Test Scores Finds Charter Schools Lagging. *The New York Times Online*, August 23, 2006.

7. Kahn & Minnich, op cit.

8. Editorial. That Promised Financial Reform. *The New York Times Online*, October 13, 2009.

9. Quirk, WJ. Too Bad Not to Fail. *The American Scholar*, Summer Issue, 2010, pp. 36-46.

10. Peet, R. Unholy Trinity: The IMF, World Bank and WTO. London: Zed Books, 2009 (Second Edition).

11. Faux, J. The Global Class War: How America's Bipartisan Elite Lost our Future-and What it will Take to Get it Back. NY: John Wiley & Sons, Inc., 2006, p 16, 157-158. Besides the books by Peet and Faux, three other excellent books about exploitative globalization are: Perkins, J. Confessions of an Economic Hit Man. San Francisco: Berrett-Koehler, 2004; Hiatt, S. (Ed.). A Game as Old as Empire: The Secret World of Economic Hit Men and the Web of Global Corruption. San Francisco: Berrett-Koehler, 2007; and Danaher, K. (Ed.). 50 Years is Enough. Boston: South End Press, 1994.

12. This is a quoted remark of Edward S. Herman, Professor Emeritus at the Wharton School, University of Pennsylvania. See Third World Traveler: Transnational Corporations and World Trade. www.thirdworldtraveler. com.

13. According to author John Perkins who once was one, "economic hit men," are highly paid professionals who do the financial skullduggery necessary in exploiting impoverished countries. See Perkins, J. op cit.

14. Guth, M. Speculative Behavior and the Operation of Competitive Markets under Uncertainty. Aldorshot, UK: Avebury Ashgate Publishing, 1994.

15. Wilson, G. The Role of Speculation in Currency Crises. *International Economics Online*, Essay 2, April 7, 1999.

16. See e.g., Rich, F. The Other Plot to Wreck America. *The New York Times Online*, January 8, 2010.

17. Uchitelle, L. Volcker Pushes for Reform, Regretting Past Silence. *The New York Times Online*, July 9, 2010. See also, Editorial. Mr. Obama's Economic Advisers. *The New York Times Online*, November 24, 2008; Stein, B. Everybody's Business: Obama's Team Isn't Exactly a Break With

the Past. *The New York Times Online*, November 28, 2008; Krugman, P. Financial Policy Despair. *The New York Times Online*, March 22, 2009; Rich, F. Has a 'Katrina Moment' Arrived? *The New York Times Online*, March 21, 2009; and Editorial. A Second Term for Mr. Bernanke? *The New York Times Online*, August 25, 2009.

18. Friedman, T. Really Unusually Uncertain. *The New York Times Online*, August 17, 2010.

19. Hartmann, T. <u>Screwed: The Undeclared War against the Middle Class</u>. San Francisco: Berrett-Koehler, 2006, p. 173.

20. Tonelson, A. & Kearns, KL. Trading Away Productivity. *The New York Times Online*, March 5, 2010.

21. Cassidy, J. After the Blowup. *The New Yorker*, January 11, 2010, 28-33.

22. Krugman, P. Fiscal Scare Tactics. *The New York Times Online*, February 4, 2010.

23. Editorial. The Truth About the Deficit. *The New York Times Online*, February 6, 2010.

24. Edwards, M. <u>Small Change: Why Business Won't Save the World</u>. San Francisco: Berrett-Koehler, 2010.

25. Kahn & Minnich, op cit. p. 4.

26. Kahn & Minnich, op cit. p. 27.

27. Krugman, P. Paying the Price. *The New York Times Online*, September 16, 2001.

28. Hartmann, op cit., p. 153.

29. See www.americanhealthcarereform.org.

30. Walsh, MW. Criticism Is Mounting Over Flood Premiums. *The New York Times Online*, September 29, 2009.

31. Herbert, B. Beyond Election Day. *The New York Times Online*, November 3, 2008.

32. Rank, MR. One Nation, Underprivileged: Why American Poverty Affects Us All. NY: Oxford University Press, 2010. See also; Hacker, JS. The Great Risk Shift: The New Insecurity and the Decline of the American Dream. New York: Oxford University Press, 2006.

33. Morin, R. What Divides America? Pew Research Center, September 24, 2009, www.pewresearch.org.

34. Rank, op cit.

35. Brooks, D. Yanks in Crisis. *The New York Times Online*, April 23, 2009.

36. Editorial. $100 Billion the Country Could Use. *The New York Times Online*, March 13, 2009.

37. Aston, AW. Fair and Full Employment: Forty Years of Unfulfilled Promises. *Journal of Law & Policy*, Vol. 15:285, April 2004.

38. Shiller, R. To Build Confidence, Aim for Full Employment. *The New York Times Online*, December 13, 2008.

39. Cooper, H. Obama Acts to Aid Small Businesses. *The New York Times Online*, March 16, 2009. But the aid is dwarfed by the amount of bailout money being given to big banks that were at the core of the financial wizardry recklessness.

40. See www.wiki.com regarding the Small Business Administration.

41. Reich, RB. Totally Spent. *The New York Times Online*, February 13, 2008.

42. Hartmann, op cit., p. 173.

43. Hartmann, op cit., p. 189.

44. Hartmann, op cit., p. 186. For a different view of the connection between wage hikes and employment see Neumark, D. & Wascher, WL. Minimum Wages. Cambridge, MA: MIT Press, 2008.

45. Greenhouse, S. Low-Wage Workers Are Often Cheated, Study Says. *The New York Times Online*, September 1, 2009.

46. Karger, H. Short Changed: Life and Debt in the Fringe Economy. San Francisco: Berrett-Koehler, 2005, p. 34.

47. Hutzler, K. Unhealthy Wages. Letter to the Editor, *The New Yorker*, February 8, 2010, p. 5.

48. Rank, op cit., 213-218.

49, Rank, op cit., 218-224.

50. Herbert, B. Peering at the Future. *The New York Times Online*, September 28, 2009.

51. Fiske, E.B. A Nation at a Loss. *The New York Times Online*, April 25, 2008.

52. Plucker, J., Burroughs, N., & Song, R. Mind the (Other) Gap!: The Growing Excellence Gap in K-12 Education. A report from the Indiana University Center for Evaluation and Education Policy, February 4, 2010.

53. Korten, op. cit., p. 170.

54. From the NGO, National Center for Employee Ownership. www.nceo.org.

55. Korten, op cit., p. 173.

56. Bowley, G. New Rivals Pose Threat to New York Stock Exchange. *The New York Times Online*, October 14, 2009.

57. Korten, op cit., p. 195.

58. Korten, op cit., p. 153-158. See also, Korten, D. Agenda for a New Economy: From Phantom Wealth to Real Wealth. San Francisco: Berrett-Koehler, 2009.

59. Editorial. The Government and the Banks. *The New York Times Online*, February 21, 2009.

60. Wagner, D. Bank Failures Top 100, Only Part of Industry Woes. Associated Press, October 23, 2009 Yahoo News. www.news.yahoo.com.

61. Grim, R. Dick Durbin: Banks "Frankly" Own the Place. *The Huffington Post Online*, April 4, 2009. See also, Labaton, S. Ailing, Banks Still Field Strong Lobby at Capitol. *The New York Times Online*, June 4, 2009.

62. Nocera, J. Only a Hint of Roosevelt in Financial Overhaul. *The New York Times Online*, June 17, 2009. See also, Editorial. Who Won Big in the Financial Bill. *The New York Times Online*, July 16, 2010.

63. Krugman, P. Rewarding Bad Actors. *The New York Times Online*, August 2, 2009.

64. Cassidy, J. Rational Irrationality: The Real Reason that Capitalism is so Crash-Prone. *The New Yorker*, October 5, 2009. p. 30-35.

65. Cavanagh, J. & Mander, J. (Eds.). Alternatives to Economic Globalization: A Better World is Possible. San Francisco: Berrett-Koehler, 2004, p. 318.

66. Rushford, G. Why Does the U.S. Keep Losing WTO Cases? Rushford Report Online, January, 2003. www.rushfordreport.com.

67. Cavanagh & Mander, op cit., p. 308-312,

68. Euroforic. NGOs Around the World Call for the European Union to

Fight for Global, Democratic Governance. November 06, 2008. www. euforic.blogspot.com.

69. Cavanagh & Mander, op cit., p. 318.

70. Watson, R. Bush Deploys Hawk as New UN Envoy. *The Times Online*, March 3, 2005.

71. Cavanagh & Mander, op cit, p. 151.

72. Cavanagh & Mander, op cit., p. 149.

73. Reich, R. How to End the Great Recession. *The New York Times Online*, September 2, 2010.

74. Zohar, D. & Marshall, I. Spiritual Capital: Wealth We Can Live By. San Francisco: Berrett-Koehler, 2004, p. 9.

75. Havel, V. Our Moral Footprint. *The New York Times Online*, September 27, 2007.

76. UN World Commission on Environment and Development. Our Common Future. Oxford: Oxford University Press, 1987.

77. Flesher, J. Nader on Energy, CO_2 and Sustainability. *The New York Times Online*, May 11, 2009.

78. Garwin, DA. Competing on the Eight Dimensions of Quality. *Harvard Business Review*, 1987, Vol. 87, p. 101-109.
79. Chan, S. Bernanke Says He Failed to See Financial Flaws. *The New York Times Online*, September 2, 2010.

80. Corporate Library. New Study Faults High CEO Compensation despite Poor Performance: Report Finds $865 Million in CEO Compensation while Shareholders Suffer $640 Billion in Losses. *EthicsOnline*, April 10, 2006.

81. Wartzman, R. Put a Cap on CEO Pay. *Business Week Online*, September 12, 2008.

82. Anderson, S. Hidden Corporate Scandal: CEOs Who Laid Off the Most Workers Rake in the Most Treasure. *AlterNet Online*, September 1, 2010. Ms Anderson was lead author of the report by the Institute for Policy Studies.

83. See the link, "take action, stop executive excess" in www.ips-dc.org.

84. Thurow, L. The Future of Capitalism: How Today's Economic Forces Shape Tomorrow's World. NY: William Morrow and Co., 1996, p. 242.

85. Personal communication with Professor Derber, March 2010.

86. Herbert, B. Beyond the Fat Cats. *The New York Times Online*, November 10, 2008.

Afterword Notes

1. My account of the Rough Riders was drawn from two sources; a *New Yorker* "briefly noted" book review (June 7, 2010) of The War Lovers: Roosevelt, Lodge, Hearst, and the Rush to Empire, 1898 by Evan Thomas, London: Little, Brown and Company, 2010); and secondly, an interview exchange appearing in Amazon.com editorial review between Mr. Thomas and author Sebastian Junger.

2. Eisler, R. The Real Wealth of Nations: Creating a Caring Economics. San Francisco: Berrett-Koehler, 2007, p. 96.

3. Ibid., pp. 213-235.

4. See www.wilpf.org.

5. Collins, J. How the Mighty Fall: And Why Some Companies Never Give In. A book excerpt featured in Business Week, May 22, 2009, p. 26-38.

6. Sherry, M. Our Madness for War. *The American Scholar*, Autumn, 2010, p. 102-104. This is a review by Mr. Sherry, a historian, of a book written by another historian, John W. Dower, entitled Cultures of War: Pearl Harbor/ Hiroshima/9/11/Iraq. NY: Norton, 2010.

7. See www.globalsecurity.org/military/worldwar; also, Marshall, MG. & Gurr, TR. <u>Peace and Conflict. College Park</u>, MD: Center for International Development and Conflict Management, 2005.

8. Editorial. Where Do We Go From Here? *The New York Times Online*, July 7, 2008.

9. See, e.g., Rutenberg, J. et al. Tax-Exempt Funds Aid Settlements in West Bank. *The New York Times Online*, July 5, 2010. Regarding Osama bin Laden's motivations see the full text of his "letter to America" in Observer. co.uk, November 24, 2002. www.guardian.co.uk.

10. Coll, S. War by Other Means. *The New Yorker*, May 24, 2010, 42-53, p. 44.

11. Etzioni, A. All Style, No Substance. *The American Scholar*, Summer 2010, p. 28-35.

12. Krugman, P. The Old Enemies. *The New York Times Online*, May 23, 2010.

Appendix C Notes

1. My account of Aristotle and his era are drawn from three sources: Professor Darel Tai Engen's paper, The Economy of Ancient Greece, EH.Net Encyclopedia, edited by Robert Whaples. August 1, 2004. http://eh.net/encyclopedia/article/engen.greece; Professor John Martella's 1992 paper, Philosophy, Economic History, and the Rise of Capitalism, www.drury.edu/ess/history/modern/econhist.html; and Professor Edward W. Younkin's September 15, 2005 paper, number 158, Aristotle and Economics. www.quebecoislibre.org/05/050915-11.htm.

2. Barnes, P. Capitalism 3.0: A Guide to Reclaiming the Commons. San Francisco: Berrett-Koehler, 2006, p. 35.

3. Personal communication with Mr. Barnes, February 18, 2010.

4. Barnes, op cit. p. 73.

5. Eisler, R. <u>The Real Wealth of Nations: Creating a Caring Economics</u>. San Francisco: Berrett-Koehler, 2007, p. 64.

6. Gates, JR. <u>The Ownership Solution: Toward A Shared Capitalism for The 21st Century</u>. Reading, MA: Addison-Wesley, 1998.

7. Hartmann, T. Screwed: <u>The Undeclared War against the Middle Class</u>. San Francisco: Berrett-Koehler, 2006, p. 14.

8. Hawkins, P., Lovins, A., & Lovins, LH. <u>Natural Capitalism: Creating the Next Industrial Revolution</u>, NY: Little Brown & Co., 1999.

9. Karger, H. <u>Short Changed: Life and Debt in the Fringe Economy</u>. San Francisco: Berrett-Koehler, 2005, p. 34.

10. Personal communication with Professor Karger, November 12, 2008.

11. Korten, D. <u>The Post-Corporate World: Life after Capitalism</u>. West Hartford, CT and San Francisco: Kumerian Press and Berrett-Koehler, 1999.

12. Terry, R. <u>Economic Insanity: How Growth-Driven Capitalism is Devouring the American Dream</u>. San Francisco: Berrett-Koehler, 1995.

13. Zohar, D. & Marshall, I. <u>Spiritual Capital: Wealth We Can Live By</u>. San Francisco: Berrett-Koehler, 2004, p. 9.

Index

About the Author

Gary Brumback received his undergraduate degree from Indiana University and his Ph.D. in organizational psychology from The Ohio State University in 1963. His doctoral dissertation was on the subject of personal and organizational values.

Dr. Brumback has had a long and varied career involving the retail industry, the insurance industry, the manufacturing industry, university teaching, the not-for-profit research sector, and the U.S. government.

He was elected a Fellow of both The American Psychological Association and The Association for Psychological Science in recognition of his outstanding and distinguished contributions to psychology. He is also a member of the scholastic honorary society, Phi Beta Kappa, and the research honorary society, Sigma Xi.

He is a prolific writer. His first book, *Tall Performance from Short Organizations through We/Me Power* is about managing performance in non-hierarchical, empowering organizations. He was invited by the U.S. government to showcase his MBR (managing behavior and results) model of performance management around the country. He has authored 50 book reviews, many articles in professional journals, and many technical reports. He has given many talks and invited addresses at professional meetings in the U.S. and abroad. His research, writings, and presentations have covered a broad array of topics.

Since retiring over 15 years ago he has gone beyond his own field to delve into economics, history, humanism, moral philosophy, political science, public affairs, and theology. He spent nearly ten years researching and writing The Devil's Marriage.

He was reared a Quaker pacifist and considers himself a free-thinking humanist. He is married and lives in Palm Coast, Florida. He and his wife have two daughters and two grandsons.